PRAISE FOR ~~ROSIE~~
A MOTHER'S STORY

'I take my hat off to Rosie Batty, who will not be silenced,
and say thank goodness for that' Anna Bligh, *Financial Review*

'A brave, resolute and heart-breaking tale'
Steven Carroll, *Sydney Morning Herald*

'[Rosie Batty's] memoir is both a tribute to her lost son and
a call to action for every reader to stand against family violence'
Lauren Novak, *Adelaide Advertiser*

'Heartfelt, honest and profoundly moving, this is one mother's
story. It is also an inspiring, extraordinary story of how one
individual can make a significant difference' *Maitland Mercury*

'Every Australian should read this book' Tracey Spicer

'She suffers, but she is not a victim. Batty is comforting and
terrifying. She is protector and avenger. Her maternal love is
gigantic, big enough to embrace "all the abused women and
children out there". She has moral authority and dignity ...
compelling' Rachel Buchanan, *Australian Book Review*

'Thank you Rosie for opening my eyes. For fighting hard for
those not in a position to do so for themselves. For honouring
your son in the best possible way. But most of all, for sharing
your son with the world' Julie Garner, Goodreads

'I do hope men read this book. It is a journey that you will emerge from a changed person. This may help change the system' David Brown, Goodreads

'A beautifully written story. Rosie has definitely had a tough life from a young age, yet she still seems to shine and rise above it to use her experiences to help others. Rosie, you are a true hero' julieg, Booktopia

'[Rosie Batty's] willingness to share her story and her pain have led to greater awareness of domestic violence and prompted reform and greater funding to assist women and children who are at risk. An important book that will enlighten, and provide a voice to those who are in this insidious position' The Big Book Club

'intensely moving … This is the story of a woman with compassion, courage, grace and forgiveness in spades' Sara Bunny, *New Zealand Woman's Weekly*

'[Rosie Batty's] voice is now the leading voice in Australia on family violence and has paved the way for other families to speak up, for the start of a dialogue about family violence – and even for a royal commission in Victoria. Her book is now another step in this important battle' Shauna Anderson, Mamamia

Family violence campaigner **Rosie Batty** is the 2015 Australian of the Year and the Pride of Australia's National Courage Medal recipient.

Born in Nottinghamshire, England, Rosie moved to Australia in the 1980s. In 2014, she rose above personal tragedy and the great loss of her eleven-year-old son, Luke, who was killed by his father in a very public assault, to become a leader in the crusade against family violence. Since then her name has become synonymous with the words 'courage' and 'resilience'.

Now a tireless campaigner, Rosie has established the Luke Batty Foundation and this year launched the Never Alone Campaign, in which she asks all Australians to stand with her and beside all victims of family violence by signing up at neveralone.com.au.

Rosie is deputy chair of the Council of Australian Governments' advisory panel on preventing violence against women. She is also Ambassador for Our Watch and the Lort Smith Animal Hospital and Patron of Doncare Community Services, and has been inducted into the Victorian Honour Roll of Women.

Bryce Corbett is a journalist and author of more than twenty-five years' experience. He is currently the Executive Editor of *The Australian Women's Weekly* and is the author of two books, *A Town Like Paris* and *Memoirs of a Showgirl*, which he wrote with his wife, Shay Stafford. Bryce met Rosie Batty not long after her son, Luke, was killed. They struck up an immediate friendship, which eventually led to collaborating on this book. Bryce lives in Brisbane with his wife and two children, Flynn and Rose.

Rosie Batty

with Bryce Corbett

A Mother's Story

HarperCollins*Publishers*

HarperCollins*Publishers*

First published in Australia in 2015
This edition published in 2016
by HarperCollins*Publishers* Australia Pty Limited
ABN 36 009 913 517
harpercollins.com.au

HarperCollins*Publishers*
Level 13, 201 Elizabeth Street, Sydney NSW 2000, Australia
Unit D1, 63 Apollo Drive, Rosedale, Auckland 0632, New Zealand
A 53, Sector 57, Noida, UP, India
1 London Bridge Street, London, SE1 9GF, United Kingdom
2 Bloor Street East, 20th floor, Toronto, Ontario M4W 1A8, Canada
195 Broadway, New York NY 10007, USA

National Library of Australia Cataloguing-in-Publication data:

Batty, Rosie, author.
  A mother's story / Rosie Batty with Bryce Corbett.
  ISBN: 978 1 4607 5262 3 (paperback)
  ISBN: 978 1 4607 0510 0 (ebook)
  Batty, Rosie.
  Batty, Luke.
  Victims of family violence – Australia – Biography.
  Abused wives – Australia – Biography.
  Family violence – Australia
  Family violence – Australia – Prevention.
  Other Creators/Contributors: Corbett, Bryce, author.
362.8292092

Cover design by Hazel Lam, HarperCollins Design Studio
Cover photography by Julian Kingma
Back cover photograph of Rosie and Luke Batty courtesy of the author
Photograph of Bryce Corbett and Rosie Batty on page iii by Michelle Holden
Typeset in Bembo Std by Kirby Jones
Printed and bound in Australia by Griffin Press
The papers used by HarperCollins in the manufacture of this book are a natural,
recyclable product made from wood grown in sustainable plantation forests.
The fibre source and manufacturing processes meet recognised international
environmental standards, and carry certification.

'To live in hearts we leave behind is not to die'

*To my little boy with the little button nose, the little dimple chin,
the little chubby cheeks and the BIG blue eyes.
You will be in my heart forever, Luke.*

*And to my mum, Sheila Mary Atkin, who I lost so long ago
but who will always be alive in my heart.*

CONTENTS

Prologue

I'm standing on a stage in front of Parliament House. A crowd of some thousand or so people stretches out before me. To one side of me is Deborra-Lee Furness – Hugh Jackman's wife! – and to the other, Dr Gill Hicks, London bombing survivor, and decorated neuroscientist Professor Lyn Beazley. To say that I am feeling overwhelmed is an understatement.

We're gathered here together as nominees for Australian of the Year. It's the end of a remarkable three days – where I've been wined and dined at the governor-general's residence, met with the prime minister and shaken hands with more truly impressive Australians than I could ever hope to have met.

The ceremony is unfolding. A huge screen to the side of the stage plays video packages enumerating each nominee's achievements – a catalogue of our triumphs, a sober recollection of what we've done, who we are and why we have come to be standing on this stage. I can't help but feel that mine is a little bit light on compared to the weighty achievements of the people standing on either side of me. But I'm determined to soak it all in and enjoy the experience for what it is.

Down in the crowd I spy old friends David, Lee, Sue and Mike grinning up at me. A little further back and leaning heavily on his stick is my dad. He's flown all the way here from the UK, just for this. I hope to God he hasn't wasted a trip. For a man who worked the land so hard and was always in my childhood imagination a pillar of strength – a stoic, unshakeable, immutable Nottinghamshire farmer – he looks suddenly frail.

As the speeches go on, I shift on the spot. I've become more used to being in the public eye these last twelve months, but it's still something with which I am uneasy. As I look out across the crowd, many of them lazing on the lawns that stretch from new Parliament House to Old Parliament House, basking in a Canberra sunset after a typically hot January day, I smile inwardly – amused at the laconic approach my adopted country folk take to this most auspicious of occasions. Back in England, this would be a ceremony leaden with pomp and ceremony.

I take in the ghost gums that line the lawns, cast an eye over my shoulder at the setting sun and think about how much I wish my son, Luke, could have been here to see this. He would have laughed. He would have poked fun at me. He would have told me to get over myself then, showing all the interest in my life that his pre-teen mind could be bothered to muster, he'd have gone back to his iPad.

I think back on the last twelve months. What a whirlwind it's been. I've met with CEOs, taken tea with premiers and ricocheted from one awards ceremony to another. The Pride of Australia Courage Award, Victorian Australian of the Year. I've done more media interviews than I can count, spoken at more events than I can remember and had the utterly disconcerting experience of being approached at airports for my autograph. And it's all happened so fast, I haven't had a chance to process any of it. Which is probably just as well. I'm not entirely sure my brain is *capable* of processing it.

There's a sudden hush from the crowd as the prime minister approaches the lectern. I'm jolted from my thoughts. This is it.

'And the 2015 Australian of the Year,' he says, pausing for effect, 'is Rosie Batty.'

The crowd rise to their feet in spontaneous ovation. There is cheering as I step gingerly forward to accept the award.

A sea of faces look expectantly up at me and the lenses of multiple cameras are trained on me, beaming this moment live around the country. I feel a wave of goodwill from the crowd, as if each one of them is silently reaching forward, holding me up. It's an honour beyond my wildest imaginings. I am overwhelmed, and truly humbled.

And yet it's all so bittersweet. Twelve months ago I was a single mum from Tyabb, a tiny dot on the map of the Mornington Peninsula. But in eighteen days' time it will be the one-year anniversary of the death of my only son – killed by his father at cricket training.

And then the sadness hits me. The only reason I am in this position, the only reason I am standing here holding this trophy and receiving this ovation is because I have endured the kind of tragedy that makes people recoil. I've become Australian of the Year because I am the person no one wants to be, the mother who has suffered the insufferable.

Taking a deep breath, and fighting back tears, I begin to speak.

'I would like to dedicate this award to my beautiful son, Luke. He is the reason I have found my voice,' I say, to a hushed silence. 'Luke, my little man. You did not die in vain and will not be forgotten. You are beside me on this journey and with me every step of the way.'

There is silence, then applause. It starts as a ripple at the back of the crowd and builds into a roar. As I turn from the lectern, I brush a single tear from my eye.

1

Luke floats out of his bedroom, late again. His hair is tousled, his mood sullen. It's going to be one of those days.

'Morning, buddy,' I chime.

It's been only a few weeks since we returned from England. Five glorious weeks at home, visiting family, catching up with friends. Forgetting about Greg. And most importantly, coming to realise that my life doesn't have to be dominated by him anymore.

Not even my son's reluctance to eat his breakfast, get in the shower and generally get his arse into gear can break my spirit this morning. For the first time in a long time there's a sense of hope, a sense of clarity. It feels almost as if some sort of veil has been lifted and I can see a future starting to take shape – a bright, carefree, happy future.

The clock is showing 8 am. At this rate, Luke is going to be late for school. I know I should probably be more worried when he acts up like this. But he is only eleven, and last year was a tough year. Despite that, Luke seems to have turned a corner. He's really settled into school and is growing into a fine young man.

As I look across the kitchen bench at him hunched over his cereal, I catch a glimpse of those crystalline blue eyes through his mop of a fringe. My baby boy. My Luke. He may be growing up before my eyes, but he'll always be my little boy.

'C'mon,' I say, rallying. 'Shower. Now. We're going to be late.'

I bundle the dogs into the car and call for Luke to hurry up. It's 8.15 am. He comes flying out of the house, slamming the front door behind him, school shirt untucked and school bag flung over one shoulder.

School is all of 500 metres down the road – even closer as the crow flies. But this has been our routine for as long as I can remember. And these days, when it's a miracle if I can get three sentences out of him in one sitting, the drive is a chance to force some conversation out of my increasingly taciturn son.

As we arrive at Flinders Christian Community College, there's already a queue of cars. I think back to my childhood in provincial England. We were lucky if our dad was even there to wave us off at the door, much less chauffeur us to the front gate of our school.

I think I do an okay job as a mum, all things considered. It's hard to know without any real benchmark to measure it against, though I do sometimes worry I am too soft with Luke. But he's a good kid. Our lives are not exactly straightforward. It's never been picket fences and a nuclear family for us, far from it. And he's my only child. I won't get another go at this motherhood thing – so of course I am going to indulge him a little.

As the car idles, we joke about having to leave home earlier to beat the rush-hour traffic snarl in sleepy Tyabb on the Mornington Peninsula. He still has a wicked sense of humour, even if puberty is starting to dull it. We are simpatico, Luke and I. When all is said and done, it's me and him against the world. Just as it has been from the start.

When we arrive at the kerb in front of the main gates, Luke gathers his school bag and opens the door.

'Bye, buddy,' I say. 'Learn lots.'

He rolls his eyes and walks off.

And so, another day begins. I have some chores to do at home, some phone calls to make for the business and an optometrist appointment to reschedule. Oh, and if I have time, the Kreepy Krawly needs servicing over in Mornington.

As I pull out from the kerb and head home, I look in the rear-vision mirror and see Luke dawdling into school. I can't believe how fast he's growing up. It's eleven years since he was born but it seems like yesterday.

2

The Beginning

People say they have memories from when they were two or three years old. I don't remember that far back. My earliest memories are mostly of my mother. She died unexpectedly when I was six years old.

It's hard to say if I was close to my mother. I was so young when she died, it's so long ago now, and my dad has never been much of a one for talking. What I do have are vague recollections of a presence in my life that was loving, warm and nurturing. And then, all of a sudden, it was gone.

My mother was born Sheila Atkin. By all accounts, hers was a typical upbringing for a girl born in the 1940s in northern England. She trained to become a hairdresser, studying in Leeds. She met my dad through mutual friends. Geoffrey Batty hailed from a proud line of relatively well-to-do farmers in a village called Laneham. His dad was a farmer, his granddad had been a farmer. They raised sheep and cattle, and I can only suppose in the eyes of a hairdressing apprentice from Leeds, my dad presented as quite the prospect.

And so, they married and moved to Laneham. You could drive through Laneham today and barely realise it. Back then, it had a corner shop, two pubs and a church. To those who didn't live there and know its tight-knit community well, its most remarkable feature, other than being on a picturesque bend of the River Trent, was that it was near the town of Retford, which is on the London to Edinburgh train line. With a population of about three hundred people, it wasn't exactly what you'd call a thriving metropolis.

But when I was small, and my parents were my world, it seemed plenty big enough to me. I was born at Willingham Hospital in Lincolnshire on 9 February 1962. I was the first born of three children. There was me, Rosemary Anne Batty, my brother Robert, two years my junior, and James, who was five years younger than me.

We had what most would consider a pretty idyllic early childhood: raised in the English countryside, with fields for a backyard, a great big rambling farmhouse and plenty of farmyard animals. We had some of the locals working on the farm – Marlene the postwoman was our house cleaner. As we got older, people used to tease us. Because our farm was the biggest one in the village, we were seen as the big farming family. Since it was around the time when Dallas and Dynasty ruled the TV airwaves, they used to call my brother Robert 'Bobby Ewing'.

One of my earliest memories is not wanting to leave Robert when I went off to school. We were as close as any two siblings could be. I can remember him playing on a plough and falling and cutting his eye open. I also distinctly remember James being born. I told Mum I wanted her to call him Paul. I seem to recall I was quite smitten at the time with a local boy called Paul Baker, the son of my primary school teacher.

Memories of my mum are scant. My first memory is of her caring for Robert and me when we got chicken pox. Sadly, though, the main memories I have of Mum are her arguing with my father. I remember her being upset and me trying to comfort her. At the time she died, their marriage was under a lot of strain.

I used to actively seek out people who had known her and could talk about her. Probably because Dad never talked about her, I made it my mission to construct my own portrait of my mum. I had the vague outline, and I used other people's memories and recollections to provide the colour and texture. She had a great sense of humour – but also a temper. I don't remember thinking I took after her, but when I was growing up, a lot of people said I was very like her.

Dad never really knew how to talk to any of his kids. He was the sort of father who was utterly dependable and stoic, but didn't know how to demonstrate his love for his children. He never discussed the topic of Mum and what had happened to her. And as a result, we never really asked him.

My brother James didn't even know how my mum died until, in the days after Luke's funeral, my dad spoke about her dying from a strangulated hernia and complications from peritonitis due to negligence. We weren't even told she was dead until after her funeral. I do remember the day she died, however. We went for a walk in the morning. James was in a pram; he wasn't even two years old. We got to the end of our neighbour's driveway, then Mum turned and went back.

The next thing I remember is her being in the bedroom surrounded by lots of people, including doctors. And I remember asking where it hurt and she showed me her tummy. The ambulance came and I have this vivid memory of her being carried down the stairs on a stretcher.

I asked our neighbour Carol, 'She's going to die, isn't she?'

To which Carol replied, 'Don't be silly.'

The last time I saw my mother, she was being loaded into the back of an ambulance. She died on 7 November 1968. She was thirty-seven years old.

When Mum went into hospital, us three kids were sent to our aunty and uncle's house to stay, in Brandesburton, a small village in Yorkshire. I remember playing with my cousins and saying, 'My mum is coming out of hospital soon,' and them reacting a little bit oddly. I didn't know it at the time, but they already knew she was dead. It turned out everybody knew she had died. Everybody except her own children.

I remember Dad bringing us back home a week or so later. I remember him sitting us on his knee and telling us that Mum had died. I remember running out to Nanna Atkin and asking if it was true and she said it was. I ran to the neighbour's house and asked my playmate, William, a boy only a year older than me, whether he knew – and he did.

And in my little-girl mind, I remember being so confused. How could Mum have died without saying goodbye? Not one last cuddle, not one final kiss on the forehead. And so I decided they had all gotten it wrong. That they were clearly confusing her with someone else's mother. And I determined that I would only believe it when I saw her name on a gravestone.

In England, the ground is left to settle for several months after a funeral before a headstone is erected, to prevent it becoming uneven. And so I floated in this kind of half-reality, acutely aware that my world had shifted irrevocably, acutely aware that there was a sadness hanging over my family but not willing to think about why. In the company of my father who, in spite of his determination not to display emotion, and even despite the fact

11

their marriage was rocky, had lost a woman he had loved. The mother of his three children; his wife. When eventually I did see the gravestone, just over our hedge – the local churchyard was adjacent to our garden – I was probably too young to process it.

From an early age I didn't really feel like I could discuss Mum's death with anyone. I remember when I was at school, Mrs Baker, the teacher, would show me extraordinary kindness. When all the other kids were out playing, she'd allow me to sneak back into the library corner and lose myself in books. It was my escape, my comfort – I would lose myself in imaginary worlds. And that's been a pattern throughout my life – I have always sought the solace of books.

Dad never did cry. Or if he did, I never saw it. I suppose in those days dads didn't have a lot of hands-on interaction with their kids like fathers today. Nurturing was the mother's role. The most emotional I have seen my dad was when he came to Australia for Luke's funeral. It was as if he used the opportunity to grieve in a way he hadn't done before. I remember him talking about my mum to people after we had laid Luke to rest, which I'd never heard him do.

Neither I nor my two brothers have ever married. My journey as an adult has been to understand why I am who I am. And I have come to understand that the depth of trauma we suffered as small kids has taken a huge toll on all three of our lives.

Without a mother around, and with a caring but distant father, I turned instinctively to my grandparents and cousins to fill the emotional void in my life. As the oldest of my siblings, and perhaps also as the only girl, I was lucky in that I was able to seek it out more readily than my brothers were. I have always felt a sense of responsibility for them.

I remember when my mum died being scared of going to bed and crying whenever it was bedtime. And I remember Dad telling me, 'Don't cry – you have to be a big girl for your brothers.' Despite the fact I was only six years old, I learned how to not cry whenever I was sad or in pain, because I didn't want to upset my little brothers, and because I wanted to please my dad. So there I was, in bed at night in a big, dark, cold farmhouse, sad, alone and too scared to get up and go to the toilet in the night. For a period of time I routinely wet my bed, which was obviously an embarrassment. After Mum died, all three of us kids went through a phase where we routinely soiled ourselves, and we were made to feel ashamed of it. Decades later, when I was studying for a community welfare degree, I discovered it was a common response to trauma. Soiling occurs whenever there are periods of emotional distress. I can talk about it now, but was so ashamed of it as a child.

Dad was just not capable of showing emotion. My dad didn't have an especially good upbringing from his parents. I think even he would admit they were emotionally neglectful. And so, Dad did the best he could with the tools he had been given.

Dad loved my mum's family. She came from a big family with four brothers, and they were all close in a way Dad hadn't experienced with his own family. They were demonstrative with their emotions, and I suppose he was drawn to them because of it. Once Mum died, Dad made sure we still spent plenty of time with Mum's family. All our school holidays were spent in Brandesburton. We would either stay with Nanna Atkin or with one or two of the aunties. All of us cousins adored our grandparents, and they ended up being a formative influence in all of our lives.

My grandfather taught me how to write letters and wrap presents. He taught me the importance of writing cards to people and the power of the written word. When later I was sent to boarding school, he would write to me regularly. He taught me things that maybe my dad was unable to.

13

But it was Nanna Atkin who made the most lasting impact on my childhood and adolescence. Her name was Gertrude Atkin, and she would go on to live to one hundred. She taught me to be curious about life and people. She taught me, above all, that family was paramount. Nanna was really proud of her family – from humble beginnings her sons all did well, building their own businesses. And of course she had loved my mum – as a mother loves her only daughter.

Nanna Atkin always had lots of friends. Life around her was never dull. Even in her sunset years, she kept her 'marbles', as she called them, by watching quiz shows and playing Scrabble. Fiercely independent, she lived in her own home to the end. She didn't go to church regularly. She was a Methodist, though, and while not a strict one, religion did inform the way she lived her life. I grew up going to Sunday School and being connected to the local church.

Nanna Atkin hailed from the era where you changed clothes in the afternoon in preparation for dinner. She never wore a pair of trousers in her life. She always wore a bit of lipstick and she never got drunk, only ever indulging in the occasional glass of sherry. She never had a lot of money and never in her hundred years did she travel overseas. For a large part of my childhood, Nanna Atkin and my grandfather ran a fish-and-chip shop, and I remember helping them with the chip machine and prepping the newspapers for wrapping.

She always had a great sense of humour. I remember sitting with Grandma and Grandpa Atkin watching *The Benny Hill Show*, *The Black and White Minstrel Show* and *Dad's Army*. Most of all, I used to love listening to their music. Jim Reeves was a particular favourite, and we'd sit together on the settee, playing Scrabble and listening to him warble, the crackle of needle on vinyl. When I was older, Grandpa would sometimes make me a 'snowball' (advocaat and lemonade). Even as a teenager, I sought out their company and enjoyed being around them. Most of the time we would just sit. It was enough to be in one another's company. Nanna would sew or embroider and Grandpa would read the newspaper or watch television.

We'd eat Yorkshire pudding at Sunday dinner. She was a really good cook, my nanna, a complete mistress in the kitchen of a very traditionally English repertoire. Nanna was never one to moan about ailments. When she no longer had the strength in her arms to mash the potatoes for dinner, she would put the saucepan on the kitchen floor and use her body weight. And she was always up for new things. She learned how to use a microwave at the age of a hundred – and very pleased with herself she was too.

More than anything else to me, she was a connection to my mum. Without ever really knowing or acknowledging it, I suppose my desire to spend time with her was borne of a desire to get to know the mother I never knew. And she would talk about Mum, reminisce about her as a girl and often remark how I behaved or looked exactly like her. And I took enormous comfort from that.

Nanna Atkin really wanted to turn a hundred – it was a milestone for her. And she made it, too. She had a lovely party, but because I had just given birth to Luke I was unable to go. Six months later we did manage to travel to England, and Nanna at last met my little boy. She got to see him roll over for the first time and that was really special and important to me. For the longest time during my adulthood, Nanna Atkin had badgered me about finding a husband and settling down. For her to see me so happy with Luke meant the world to both of us. I suppose she knew – just as I was beginning to understand – how becoming a mother would so utterly fulfil me.

3

Growing Up

I don't know if it has anything to do with losing my mum at such a young age, but I was a tomboy growing up. I spent most of my spare time playing with my brothers and the boy next door, William. Being tough and able to hold my own in the fights that invariably broke out was really important to me. I focused more on trying to be the toughest I could be rather than a really feminine girl.

But I did like playing with dolls. I received my favourite doll from my godmother when my mother died – her miniature clothes had been made by Nanna Atkin. Her underwear was fashioned out of a dish cloth and her outfit was hand knitted. The doll was very pretty, with lovely long blonde hair and blue eyes. I found her recently in the back of a cupboard, and I remember as a girl keeping all my most treasured possessions in a little cupboard in my bedroom.

For a long time when I was growing up, I remember being ashamed I didn't have appropriate clothes. Because the job of buying our clothes fell to Dad after Mum died, my wardrobe could best be described as 'function over form'. Let's just say there wasn't much in the way of pink – or even dresses, for that matter. Of course, there wasn't the same focus on looking presentable or being fashionable back then. It wasn't a part of village life, and it wasn't really a part of a kid's life in 1970s Britain.

Not that I was overly fussed. It was all about sport for me at school. At my primary school, I was the best at sport by a long shot for quite a few years. Of course, it never occurred to me that this might have something to do with the competition at my tiny village school being not all that impressive. I was quickly cut down to size when I went to high school, no longer a big fish in a little pond. But I still managed to hold my own. Running was my sport, and my fondest memories of primary school were sports days where I won every race, be it running, egg and spoon or sack races.

When I was old enough for high school, Dad decided that it would be best for me to go to private school. I was devastated. Not only were all my friends going to the local public high school, but the new school was a Catholic school, while we were Church of England. And in those days, that meant something. So, at the age of eleven, and with nothing but fear and resentment in my heart, I was dispatched to St Joseph's Convent in Lincoln. In truth, Lincoln was only across the bridge from Laneham – not far away at all. But when my life had been defined by the boundaries of a couple of fields and the banks of the River Trent, it felt like another world.

My friends in Laneham were all horrified I was being sent away to become a 'nun'. I was just really angry and, once again, forced to deal alone with what was a fairly traumatic experience in my young life. To make things worse, being Anglican in a Catholic school in those days meant the nuns went out of their way to remind me how spiritually inferior I was to the other students, making little comments all the time about me being there at their indulgence.

I tried really hard at school the first year, and I won the class prize. At the end of first year, we staged a nativity play. I had been chosen to play an angel.

My teacher told everyone in the cast to get their mothers to help them sew their costumes.

'Please, miss,' I said timidly to the teacher, fighting back tears. 'I don't have a mum.' Not having a mum made me feel different.

After passing a nasty note in class to one of my friends, I was hauled before the headmistress, who promptly informed me, 'You are only at this school because you lost your mother, not because we want you here.' At that point I shut down completely. By the time I reached my third year at high school I was a full-blown delinquent.

When I was twelve, Dad announced he was remarrying. As it turned out, I had met my new stepmother, Josephine, months before. She was from Dunedin in New Zealand and had met my father through a mutual friend while working in London as a nanny. That first time we'd met we got on really well. Josephine was kind and young (at twenty-eight she was almost closer in age to me than my dad, who was forty-two at the time), and in the confines of the village she was a breath of fresh air.

But when Dad told me he was getting married I laughed. I knew he'd had girlfriends, but it never occurred to me he would actually remarry. I had become used to being the only female in the house and now my status was about to be overturned. More significantly, I felt that Mum was about to be replaced, and that Josephine would take my dad away from me.

When Josephine first arrived, it was a huge adjustment for us kids. I'm old enough and sensible enough now to look back and see that it must have been just as difficult for her, moving in with three children and becoming a step parent overnight. But, over time, Josephine introduced some much-needed discipline and structure into our household.

I started to ride horses around this time. At the end of school each day, I would go straight to the riding school. I've always had an affinity with animals. Whether it's a consequence of having been raised in a rural setting or whether I gravitated to the company of animals to fill the void in my emotional life, I can't say. All I know is, as long as I can remember, I have had a host of pets – rabbits, dogs, goats, cats, chickens and donkeys. There's something uncomplicated and wonderfully straightforward about the love of – and for – an animal.

Love for a different kind of animal reared its head in my early teens too: boys suddenly became far more interesting as I reached the ages of thirteen and fourteen. The timing may purely have been coincidental, but it was also around this time that I started to get into trouble at school.

Looking back, I am sure becoming a troublemaker was in no small part in reaction to my unhappy home life. I was confused and scared, and I felt I was having to navigate it all on my own, so I acted up at school. At the end of my third year, I received a report that was so appalling I didn't have the gumption to show it to Dad and Josephine. Instead, I began petitioning to become a weekly boarder.

And so, for the last two years of my school life I spent the week at school and the weekends at home. It was the best thing I could have done. The sisters ran a tight ship, with Sister Winifred waking us each morning at the crack of dawn by ringing a big bell, whereupon we had to sit bolt upright in bed and start reciting the Hail Mary. Despite being an Anglican, not only had I picked up the arcane rituals of the Catholic Church with startling alacrity, but I threw myself into them, relishing the structure and certainty they seemed to provide. And while I wouldn't describe myself as a religious person now, I developed a spirituality that I cherish and that nourishes and comforts me to this day.

We would study before breakfast, then trot off to class. For reasons I'm still not entirely sure about, we were not allowed to shower mid-week, and were allowed only one bath a week, so my hair would become so greasy.

Despite enjoying a marked rise in my academic fortunes, and starting to take home impressive grades, I nevertheless determined to leave school at the age of sixteen, having passed a handful of O levels. The declaration that I'd had enough of schooling went largely unchallenged as I had secured myself a good job.

Not even Sister Winifred had the energy to oppose me, a decision made easier, I daresay, after she caught sight of my latest hairdo. Deciding it was time to up the fashion ante, I had gone off and gotten a perm at the local hair salon. They were very fashionable at the time, difficult though it is to believe now. My head turned into a frizzy mop. Dad didn't recognise me the first time he saw me with it. Sister Winifred took one look and declared, 'Batty, you look like a washer woman.' It took a month for the perm to 'settle'.

Months later I started working as a junior bank clerk in nearby Retford. I probably thought at the time that I was the very model of a modern working girl, revelling in the independence and what I can only imagine now was a piddling weekly pay packet.

Meanwhile, back on the home front, things were about to take a dramatic turn. Five years into their marriage, Dad and

Josephine welcomed my half-brother, Terry, into the world. We all adored him. I couldn't stop hugging him. I was seventeen years old and suddenly helping to care for a newborn, and I couldn't have been happier. I would come home from work and immediately take him off Josephine's hands. And over time, caring for Terry served to bring us closer.

Perhaps unsurprisingly, the world of high finance in the rural branch of a small bank failed to fire my imagination for too long, and so I began to wonder what lay beyond the stone walls and green fields of English village life. It was this natural curiosity that Josephine had always fostered, that led me to a new life in Austria. I had spied an advertisement for an agency placing English au pairs with European families, and I recognised it as my ticket out of there. And so, with only a backpack and a hopelessly inadequate grasp of German, I decided to head to Innsbruck to work as a live-in nanny.

I spent the first few weeks after arriving crippled by homesickness. By day I was looking after a two-year-old and a four-year-old whom I couldn't understand, and by night I cried myself to sleep. But I was too proud to tell anyone, a trait that would prove hard to shake later on in my life.

My employees were a wonderfully stereotypical Austrian family who were kind enough in their way but perhaps a little dull for my adventurous twenty-year-old spirit. Mercifully, not long after arriving I met Sue, another young English girl au pairing for a local family. We hit it off immediately and set about exploring Innsbruck by night, a far more interesting and entertaining place than you might imagine. Mind you, coming as I did from the bustling metropolis that was Laneham, an outpost of the Soviet Empire in Siberia would have looked cosmopolitan. I was so fantastically unworldly that I used to wait for Sue outside her apartment each night wondering what all the scantily clad women were doing lounging against street lamps. Sue and I would go to the nightclubs of Innsbruck until five in the morning then come home, get the kids off to school and sleep until their pick-up time.

It shouldn't have come as a huge surprise (and yet it did) when the family and I had a falling out. I discovered they had been phoning home to my parents, complaining about my extracurricular activities. I threw an impetuous strop of the kind only a twenty-year-old in a foreign country who doesn't know a soul would, and packed my bags and left. I was furious, I was homeless – and I was determined more than ever not to go home.

Not long after, I was placed with another family in the even smaller Austrian town of Thaur. It was a pretty little Austrian village, but even more isolated than Innsbruck. I read a lot and smoked a lot of cigarettes. As my language improved, I got to know many of the local Austrians around my age, including Richard. He was a few years older than me and rather conveniently lived in the apartment downstairs. He was extremely good-looking, didn't speak a word of English and took me out a lot. We found ourselves conducting one of those wonderfully wordless romantic affairs that are the exclusive preserve of young travellers everywhere.

Richard had a false leg, having lost one of his limbs in a motorcycle accident, but he was one of the best skiers I had ever seen. I liked him because he never moaned about his disability. If he wasn't skiing, he was rock climbing or dragging me to Munich for Joe Cocker, Chris de Burgh and Supertramp concerts. (It was 1982. They were the height of cool back then.) In Thaur I also met Coleen, another nanny who lived a few doors down. Coleen was from Vancouver and we became good friends. Together we would travel down to Riva del Garda in Italy's lake district, hunkered down in my tiny Renault 5. I loved Austria for its neat collection of cookie-cutter buildings and general orderliness, but the ruggedness of Italy – the unkempt houses, the comparatively impetuous and passionate people – also really appealed to me.

Once my Austrian nanny contract came to an end, I bade farewell to Thaur and Coleen and met up with my friend Alison in Geneva. We spent two or three months driving around Europe together. Through the French Alps, across what was then called Yugoslavia and down along the Adriatic coast my little Renault faithfully carried us. We had about two pennies to rub together between us, so a lot of time was spent eating bread and sleeping uncomfortably in the front seats of the Renault.

Whenever we could, we would find an out-of-the-way campsite and pitch our little two-man tent. On one occasion, we arrived at dusk, put up our tent and only discovered it was a nudist camp when we woke in the morning to the sight of countless naked middle-aged German people hunched over campfires, cooking their breakfast. We went topless as a gesture, but were too self-conscious to join the crowd.

By the time I returned to Laneham, I was twenty-one years old – and a whole lot more worldly and experienced than when I'd left. All roads in town traditionally led to the Butchers Arms. It was the pub to which everyone my age gravitated. Walking into the Butchers and ordering a gin and tonic was always, for me, when I knew I was home.

I had been back from Europe only a day or two when, one evening, I recognised a bloke I had once had a serious flirtation with. Nothing untoward, of course, because I had become a good Catholic boarding school girl, but there had always been a mutual attraction. His name was Phil, he was my age and he was an uncharacteristically good-looking farmer from the local area.

Before I had gone overseas, Phil had had a serious car accident. The passenger in the car he was driving had been killed, and Phil had ended up on life support. He lost his arm in the process. He was still the same cheeky, flirtatious guy that I remembered. As he chatted me up, I was impressed that, in the face of something that could have knocked him down, he had picked himself up and was forging on with life. Phil had been brain-damaged in the accident, which had slowed down his speech. He wasn't the same bloke I had known two years previously, but he still had the same glint in his eye – and he was still good-looking. So Phil and I started seeing each other.

It would become something of a pattern in my life to be attracted to the underdog. I had a desire to care for and rehabilitate those who are damaged. If a bird has a broken wing, I will always feel compelled to nurse it back to health.

I soon realised, however, that Phil was a slow learner. Despite having lost an arm and a friend to a wholly avoidable driving accident, he still drove like a maniac. And so I called it off.

Not long after, William came into my life. He was another local lad and had always had a crush on me. He was short, and I was shallow, so the interest had never been reciprocated. But as with many good relationships, he persisted and wore me down. We ended up going out together for about three years. Looking back, William was the guy I could – maybe should – have married. He was just a lovely man. He had his own business, and he was loyal and adoring. He was also possessed of the unique skill of falling asleep propped against the bar, a trick he used to pull quite regularly in the Butchers.

I've often wondered how different my life would have turned out had he and I married, and never more so than in the last eighteen months. But William needed someone who was going to keep him on a short lead, and I was never going to be that for him, or anyone. Besides, my time in Austria and subsequent European jaunt had expanded my horizons. I'd had a taste of how big the world was, and how far it extended beyond the Laneham village limits.

Back in those days, Australia was one of the few places to which you could get a six-month working visa. And so, for no other reasons than the suitability of its visa arrangements and the fact that it was about as far removed from Laneham as possible, in 1987 I bought a round-the-world ticket to Australia, never expecting that I would fall in love with the place.

I arrived in Brisbane on Melbourne Cup Day. I distinctly recall complete strangers passing me in the street and being so overtly friendly I wondered if we had met before. They couldn't have been more hospitable. And to a person, at the end of every conversation, no matter how short, they'd say, 'See you later.' It confused me, because I had only just met them and couldn't work out where or why they thought they were going to see me again.

I picked my way up the east coast, joining the throng of backpackers from all over the world doing likewise. There was whitewater rafting in Tully and deep-sea diving in Cairns, and a stint spent working as a cleaner in a hostel on Cape Tribulation (where the resident bush pig, Lola, would sleep under my bed).

I was meeting all these young English people who hated England and were busily working out ways to stay in Australia. One guy, Nick, had even been creative enough to scan the obituary pages of a local newspaper and assume the identity of a recently deceased local. But I liked England and wanted to go back. To my mind, I was just having a lovely holiday. It was all a great experience, but I certainly had no intention of living in Australia. The weather and the people – or at least those I had met in far north Queensland – were too extreme. The mosquitoes alone were enough to drive me south. And so, when I met Janet, I took up her invitation to head back down the coast.

Janet worked for a TV network as a set designer. Within a week or so of arriving in Melbourne, she invited me to an engagement party for someone called Leonie.

From the first time we met, Leonie and I hit it off. We had similar outlooks on life and a similar determination to wring every ounce of enjoyment out of each day. Leonie was there at the very beginning of my Australian experience and remains one of my dearest friends to this day.

At Leonie's party I also happened upon a charming bloke who I will call Jake. He worked as a stage hand on various TV shows. Almost immediately I found myself part of a group of like-minded friends enjoying life in our mid twenties. Not long after the party, I accepted Jake's invitation to join his share house, where I cleaned and cooked for him and his flatmates in return for a room.

I found a temp job, working in the office of a cemetery. I was the typist, incredibly timid – and the only female in the workplace. It was just me and the gravediggers. I wanted to do the job well, but I was scared to ask any questions. I was there for a whole week before I dared venture into the tearoom to make myself a cup of coffee, only to turn promptly on my heel at the sight of a wall plastered with Playboy posters and a toilet that looked like something out of *The Young Ones*. Despite travelling to the other side of the world and fending for myself, I was still a sheltered country girl at heart.

When I first arrived in Brisbane, I was too scared to ask people for directions, too intimidated to go into trendy boutiques and much too scared to set foot in a flash restaurant. People often think I am this tower of unshakeable confidence, when the truth is I have a lot of self-doubt and need a lot of reassurance. Over the years I've had to force myself to act confident and self-assured.

With my round-the-world ticket about to expire, I said goodbye to Jake, the housemates, Janet and the gravediggers, and set the compass for home via New Zealand and a brief stopover in Canada to see my old friend from Austria, Coleen.

Arriving back in Laneham, I was immediately struck by how small it seemed. And so I was torn. Did I tend to the itch in my feet and return to Australia? To give a nascent romance with Jake a proper go? To try my hand in a country where I had to admit I felt completely at ease? Or did I stay in my homeland and put down roots? I half-heartedly applied for university and was accepted into a polytechnic to do business studies in Cardiff.

And so I had to weigh it up: return to sunny Australia and throw my fortunes to the wind or study business school in Wales's blustery capital. In the end, the decision was not so difficult to make. And yet, in years to come, I would look back on it and recognise it as one of many 'sliding doors' moments in my life: where a decision made at a crossroads would alter the entire course of my life.

I bought an airline ticket and flew back to Melbourne.

4

A Fateful Meeting

As the plane touched down in Melbourne, following a frantic couple of months working at a motorway diner near Retford to earn the money for my fare, I was filled with a sense of trepidation. Here I was, aged twenty-five, once again on the other side of the world, having made a conscious decision to return for a relationship that was embryonic at best, in a country where I had no family or any obvious prospect of gainful employment. But, like many thousands of my country folk before me, I was ready to take a chance on this bright and shiny new land.

I moved in with Jake pretty much straight off the plane, an arrangement that would last, as it turned out, for the ensuing five years. For the first few weeks, life was idyllic. Almost immediately, I lodged an application for residency on the grounds of being in a de facto relationship. I wanted time to explore the relationship with Jake, which I felt had enormous promise, without the added pressure of feeling we needed to get married. I started working as a temp, doing secretarial work in the city, and Jake continued to work at the TV network.

Over the next few years, we were part of a group of friends who went out a lot. There always seemed to be a dinner out somewhere or a house party at someone's place. And with every occasion there was alcohol. I liked a drink as much as the next person, but always knew my limits. Jake, on the other hand, began to drink more and more heavily. And, after a while, it started to impact on our relationship. He was never violent when he drank, but he would turn to the bottle whenever life started to become a little difficult for him. It was his coping mechanism – his crutch, if you like.

At work, his boss would try to cover for him and help him. For a long time, I didn't realise the extent of his alcoholism. You just think someone is drinking a little more than usual but that the incidents are isolated. And then you come upon, as I did, empty scotch bottles in the neighbour's garden. And you start to monitor more closely the rate at which they are drinking and the occasions on which they are drunk.

One evening, we had invited people over to dinner. I was driving home from the hairdressers when I saw a man struggling to stay upright as he staggered, clearly drunk, along the footpath. It was Jake. It was the middle of the day and he was lugging a joint of beef he'd picked up at the butcher's. He'd also clearly stopped off at the pub. I was disgusted. For him to write himself off like that when we had friends coming over was the last straw for me. There had been times in our relationship when we'd had troubles because of Jake's drinking. He would invariably straighten himself out for a while before falling off the wagon again. But it had gotten to the point where I was too frightened to go to sleep next to him at night, because I worried he was going to fall asleep drunk with a cigarette and set the house on fire.

I pulled the car over, wound down the window. 'I hope you enjoy it,' I said, pointing to the joint of beef he was carrying. 'Because I won't be around to eat it with you.'

I went home, packed my bags and left.

I moved out to a friend's place in Richmond and set about starting over. It was 1992, and I was about to turn thirty. I was determined to get on with my own life, but I still cared for Jake and couldn't just abandon him. And so I would visit him regularly to see how he was doing. He was on a path of self-destruction, drinking heavily and hating himself for it. One time I found him at home nursing a huge scar on the side of his face. He had fallen in the night and cut his face on the kitchen bench. In his fridge was a bottle of Coke and a bottle of milk. On the kitchen table was an empty bottle of scotch.

He had lost his job and sold everything we owned. The rent was in arrears, and I was liable for it because my name was on the lease. He was at the point where he needed someone to take him to rehab, and so I did. From rehab, he ended up going home to live with his mum. Jake was a lovely guy but clearly damaged and susceptible to the ravages of alcoholism. It was, for me, another chapter in my already chequered romantic story.

When Jake's problem with alcohol first became apparent, I suppose I kidded myself that I was going to be his saviour. And so I was gratified when he started to make positive changes in his life, and I believed I was helping to turn him around. But ultimately you can't turn alcoholics around. Nobody can help them until and unless they want to help themselves. Jake used to beg me to stay, telling me I was the only thing keeping him from going completely over the edge – and for the longest time I allowed myself to be emotionally blackmailed like that. When you are young and in love, you make all kinds of excuses for behaviour that frankly should never be indulged. If only I had been clever enough to learn from that situation. If only that was the only instance of emotional blackmail to which I would be exposed in my life.

I decided to treat myself to a season of skiing at Mt Buller that year to clear my head and to put some space and untouched powder between Jake and me. And it was like a tonic. Weekends that winter were spent happily schussing down the slopes and letting my hair down on the après-ski scene. It was just what I needed.

Towards the end of winter I applied for a job at a recruitment company. The job was in sales and it saw me undertake a daily commute to the company's headquarters in the Melbourne CBD. As it was my first sales job, I was nervous. But there was rent to pay and a new life to forge, so I threw myself into it.

Because of the recession there was a lot of uncertainty in the sector, meaning it wasn't long before I was asked to take on extra duties and become an account manager.

It was in this capacity that I first met Greg Anderson. He was one of the members of the sales team with whom I had contact. He was good-looking, tall and extremely well-groomed. He was also charming in his way, a great bear of a man with a quick (if occasionally off-kilter) sense of humour. We hit it off straight away.

With a romantic past peppered with alcoholics, one-legged Austrian skiers and one-armed farmers, I was open to the idea of embarking on a relationship with an urban sophisticate. And while few others would ever have described Greg as urbane or sophisticated, to my country-girl eyes he presented as eminently more corporate and together than my previous boyfriends. He wore a suit, and he appeared – to all intents and purposes – to have a job about which he was serious. He had, at least at first glance, what might be referred to in the classics as 'prospects'.

I bumped into him one day when we were both cold-calling a client and he asked me if I wanted to go for a drink. I did. But instead of meeting at a bar for the customary first date, I invited Greg to join me for a drive out to the Dandenong Ranges where I had only recently put a down payment on a house. And so we set off, driving through the mountains to the small community of Belgrave on Melbourne's outskirts, taking in the tiny cottage on acreage that I had just committed to. It was a day in the country in the company of a man who was clearly intent on impressing me. It was very pleasant.

Greg was charming. It was clear he could hold a conversation, and he managed to put me completely at ease. He told me he had been married, but that the marriage hadn't worked out and he was now estranged from his ex-wife. He gave the distinct impression that the situation had been beyond his control. He also told me he had a son but was estranged from him too. I felt sorry for him.

I was always so nervous whenever I went on a first date with someone. I had a bad habit of drinking more than I should, to ease the nerves. And so, midway through the drive back home to Richmond, I was gripped by an overwhelming desire to go to the toilet. We finally found a place to pull over so that I could whip inside and use the facilities. But I got caught short, returning sheepishly to the car. I spent the remainder of the trip back to Richmond with this man I barely knew – a man I worked with, no less – panicking about how I was going to exit the car without him seeing I had wet myself.

Upon arriving home, I somehow stage-managed it so that he would enter the house in front of me. As I left him in the living room, chatting to my flatmate, I snuck into the bathroom. That would have been the end of it were it not for the fact that I needed to change my trousers quite urgently – and between the bathroom and my bedroom rather inconveniently lay the living room. So, in a scene reminiscent of the worst sitcom, I crept out of the bathroom, around to the back of the house and back up the side of the house, where I got down on my hands and knees and crawled under the living room window to access my bedroom – then sauntered into the living room as if nothing had happened. I was mortified, but Greg didn't say a word.

A week later he asked me to go for a coffee with him. We sat down over flat whites and started chatting about nothing in particular until, at a certain point, he said, 'So, how long have you been incontinent?' That was the thing about Greg. He could be charming and funny. And in the next breath, he could be rude or inappropriate.

For instance, he arrived on our first date with a bunch of flowers and made certain I knew he was really keen on me. But then he would go for days or even a week without contacting me. After the emotionally draining experience of Jake, and after feeling so suffocated by that relationship, I think I quite liked the fact that Greg was occasionally aloof: that he appeared to be the master of his own domain and slave to none.

What was less appealing was his habit of saying things in social situations that were either provocative or wildly inappropriate. I remember one instance where we were having drinks with a friend of mine and, out of nowhere, in the middle of our conversation he pointed to my friend's legs and said, 'How long have you had those veins on your legs?'

I invited him to my thirtieth birthday party to introduce him to all my friends. And at first, they were all excited for me, impressed at the handsome specimen I had landed. But as the night wore on, almost to a person my friends took me aside and told me Greg was a dickhead who needed to be dumped immediately. Apparently, after making such a good first impression, he had proceeded to deeply offend every person in the party, making remarks that were either deliberately provocative or just plain rude.

In retrospect, it should have been grounds for dumping him. But I didn't, not least because we were never technically going out with one another. We would see each other sporadically, but I was never really sure where I stood with Greg – and I was even less sure when I learned that, while he was seeing me, he had also made passes at other women at our office.

As I write these things, I see them in black and white, and I see how dreadful they look when they are committed to paper but, at the time, in the circumstances, I found myself creating excuses for Greg's bad behaviour. Besides, I had just come out of a bruising five-year relationship and wasn't keen to jump straight back into another one. I decided to enjoy whatever attention Greg showered me with.

All of which would have been fine were it not for the fact that Greg soon after asked me outright to be his girlfriend. And the inference was very much that we be exclusive. We were, he had decided, at some sort of a crossroads, and I needed to decide whether I was interested in a relationship with him. And so I decided, on balance, yes, I was sufficiently flattered and sufficiently interested to give it a go. Again, sliding doors.

The following weekend, I had a trip planned to Sorrento with a girlfriend who Greg had decided he didn't like, and he made sure I was aware of his displeasure. But I wasn't about to let anyone tell me who I could or couldn't spend time with, and so I went. When I returned, he was really off-hand with me, acting aloof and indifferent. I challenged him, saying, 'Either you're being like this because you're seeing someone else or you don't want to see me anymore.'

He promptly replied that he was seeing someone else, alluding to the fact that she was some sort of sex goddess. I was hurt, because he'd lashed out and wounded me in the one part of my life he knew I was especially sensitive.

I don't know if it was because I had lost my mum at six and never really had a role model for relations with members of the opposite sex, but I had never been totally at ease – or especially confident – about sex. I remember being fourteen years old and having boys wanting to kiss me or hold my hand, and I always pushed them away. My nickname in the village among boys of a certain age was 'untouchable'. In that sense, my being sent to boarding school was quite a relief, because I didn't have to deal with any of that stuff.

And so when Greg sought to hurt me with that comment – the truth of which was anyone's guess – I thought to myself, he can go and get stuffed. I had spent all those years in a small village dealing with abandonment and rejection issues, always being especially careful of giving too much of myself away for fear of being rebuffed, and here was Greg repaying the trust I had begun to place in him by treating me like dirt.

Looking back now, it was the first really obvious sign of his need for power and control in a relationship – two qualities that would go on to become a hallmark of all our interactions. But, of course, I didn't recognise it at the time.

5

Isolation

Later in 1992 I moved into my new place in Belgrave, out to the east of Melbourne. It's a beautiful part of the world – famous as the home of the Puffing Billy steam engine. Perched on the edge of the Dandenong Ranges National Park, it's green and covered in bushland. It was, I had decided, the perfect bolthole for a girl from the country: close enough to commute to work in the CBD and just far enough away to feel like I was out in the country.

My house was a little run-down shack of a place – no more than a wooden cottage in the hills. At the time, I was just excited at how much land I was able to purchase for the same amount it would have cost to purchase a shoebox in Richmond, which had been my alternative option. Nottinghamshire, from whence I had come, is really flat and mostly featureless. The Dandenongs by comparison are undulating and covered in the most gloriously unkempt bushland and forest.

But from the moment I moved in I was miserable. I soon came to hate the house and I started to feel increasingly lonely. I now lived a long way from my friends, and there were no close neighbours.

The financial pressure of the mortgage, combined with an increasingly precarious work environment, made me anxious as I had never been before. I had a job I was struggling to master and a work environment that was not particularly nurturing. I would return to my shack at night, close the door against the winter cold and think about how much I missed my family.

I became very distressed by the number of people being summarily dismissed at work and was convinced I was on the chopping block, so I worked even harder. Selling a service, as it turns out, is really difficult. Having to cold-call companies that have no desire to speak to you can be soul-destroying. I was way outside my comfort zone. Sales, I have since come to understand, is not a great profession for someone who has issues with rejection. I nevertheless stuck it out at the recruitment company for almost three years. Those of us who survived – and I use that word deliberately – developed a kind of 'in the trenches' mentality, but none of us left there without scars.

I remember going to someone's leaving lunch and feeling so anxious I couldn't sit through the meal. A friend who knew me well suggested I go see a doctor, who promptly informed me the three most common triggers for stress and anxiety are money worries, men trouble and job insecurity. I had hit the trifecta.

Meanwhile out at Belgrave, I had embarked upon a pet-accumulation spree in an effort to introduce some companions into my life. And so the household grew with the acquisition of Gordon the Brittany spaniel, Lola the springer spaniel and two cats, William and Henry. Their ranks were soon bolstered by the arrival of a goat called Gilbert and a sheep called Rodney. They all did their darnedest to keep me company, but I was still too young to become a confirmed cat spinster, so I took in a lodger to help with rent and provide a bit of human company. Mark was the brother of one of my neighbours, a really nice bloke who liked to keep to himself. We became good friends.

It was around this time that Greg started making impromptu house calls. Since the time he'd hurt me, I had never allowed things between us to escalate beyond a vague friendship. He had gotten the sack months earlier, because he was consistently missing sales targets, though, if you asked him, he was the greatest salesman in the world and solely responsible for landing the biggest deal in the company. He was deluded like that.

The house calls started on weekends. He would appear unannounced and offer to help out in the yard – taking to the undergrowth with the whipper-snipper, moving logs, you name it. I was wary but happy to see a familiar face. And being on my own with a vast yard and expanding menagerie to manage, I was grateful for the extra set of helping hands. On the odd Saturday night, Greg would stay over, always sleeping in the spare room. He would often joke to Mark and me what a perfect couple we made, and loudly predict that we would end up together. It was all very jocular, and to my mind, at least, spoke to the possibility of Greg and I having a perfectly normal platonic friendship. I think he genuinely liked me but, in retrospect, part of his attraction to me lay in the fact that he saw me as vulnerable and easy to manipulate.

One evening I got a phone call from Greg saying he had to move out of his house and could he stay with me. I felt sorry for him and was so lonely, I said yes. And so, for what would be the first of many times, Greg moved in.

Greg had an arrogance about him that I found offensive. He took a keen interest in alternative medicine and there were always pots of Chinese herbs bubbling away on the stove, stinking the house out. I started to notice the books he was reading – most of them about Eastern philosophy and religion. I'm not sure that he ever read a complete book. He would read a chapter here and a chapter there and cherry-pick from each of them the bits he liked the sound of.

That first time he stayed at my place for about ten months. As time went by, we found ourselves in a sort of relationship. He was quite removed and didn't have a lot of friends. He would have a job for a few weeks here and there, but they never lasted. He never seem fazed when he lost a job, and was always ready to blame the company or a colleague rather than admit any shortcomings of his own. Greg was always good at paying bills and making a financial contribution to the running of the household. Despite his frequently stated conviction that Mark and I were a match made in heaven, Greg and I were intimate on and off. It was always random, and never seemed especially meaningful for either of us.

I began to see a pattern emerge in our relationship (if indeed you could have called it that). If he thought I wasn't interested in him, he made an effort to engage with me. If I showed interest in him, he would pull back and become aloof.

We kept separate bedrooms, and I made a conscious effort to keep things between us as casual as possible. It was only after a trip back to England later that year that I realised how much living with Greg was dragging me down.

I had left Greg with the use of my car and care of the animals. Back in England, I spent a solid few weeks in the company of my younger brother James, visiting a succession of local pubs and essentially letting my hair down. The pressure of work, the mortgage, the uncertainty around my relationship with Greg – it had all built up without my realising. And back in the bosom of my family, I felt finally able to let go. It also afforded me some much-needed perspective. I accepted that I needed to make changes in my life, and the two things I needed to do most urgently were to get out of the recruitment company and get rid of Greg.

I returned to Australia with a sense of resolve. I quit my job and soon after found a new gig with a major computer company – one that would prove to be both challenging and rewarding.

Getting rid of Greg was not so straightforward. He had become very comfortable at my house, driving my car and using all my things. He was not disposed to being turfed out, and he made his feelings clear. He had developed a sense of entitlement that was hard to crack – no matter how many hints I dropped about him needing to find somewhere else to live. I remember Mark saying, 'He's dragging you down, Rosie. You came back from England in a really good place, but with every day that passes and he's still here, he's eroding your confidence.' Mark was right, but the thing about being undermined on an almost daily basis is that when finally you find the resolve to do something about it, you don't have the confidence to see it through.

One evening, a mutual friend of Greg's and mine came to visit me. Greg was out for the night. She listened to me talk about Greg and how I felt confused and somehow at fault for creating my situation. And she said, 'Rosie, this is not your fault. You're not to blame. I have to tell you something. Greg tried to rape me in my house. I had to fight him off. I don't want you to tell anyone. It's important, though, that you know.'

I was horrified. My friend was a confident, assertive woman and he had tried to sexually assault her. And here she was embarrassed to report the attack for fear of being blamed for having somehow incited it. Whatever had happened on that night, she said, she ended up having to talk Greg down. Something had seemed to switch in his personality and she realised she didn't really know who this person was or what he was capable of.

Suddenly Greg's behaviour over the previous ten months was cast in a new and sinister light. Sex between us – on the odd occasions it had occurred – had always been confusing. His behaviour towards me sexually was nothing short of deviant. In many instances I would wake up in the middle of the night and find him having sex with me, having let himself into my room and bed. I would be too shocked to do or say anything, and he would gratify himself and then leave. For reasons I still don't really understand today, I never considered it rape. I think I was just so confused by him and this ill-defined relationship we had. He didn't ostensibly force me to have sex with him, but it was all just so furtive and abnormal.

Talking to my friend that night, something in me snapped and I thought, you bastard! I was furious with him – and with myself. It made me realise the emotional and physical abuse to which he had been subjecting me, and I resolved to cut him out of my life.

Later that evening, Greg tried to come into my bedroom. I told him to fuck off and make plans to leave my house immediately. 'If you don't leave,' I told him, 'I will be calling the police to have you removed.'

He sensed that something had shifted in me and backed off instinctively.

That weekend I went away with friends for a couple of days. I returned to find Greg gone. He had taken everything he owned and only left behind two gifts I had given him: a mug and a souvenir from England.

With Greg excised from my life, I felt a huge sense of relief – a lightness. I began kicking goals on the work front and my reputation for excellence grew. Eventually, I moved to another computer company into what would become the best job I have ever had. As a business development representative, I looked after major channels, including Harvey Norman and Myer. The job required me to travel extensively and, in turn, meant the sense of isolation I felt living at Belgrave was significantly reduced. I was happily single and in something of a purple patch.

When I was offered a promotion, I was ecstatic. When it became clear the new job would be based in Sydney, though, I was hesitant. It was 1995 and I had just spent the better part of the last decade getting myself established in Melbourne. All my friends were there, my home, my network. But it was an opportunity too good to refuse, and so I packed up my life, sold my property in Belgrave, and headed north.

At first, the bright lights of Sydney were intoxicating. I loved the harbour city – I loved its energy and I loved the opportunity to explore a brand-new town. The dogs and I set ourselves up in Castle Hill, on the Sydney's north-western outskirts. My new workplace was in Lane Cove. True to Sydney form, I took up daily exercise with a vengeance, waking every morning at five-thirty with the dogs.

The new job – my first in a management position – was demanding. It was not uncommon to turn in fourteen-hour days, leaving the office sometimes at 10 pm. The office environment was relentlessly competitive – which could have been good were it not for the fact it was a bit of a boys' club and I was the only woman. The discrimination was never overt. It was made up of simple things, such as all the male managers – my colleagues – going for lunches and forgetting to invite me, or playing golf together and never thinking to include me. I see it now for the workplace discrimination it was but, at the time, it dented the self-confidence of a girl who had never really dealt with her rejection and abandonment issues.

Nevertheless, I threw myself into my job, determined to prove my worth. But it was all to no end. The division I was in was earmarked for restructuring and I was one of the first to be retrenched. I had given my heart and soul to that job only to be escorted from the premises with a box full of personal effects.

I went to bed for three days and didn't get up. I had given everything to that job to the exclusion of all else in my life. I had moved to Sydney, left behind friends and lived and breathed the role. I had allowed my sense of self-worth to be defined by the job, and now I didn't have it anymore. I felt desolate and so very alone. I understood for the first time why people commit suicide. I thought I was a failure.

I picked myself up and, a month or so later, I got a great new job working for another computer company. My self-esteem and confidence returned.

But eventually a turning point came when I returned to Melbourne one weekend for Leonie's wedding. There, in one room of nuptial-inspired bonhomie, was everything I had been missing in Sydney. These were my friends and I realised how much I needed to be near them.

I made a checklist of the pros and cons of another move. Having sold my Belgrave property when I moved north, I had prevaricated and hadn't invested the money straight into a property in Sydney. Now the market had moved on and I'd missed the boat. The only place I could afford to buy was on the Central Coast, more than an hour's drive north of Sydney. A quick scout of the Melbourne market showed me there were homes available, in my price range, within striking distance of all my friends. In all my time in Sydney I had never really put down roots. I decided to head back south.

6

Turning Point

During my online real-estate fossicking while still living in Sydney, I had come across a property in Menzies Creek, a tiny township in the Dandenong region not far from where I had previously lived in Belgrave. I asked my former Belgrave neighbours to give it the once-over, and they came back with generally positive reviews. I bought it, sight unseen.

When I arrived to see it for myself a few weeks later, it was ten-thirty at night. I loved the place. It was essentially a log cabin with pine-panelled interiors. I thought it was rustic and charming, and a perfect antidote to my three years of city living in Sydney. I sat in the empty living room, opened a bottle of wine and had a toast to whatever lay ahead with my old neighbour, Carrie, and friend Chris, who had brought my furniture from Sydney. The next morning, I returned to see it for the first time in daylight and it was even more spectacular. Nestled in the midst of dense eucalypt forest, with ferns and bracken in the thick undergrowth, it was rugged and private. My own little bush hideaway in the mountains.

Not long after my return to Melbourne, I landed a job with a trade marketing company in St Kilda. The commute – some 50 kilometres each way – was manageable at first, but soon became tiresome. The more hours I spent at work or on my commute, the fewer hours I had to maintain my house and property. So I left my job for a role as a sales representative with a telecommunications company, which, I figured, would at least cut out the daily commute to an office.

The decision to move back to Melbourne had been motivated by a desire to be back in the circle of friends I had known for over a decade. What I hadn't taken into account was the fact that, during the three years I had been in Sydney, most of them had married and had children. I had come back to rejoin the tight-knit Melbourne crew that had once nurtured me, but that crew no longer existed. Or if it did, its members were all busy changing nappies.

Out of the blue one day, a friend called me. 'You'll never guess who I just bumped into in the city,' she said.

'Greg Anderson?' I guessed, without knowing why.

'Yes! How did you guess?' she replied. 'And he asked me all about you. Whether you were married, whether you had children.'

Almost eight years had passed since I'd seen Greg and we'd had no contact at all in that time. I was bemused that he would ask after me. What would he look like? Would he have met someone and married like everyone else? Was he still the arrogant tosser I had thrown from my house all those years ago?

The intense anger I had felt towards him had faded over the last eight years, and I was intrigued to catch up and see him. What harm could it do to meet for coffee? So I called Greg and we organised to meet in the city. Coming back to Melbourne had given me the perspective necessary to reflect on my time in Sydney, and I felt good going in to meet Greg, thinking about how I'd lived independently and built on my career up there, despite the way things had ended.

I fronted up to the café and breezed in. Greg had less hair and his face had a few more lines but he was still the tall, imposing figure he had always been. He was the Greg I remembered, but not quite the same.

When I look back now, knowing what I do, our reunion happened around the time Greg was living with the Hare Krishnas in St Kilda. He was, for all intents and purposes, homeless and without a job. He tried to give me the impression he was on a spiritual path. He mentioned also having spent time exploring the Mormon faith and told me he was involved with a Russian Orthodox monastery near the NSW–Victoria border. It all sounded a bit odd. But he'd always been so quirky, so borderline unusual, that I just took it at face value and didn't think too much about it.

Greg told me he hadn't slept with another woman since me. And even though I had left our relationship – such as it was – utterly confused about the sexual side of it, I was nevertheless flattered by this. One of the tenets of his spiritual quest, he would later tell me, was to wean himself off a need for sexual contact with women. In retrospect, who knows whether there was any truth to it.

We talked about old times, and laughed about shared memories. Here he was, calling me McBatty – his nickname for me – again. It felt familiar and, in spite of my better judgement, it felt good. I remembered how he would pick me up and spin me around, and it was a good memory. We reminisced about the work we had done together on my property in Belgrave.

So when he expressed an interest in seeing my new home in Menzies Creek, I invited him back to see it. That afternoon we chopped wood together and made a lovely fire. He seemed to have changed for the better, and appeared to have genuinely realised how much he'd thought about me during the past eight years. I was flattered and intrigued.

And so began a pattern of him reclaiming a place for himself in my life. Just as before, we were never really 'going out' in any conventional sense, but he became once again a kind of fixture in my life. He would show up at my place most weekends, and he did a lot of work on the property, clearing brambles, chopping fallen trees, laying sleepers to create a path. He was, it must be said, really good to me in this way.

One weekend, we worked together restoring and repainting an old garden bench that we'd picked up from someone's throw-out pile. It was a rickety old thing, but it seemed to suit the ramshackle nature of the house – not to mention the ill-defined, slightly odd, but nevertheless vaguely comfortable relationship that was developing between Greg and me.

My property was on a hill, and sometimes I'd look down and see him working on my garden. He was going bald and looked like your average mature middle-aged man. But he still appeared strong and I remember regarding him with a degree of fondness. I was lonely, but now I had someone to help build something at the property. I felt that there was a connection between us.

Sometimes Greg would stay overnight, and sometimes he would go back to where he was living in St Kilda. I even went so far as to buy him a pair of slippers to wear on the nights we would sit in front of the fire, watching the wood we had chopped slowly burn to cinders. There was a sense of rekindling a relationship that hadn't worked out before, of two kindred spirits who had gotten to a more mature point in their respective lives.

I was thirty-nine years old and in a period of reassessing my life. I didn't have the same desire and drive to get ahead at work. I'd had years of being all-consumed by my job, but I had lost the passion for that. I remember watching the film *High Fidelity*, with John Cusack, around that time and really relating to it. It was about a guy about to hit forty taking stock of his life and realising everything he had held up as important ten years previously really didn't matter in the grand scheme.

And so, in many respects, the reappearance of Greg in my life was just a matter of timing. I hadn't had a relationship for years. Now I wondered whether I should go back on the Pill, even though I didn't feel comfortable taking it. But I didn't want to fall pregnant, either.

When I told Greg this, he protested. 'I'm not having sex with you if you're on the Pill,' he said. 'It's not good for you.' Greg was in the midst of his alternative medicine phase. He was virulently anti-vaccination and thought the Pill – like many modern medicines – was a kind of poison.

Now that I think about it, the fact he was purporting to care about my health, when he had never shown any interest in my welfare before, should have been a red flag.

I was still confused about sex with him, as I had always been. He seemed to put himself on this spiritual pedestal. He had a firm belief that he was spiritually superior – not just to me, but to everyone around him. He truly felt he had complete control over his sexual desire, to the point where, if we did have sex – which happened infrequently – he would control whether or not he came. I often felt rejected because, for the most part, he didn't want to have sex with me.

I can now see that, for him, sex like everything else was about power and control. And on the odd occasions we did have sex, there was never any suggestion of him satisfying my needs. Once he had gratified himself, that was it. I remember once, after we'd had sex, indicating to him that perhaps I would like to be sexually gratified too. 'You had your chance,' he said.

One week, Greg took himself off to Queensland on a spiritual retreat of some kind. When he returned, it was like he was a changed man. He was invigorated in a way I hadn't seen him for a long time. He was affectionate and attentive, and suddenly very interested in being intimate and wanting to spend a lot of time in the bedroom. I was only too happy to have this normal, loving man in my life – and I thought that whatever issues he'd had he must have resolved. For a day or two, there was a lot of sexual activity between us – a renewed affection, and what I foolishly believed might even have been a new beginning.

I can pinpoint the day that Luke was conceived. And though Greg would never have admitted it, I am now convinced he contrived the whole thing. Years later, he would tell me how he knew from the first time he saw me that I would make an excellent mother for his child.

I don't mean to say that, from the moment he met me all those years previously, he plotted to impregnate me so I could produce an heir for him, but, looking back, I think his conceiving a baby with me was no accident. The insistence on me not using contraception, the sudden change in mood the weekend he returned from Queensland, the attentiveness, the affection: it was all part of him grooming me for the express purpose of making me fall pregnant with his baby. And, of course, a part of me wanted to be pregnant too. I was almost forty and thought that if it didn't happen now, maybe it would never happen.

I remember in the following weeks becoming quite sure I was pregnant and feeling uneasy at the prospect. Following a couple of weeks of behaving like a normal human being, Greg had since returned to his hot-headed, unpredictable self. He affected an arrogance and treated me with low-level contempt, reminding me of all the reasons I had pushed him away in the first place.

With a certain amount of trepidation, I bought a home pregnancy test. When it confirmed I was pregnant, I felt mixed emotions. I was carrying Greg's child and things were weird between us, and while I was pretty certain I wanted a child, I was absolutely certain I didn't want to co-parent a child with Greg.

And so I started to weigh up my options. I could terminate the pregnancy – and give up what might be my only chance of being a mother. Or go through with it and endure a future in which Greg would always play a significant role. I didn't know what to do. I went to see Jan to ask her advice. Her son was also visiting and he asked me, 'Rosie, what did you feel when you found out you were pregnant?' I thought about it, and I eventually replied I would have been disappointed if the pregnancy test had come back negative. It made me realise that, above all else, I did want a child.

I spoke to my friends and told them about my misgivings, but almost to a person they advised me that, had I not fallen pregnant like this, I would never have had a child. Besides, they said, Greg might technically be the father, but there was nothing stopping me from raising the baby on my own.

I remember telling Leonie – who had never liked Greg. She knew me better than anyone and I valued her opinion. I told her I had never wanted a child up until this point, because I was just so scared that what you love the most in life, you ultimately lose. My life up to that point, I said, had been about avoiding putting myself in a situation where I loved something so much it would break me if I were to lose it. I had spent thirty-odd years protecting myself from those deep-seated feelings of abandonment and rejection. It was why I had never been married, why I had only ever been in self-destructive relationships and why, up until now, I hadn't had children. For me, the fear of having a child and then losing it was greater than any desire to become a mother.

'But Rosie,' she replied, 'it's better to have lost in love than never to have loved at all.' This was probably my one and only chance to know motherhood, Leonie said, and the life-affirming, transformative experience it was. I finally decided she was probably right.

And so, when the time was right, I broke the news to Greg. He could not have been more pleased. It seemed to trigger in him a rush of paternal instinct, and – much to my concern – he set about trying to reinsert himself more permanently in my life. He seemed to want to nest, to prepare the house, to shepherd me through the pregnancy.

I had pretty much decided that I was going to do this on my own. And yet Greg *was* the father. Shouldn't he perhaps have some involvement in the pregnancy and rearing of our child?

However, just as I was starting to wonder if there might be some kind of a mutual arrangement between Greg and me, warning signs once again emerged. The first was when we went to a garden centre together in Emerald. Everything was great, we were wandering around looking at plants to buy for my property when, all of a sudden, he turned. It was as if someone had flicked a switch – his mood darkened and suddenly he seemed to be on edge. As we walked back to the car, he started ranting about 'all these fat people everywhere' and how disgusting he found them, saying nasty things about how dirty they made him feel and how their presence was offensive to him.

As we were driving home in the car, I challenged him about it. I told him to stop being so judgemental and asked why on earth it should be of any concern to him. All of a sudden he started shouting at the top of his voice. He wasn't necessarily shouting at me – it was just irrational screaming, a violent outburst of anger. I went really quiet, tried to focus on the road ahead and burst into tears. I was shocked. Who was this man? I couldn't understand why he had flipped so suddenly – and over something so seemingly inconsequential. I sat there sobbing quietly as I drove.

After a while, he reached out, put his arm around me and apologised.

Afterwards, I tried to analyse it. Why, just as suddenly as he had become angry and irrational, had he returned to his usual rational self? But then life returned to normal, and soon I began to question whether I had remembered it properly – or if it had happened at all. But, somewhere deep inside, my doubt began to fester. A question began to take shape: how well did I really know this person?

Weeks later, I took part in a protest march in the city with a friend. Greg came to collect me afterwards. In the car on the way home, he turned to me, apropos of nothing, and said: 'Now then, McBatty, should we get married?'

I thought he must be joking and just laughed in response. I was dumbstruck but still not entirely sure he was serious. 'Don't be ridiculous,' was all I could manage in reply. We had only just rekindled our relationship, we had no security, he didn't have a job – and I was starting to have worrying doubts about his behaviour and state of mind. And, besides, if he had been serious about proposing marriage, surely he would have had a ring and gone in for something a little more romantic than throwing the question at me as we drove home along the Dandenong Road. So I laughed it off and changed the subject.

I don't recall Greg being especially surprised by my answer or in any way disappointed. Later, however, I would learn he had been deeply wounded by my rejection, and it was something he would carry with him for a long time. During an access visit with Luke ten years later, he told Luke that I had laughed at him when he asked me to marry him. And I remember Luke berating me afterwards, saying how mean it was of me to react to his dad's marriage proposal in that way. But at the time, and in context, it was the only feasible reaction.

The morning of 11 September 2001 was something of a benchmark in our relationship, at least from my point of view. A friend phoned me in the middle of the night and told me to turn on the television. I watched, horrified, as the second of the World Trade Center towers came crumbling down in New York.

I yelled at Greg to get out of bed and come and watch. But he ignored me, so I just sat alone in the dark watching the horror unfurl. Greg got up to get a glass of water at some point and saw me in front of the television, clearly upset, and he said, 'What the fuck are you doing? Get to bed.'

I just figured he hadn't grasped what was going on. An hour or two later, as I went to bed, exhausted and upset at what I had just seen, I said to him, 'Do you have any idea what's just happened?'

'I don't give a fuck,' he said. 'Just go to sleep. The Americans had it coming to them.'

'But that was someone's mother, brother, father, sister,' I replied. 'And all they did was go to work. They didn't deserve that.'

He had no empathy or compassion for the victims. I went to work that day thinking, What are you? How could you not care?

When I got home, he'd obviously registered how upset I was – and no doubt had taken cues from a day's worth of news reports and seeing the world around him in a state of shock and mourning – so he made a few token comments about how awful it all was. But he didn't mean it. He didn't feel a thing. Not a single thing.

And so I started to consciously distance myself from him. Knowing that, with Greg, knowledge was power and power meant control, I learned to drip-feed him information about my life. I was careful not to give too much away. He always wanted to know exactly how much money I was earning, and I made a point of remaining vague about it. Any information he gleaned about me, he would invariably use against me. It was better, I decided, to limit my exposure and vulnerability.

Another red flag was raised not long after when Karena came to visit. Years previously, I had taken part in the Big Brother, Big Sister mentoring program, signing up to mentor a young person from a disadvantaged background. I had been paired with Karena. She was a lovely girl, sweet and good-natured, but deeply scarred after having been abandoned by her mother when she was only thirteen years old. When her mum got a new boyfriend, she suddenly didn't have room in her life for Karena anymore, so she left her in the care of the local youth centre. By the time Karena came into my life, she had been through several foster homes, none of them very harmonious. For the ten years we had known each other, I had been one of the few constants in a life otherwise filled with uncertainty. I was about as close to her as anyone had ever been.

Karena had made her way to Melbourne and found accommodation in a boarding house, but it was an awful place, so she asked if she could stay with me for a while. I was more than happy to have her.

But the first night, over dinner, Karena was being her cheeky, bubbly self when, out of the blue, Greg's mood darkened and he threw a couple of books at her across the dinner table, muttering under his breath. He seemed to have taken an instant, irrational dislike to her for reasons I couldn't fathom. The dislike turned to distrust, and a few days later he told me he was convinced that Karena was looking through his stuff when we weren't at home. He had these paranoid delusions that she was spying on him.

One morning Karena and I went to the supermarket. As we pulled into the driveway at home, Greg came running out to the car and accused Karena of having locked him out of the house. He was really aggressive, right up in her face, shouting abuse.

I intervened, trying to calm the situation. I didn't like the way he was talking to Karena and told him so in no uncertain terms. I went inside to take a bath, whereupon Greg barged into the bathroom and started arguing with me about Karena, smacking the wall in frustration. I told him to get out, but when I emerged from the bathroom minutes later Greg was once again laying into Karena, accusing her of all manner of ridiculous things. I told him he had to leave.

Somehow, I managed to coax him into my car so I could drive him to the railway station. He spent the whole journey smacking the dashboard, repeating over and over, 'Why am I the one who has to leave? Why not her?' To Greg's way of thinking, I had chosen Karena over him, and he wasn't happy about it. Since I had shared with him the news of my pregnancy, he had started to construct a happy family fantasy – an expectation that, despite all of his odd behaviour and our clearly dysfunctional relationship, we were somehow going to be the perfect family unit.

The following day he came back to collect his things. I was at work, but Karena was at home. She stayed in her bedroom, so as not to cross paths with Greg. When I returned that night, she told me how he had come into the house and cut up the slippers I had given him as a present. Then he had gone out into the garden, taken an axe and smashed up the garden bench we had restored together. It was now just a pile of tinder, a terrifying symbol of his strength and anger.

Karena stayed with me for a couple more weeks, until she had to go into hospital. Unbeknown to me, she had become addicted to prescription medicines. I only realised after she had left that every aspirin in my house had disappeared.

Some weeks later, Karena left hospital and found a small house in Belgrave. She agreed to go to Narcotics Anonymous, and I offered to accompany her. She was determined to turn her life around – or at least that's how it appeared from the outside.

Christmas came around and I invited Karena to join me and my cousin, who was visiting from the UK, for Christmas lunch. But as midday came and went with no sign of her, I began to worry. She had been unreliable, and so I assumed she'd simply decided at the last minute that she couldn't be bothered and hadn't thought to call. She wasn't answering her phone, and so I told my cousin to start cooking lunch without me while I went to check on her. I got to her house and saw her cat sitting in the front window. I knocked on the door and received no reply. I went around to her bedroom window and smelled something bad. My stomach sank. I had a bad feeling.

I got on the phone to my friends Carri and David, who also knew Karena. They came straight over. The cat inside the window seemed agitated, desperate to get out or for us to get in. We called the police, who arrived soon after and climbed into Karena's apartment through the roof. They found her decomposing body in the bedroom. She had been there for five days – dead from a combination of prescription drugs. She was twenty-three years old.

The police let us into the house, not saying what they had found. The smell was overwhelming. At first, I thought it was the kitty litter tray, but a police officer sat us down and broke the news. As we sat there, trying to take it all in, Karena's mobile phone started ringing. It was her mother, phoning to wish her daughter Merry Christmas. I told her Karena was dead and she started screaming hysterically. In a state of shock myself, all I remember thinking was, my cousin has come here on holiday and I have left her at my home cooking Christmas lunch.

The police wanted someone to identify the body, and I thought, I cannot desert her now. So the practical side of me kicked in and I walked into the bedroom. In the end, when something bad like that is happening, you don't want pussyfooting around and mealy-mouthed language. You don't want people sugar-coating things. You just want facts, so you can make decisions. If she was dead, I needed to see it, identify the body and get on with dealing with the consequences.

I went back home, deeply shaken. But I didn't want to have the day ruined for my cousin. Later that evening, we went to a friend's house for Christmas dinner. We were all really sad and in shock, but it was Christmas day and I was determined to maintain the plans we'd made.

I spent the next couple of days phoning all the people in Karena's address book to break the news to them. I spent a lot of time on the phone with her mum, who, despite her obvious shortcomings as a mother, was nevertheless devastated by the death of her child. It was not my place to judge her mother. I had known Karena for ten years and she had loved her mum, even if she had never recovered from being rejected by her.

Between Karena's death and her funeral, I travelled to Sydney with my cousin and we did the Harbour Bridge climb. My pregnancy was starting to show, but it hadn't slowed me down. And I had never been one for histrionics. My template in life when confronted with tragedy had been to push down the sadness, draw on my reserves of country English stoicism and do what must be done. It didn't mean I wasn't devastated at my loss or profoundly sad for the waste of a young life. It simply meant I was going to mourn Karena's death in my own, private way. In the meantime, I would honour my obligations to a cousin who had travelled all the way from the UK to visit me. So I put my head down and got on with it.

At the funeral, I was determined to be the peace broker between Karena's mother and those, including youth workers and foster carers, who had taken in Karena and had nothing but contempt for her mum. I stood in the funeral parlour, staring at the coffin and feeling an overwhelming desire to howl: to scream at the gods at the senselessness of it all. But I held it in. I had a pregnancy to concentrate on and a baby on the way.

7

In a boarding house in Frankston South, 16 kilometres from Tyabb, Greg is in his room, packing almost all of his belongings into a black backpack. Leaving behind the sparsely furnished room that had been his temporary home, he visits the kitchen of his share house and places a large, black-handled knife into his bag. He sets off, bound for Tyabb. It's a journey he has made many times before. The route, the modes of transport, the semi-rural Mornington Peninsula landscape through which he travels that afternoon are all familiar to him. He would have boarded the Frankston-Tyabb bus shuttle, paid his fare and taken a seat. There would have been nothing unusual about his appearance. Just a man with a backpack going about his business on a summer's day in Frankston.

Sometime around 2.30 pm, the bus would have dropped Greg near the train station in Tyabb. He would have been oblivious to the locals scurrying about their business – heading off to collect children from school, preparing to drop them at after-school sporting activities, popping in to the local IGA for last-minute dinner supplies.

He would have walked past the tiny strip of shops that serves as Tyabb's town centre – past the pizza restaurant, past the little cafe.

His destination is little more than a half a kilometre away: Bunguyan Reserve, home of the Tyabb Cricket Club and the Tyabb Yabbies junior AFL club.

He would have arrived at the oval long before any of the parents or children started to trickle in for cricket practice. He may have taken shelter from the afternoon sun under the aluiminum awning of the cricket club; he may have waited in the shade of the trees that encircle the oval. It's the second-last training session for the year. Only Greg knows what he is thinking. Only Greg can attest to his state of mind that afternoon.

I choose not to think about him, full stop. I choose not to reflect on what went through his mind when he saw my car pull up, when he saw Luke bundle out of the car and hurry over to his team to join in the training. Was it excitement at seeing his son? Was it a feeling of foreboding, knowing what he was about to do? He was Luke's father. No one loved Luke more than Greg or I did. What does a father think about in the hour leading up to murdering his own son?

8

A New Life

I thoroughly enjoyed being pregnant. There is a shine and radiance to a pregnant woman that everyone seems to notice and revel in. And I loved the attention. Then there's the not insignificant excitement of beginning to plan for a new life.

I felt really healthy. I had next to no morning sickness, ate a lot and put on weight. I was careful to exercise as much as possible, but as I lived by myself on a large, hilly property with three dogs and two goats, I didn't have much of a choice when it came to staying active. I was still working full-time, but I felt really invigorated by my pregnancy and, perhaps mindful that this was going to be the only time I would experience being pregnant, I resolved to savour it all as much as I could.

It had been so exciting to go to the six-week scan and see a tiny human being moving around inside me. I looked enraptured at the ultrasound monitor, hardly believing that a little person was taking shape inside me and, at the end, I was going to end up with a baby in my arms. My baby.

When it came to finding out the sex, I wanted to know simply because I could. I had been secretly hoping I was carrying a little girl. Coming as I had from a house full of brothers, and never really enjoying a close relationship with a mother figure of my own, I hankered after a little girl. With my being a single parent, I figured, the chances of a daughter looking after me in my dotage and being a lifelong friend and companion were going to be manifestly greater than if I had a son.

But the doctor soon set me straight. I was carrying a little boy. And I couldn't have been happier. I immediately started thinking about names. I liked all the Old Testament names. There was something solid and classic about them. Matthew was a name I especially liked, along with Trent, after the river next to which I had been raised. Particularly important was that I choose a name that worked well with my surname, Batty, a name that had been a source of great amusement to various people throughout my life. (Greg wanted the baby to have his surname but I insisted it be Batty.)

When I mentioned the name Trent to my cousin and grandmother in England, they were horrified. They thought it was a terrible idea. I decided at that point it was better not to involve others in the name deliberations. And so, whenever anyone asked, I would simply tell them I was planning to call my child Norman. It usually shut them up.

While I loved being pregnant, there were certain things that made me feel sad. My pregnancy, while pleasant, was not like the ones my friends had had. I was under a lot of financial pressure. On a single income, pregnant and with a mortgage to service, I was never going to be able to afford to take much in the way of maternity leave. I looked into refinancing the mortgage and my car loan. I did the sums and determined the longest maternity leave I could afford to take was going to be four months. I couldn't even afford maternity clothing. Everything was given to me by friends – even my maternity bra.

Greg, who continued to visit occasionally and help out where he could around the property, didn't help matters. When I mentioned I was worried about taking time off to have the baby and wished I was financially secure enough to take a proper amount of maternity leave, he retorted, 'If you think I'm going to work while you sit on your fat arse having coffee with your friends, you have another thing coming.' This made me really upset, and I vowed to never ask him for anything again. It served to confirm what I already knew only too well: that I was going to be dealing with this baby alone, financially and emotionally.

I can't remember any violent outbursts from Greg as the pregnancy progressed. I was starting to get the impression that he responded violently or with abuse only when he was made to feel inadequate. He used his so-called spiritual pursuits as a convenient excuse for the fact he couldn't hold down a job and therefore buy any of the things a normal father might seek to buy for his unborn child. Rather than admit he was incapable of providing for his child, it was more convenient for him to say he was not interested in material possessions.

We never had a specific discussion about the role Greg would play in the baby's life, but it was always clear that Greg would be involved in his son's life. I continued to make it clear to him that I had no interest in us being a couple, that, while I welcomed his interest in the pregnancy and would always encourage him to have a relationship with his child, there was no question of us pretending at playing happy families. What had gone on between us already made me certain that the best relationship to have with Greg was one at arm's length. We were friends; we had inadvertently created a baby that I had decided to keep and intended to raise on my own. It seemed simple enough to me.

Greg accompanied me to parenting classes, which I was happy with. He was the father and he clearly wanted to have an active role in our baby's life – and I had no objection to that. He was jobless around this time, still based in St Kilda and floating between the Hare Krishnas and the Mormon Church there. He seemed to spend a lot of our time together ensuring I understood how spiritually superior he was to me. I would have preferred he focused less on his religious enlightenment and more on getting a job.

Since I had fallen pregnant, Greg had taken an unusual interest in the food I was putting in my mouth. (It is perhaps noteworthy that he had no similar concern for whether I was exhausted or stressed from having to work every hour God gave to keep up mortgage payments and singlehandedly maintain a household.)

'Are you eating properly, McBatty?' he would ask me. 'Plenty of fruit and vegetables and iron?' He wanted to make sure his offspring was being properly nourished. On the odd occasion he had money, he would run out and spend it all on organic fruit, which he would proceed to juice for me to drink. And that was fine, except that there were so many other things the baby needed before organic fruit juice. My dad gave me money for my fortieth birthday, which came and went with a whimper. I used the money to buy a change table, high chair and all the other equipment necessary for a baby.

Greg was always obsessed with purging himself. He seemed to be detoxing all the time, as if he was always trying to expel something from himself. It was always done to extremes, whether it was with organic fruit cleanses or with substances altogether far less suited to polite society. One afternoon he phoned to say he was on his way to Menzies Creek and would swing by the fish markets. I assumed he was stopping to collect a couple of nice salmon fillets for dinner. But when he arrived, he pulled out a bag of fish guts, which he promptly proceeded to burn on an open fire in the yard before stripping down and smothering his naked torso with the ashes. He told me it was some sort of cleansing ritual. I told him he was an idiot, and that there was no way he was coming in the house smelling of burnt fish gut. He would laugh at himself, half-realising how odd he was being.

But behind the quirkiness, something deeper and more sinister was simmering. And as the months passed, his behaviour became more and more disturbing. One evening he showed up at my house wearing a pair of goggles. It transpired that he thought the wire frames of his glasses were interfering with his brain waves, so he had removed the lens from the frames. He looked ridiculous but, coming as it did after the fish gut episode, I wrote it off as another one of his strange eccentricities.

Every now and then I would be afforded a glimpse into just how troubled his mind was. But it would only ever be a fleeting glimpse – and usually only ever hinted at in a throwaway comment. Because he was convinced that everyone was out to get him, it was rare that Greg confided in anyone. So for him to tell me one afternoon that he sometimes heard voices was a major admission. It set off alarm bells, but because he would offer something up and then shut down completely – refusing to elaborate and making it clear it was not a topic for further discussion – I was left unsure how serious he was or whether in fact I had even heard it.

I came to expect the ridiculous from him – and not knowing how else to handle it, I would just treat it with humour. One evening he came to me in the living room, holding a glass of water. 'Have you put something in my water?' he asked. 'It tastes funny.'

'What would I have put in your water, Greg?' I asked, part-exasperated, part-amused.

'Rosie,' he asked in all seriousness, 'are you trying to poison me?'

I laughed it off. It was, I was almost certain, just another example of his odd sense of humour.

I can remember him getting cross with me on another day because I reacted to one of his moments of madness by exclaiming, 'You do know you are totally bloody deluded?' He remembered that and brought it up years later.

The confusing part was that when he wasn't being barking mad, he had a sharp wit and we shared a good sense of humour. He never appeared to let things bother him. He lost jobs within weeks of getting them, he never had any money, he was living to a large extent relying on the kindness of strangers – and he would just potter around as if he had no cares in the world. It was only when I ventured a comment about how nice it would be to have a longer maternity leave that I discovered the insouciance was all a façade. He took it as a slight and arced up. At a fundamental level, he hated feeling inadequate.

Was it wrong for me to want to be a full-time mum? Was I a bad person for wishing the father of my child was more conventional – more capable of being the breadwinner I needed him to be?

I did feel I had Greg's loyalty. He was no longer interested in chasing other women. I had the distinct impression he thought he was connected to me. He saw me as this woman he had chosen, and with a baby on the way, we were meant to be together. But I was the one with the house, the car and the career. The sum total of what he was bringing to the partnership was pretty meagre.

It was also telling that I avoided exposing my friends to Greg. As long as he was around, there was no fear of me inviting my friends to come and visit me – Greg was too unpopular with them and his behaviour far too unpredictable. And so, without even noticing it, I became increasingly isolated. Greg, for his part, had never introduced me to a single friend in all the time I had known him. He always fell out with anyone he got even mildly close to, another symptom of his paranoia that everyone had an agenda to bring him down.

The only friendships he maintained were with his brothers, who I hadn't met. He had three brothers, and he was the second oldest. Years previously, in Belgrave, he had shared with me stories about growing up. Because his dad had a career in which they had to move all the time, they changed schools so often he didn't really form any lasting friendships in boyhood. So he and his brothers became a tight-knit unit. He felt his father didn't like him. He used to say he'd wished his mother would leave the marriage and take Greg with her. When I met his parents, they appeared to have a loving marriage, so I assumed it was just Greg being Greg.

*

Greg assumed he would be present at the birth but I had always had my misgivings. And as the pregnancy progressed, I became more certain I didn't want him anywhere near me during labour. I resolved that, when the time came, I would simply get through the birthing process alone. As a girl, I had been sent to the dentist alone to have teeth pulled. Taking on something like this by myself didn't seem like such a big deal. After all, my mum – and countless women before me – had managed on their own, and so would I. As the due date loomed, however, I started to worry about how I'd get to hospital, and so I reached out to my friend Carri. She fell over herself to help, offering to be on standby in the event I needed her.

I had chosen Monash Hospital for the birth, because it specialised in difficult and premature births. Because I was forty and this was my first pregnancy, I figured it was better to be in a place prepared for anything. I had no reason to be concerned – my doctors had been pleased with my pregnancy and all the signs were for a normal birth – but it was 2002, when having a baby at forty was still considered high-risk, as every medical professional I encountered seemed to take delight in reminding me.

A few weeks before my due date, Greg headed north for one of his semi-regular retreats at the Russian monastery, where he would help around the property with manual labour in return for food, lodging and inclusion in some of the monks' prayer sessions. Greg would sometimes describe it as the only place he could go for solace and respite. This time, his visit was scheduled to finish long before the baby was supposed to arrive.

I finished work four weeks before my due date. Because Greg was not around to help, I bustled awkwardly about the property tending to my animals. I remember picking up a 30-kilogram bag of meal to feed the goats, not realising what effect that may have.

I went to my weekly doctor's appointment a few days later, but I had to wait to see a doctor. Suddenly I became aware that I was wetting myself. When eventually a doctor saw me, he told me my membranes had ruptured, but to go home and return in the morning when they would induce me. I headed home, packed my bags and readied my little house in Menzies Creek for the arrival of my baby. Contractions began early the next morning, so I called Carri, who came to collect me. I tried reaching Greg at the monastery, but to no avail. I felt relieved that he was out of contact.

As I slung my meticulously packed overnight bag over my shoulder and made final arrangements for the dogs, I looked around the house, my emotions a mixture of anxiousness and excitement. The next time I would cross this threshold, I would be a mother; I would be carrying a baby, and a new chapter of my life would begin. Nothing would ever be the same.

Upon arriving at the hospital, I was immediately admitted and induced. Another friend, Sharon, was there, and both Carri and Sharon stayed with me until my baby was born.

The nurses were all convinced it would only be a matter of hours. Five shifts of midwives and sixteen hours of labour later, I was only 4 centimetres dilated. The decision was made to admit me for an emergency caesarean.

When they finally handed my little boy to me, I was beyond exhausted. The labour had taken its toll on me physically and emotionally, and I was drained after the stress of emergency surgery. But the moment I took the tiny bundle, wrapped in a silver foil blanket, and put him to my chest, I was overcome with euphoria. It was a feeling of complete joy like I had never felt in my life before. There was relief that he was okay, and that the ordeal was over, but mostly it was just pure happiness. A kind of bliss.

The next day, I couldn't move – I was utterly immobilised from the caesarean. Friends visited throughout the day. In between, the new little man in my life and I snatched moments together in our bliss bubble.

Greg phoned, and I told him that he had a son. But because I couldn't see him, it was hard to really gauge his reaction. As he had missed the birth, he decided he would wait until I returned home before leaving the monastery. I was relieved because I didn't want to have to worry about him doing something weird in front of the nurses. So I settled in and enjoyed three days of getting to know my baby. Flowers and cards and visits from friends reminded me how much I was loved and, for the first time in a long time, I could let go and let someone else take care of me for a change. I felt nurtured and cared for. I felt safe.

If there was a bittersweet note to any of it, it was that I didn't have my mum there to share in the joy. I felt as though I had been admitted to a secret club, a club that I realised now my mother must have known. And I so wanted her counsel on how to behave in that club, what to expect. I wanted her advice, I wanted her to come and see the little boy I had brought into the world, and I wanted her to be proud. I wanted her to know him.

I had decided to call him Luke. Luke Geoffrey Batty, born 20 June 2002. The Geoffrey was after my father. And Luke seemed to suit him perfectly: his shock of brown hair, his blue eyes. He looked at me as I cradled him in my arms, and it was almost as if he could see right through me – as if he knew me.

Because he was three weeks premature, Luke weighed only 2.7 kilos at birth and was jaundiced. He spent the first few weeks sleeping a lot, which – when finally we returned home together – gave me time to continue nesting. There was a lot of cleaning kitchen cupboards, as I recall, a job I never usually did, but somehow felt compelled to undertake now I had a newborn in the house.

Our first weeks together were a comedy of errors. Like all new mums, I was feeling as I went. Was I supposed to bathe him every day? Was once a day sufficient? And what about feeding? How often and how much? We fumbled along together, finding a rhythm. It was June in Victoria, so bitterly cold at night. I would snuggle with him in my bed, exhausted but very happy. I had never been more fulfilled in my whole life. Here was a little human being who was completely dependent on me – and I thrived on it.

Dad and Josephine were due to visit from England any day. Their excitement over the phone had been palpable, and I couldn't wait for them to meet Luke. I had been home a few days when Greg returned from the monastery. He was over the moon. He was so gentle and nurturing with Luke. There was a kind of wonder in his eyes as he nursed him. This great hulk of a man was reduced to jelly by the slightest smirk or facial tic of his newborn son. I remember thinking, whatever Greg was, whatever problems he had dealing with life in the adult world, he clearly had the capacity for unconditional love. Here was a man with his son – and it looked for all the world like he would do anything to protect him from harm.

He asked if he could stay with us for a couple of nights. Because I'd had a caesarean and was having trouble moving around, much less carrying Luke, part of me was secretly relieved. He began to help out by chopping firewood, keeping the wood stove fed and making sure I was eating properly. He had attended enough birthing classes to know that the father could help during the night by waking when the baby woke, changing its nappy and bringing it back to the mother for feeding.

After a few nights of not much sleep, I awoke one night to Luke wailing in the crib next to me. Greg decided Luke was waking up not because he was a newborn and was hungry or lonely, but because he was cold. And so he wanted to take Luke into the living room and sleep with him next to the wood stove. I wasn't having any of it. I was adamant that Luke remain in the bedroom with me.

Before I knew it, the disagreement escalated into a full-blown argument, with Greg shouting that he knew what was best for him. I tried to defuse the situation, telling Greg we were both tired and we would talk about it in the morning. But just as I turned to walk back into the bedroom, he picked up the big tea chest that I used as a coffee table and lifted it above his head, threatening to throw it across the room.

I raced over and started grappling with this six-foot-two man, screaming at him to put the tea chest down, even though, upon my release from the hospital, doctors had advised me not to strain myself for fear of tearing my stitches. I didn't think at any point that either Luke or I were in danger. It never occurred to me that either of us might get hurt. Greg was quite simply angry and this was his response.

The next morning I told him I wanted him to leave and that he wasn't to return unless at my express invitation. He seemed confused. He was aware my parents were arriving within the week – and really wanted to meet them.

I was incredulous. He had never contributed anything financially to the costs of Luke's birth. He had no job nor any prospect of one, he had watched as I had been forced to ask my father for the cash required to tide me over until I could return to work – Dad has always ensured my financial security, and I am so lucky and very grateful for that – and yet Greg wasn't even remotely ashamed at the prospect of meeting him. I told him it was quite simply not going to happen. That even if he had no shame, I certainly did, and there was no way I was going to present him to my family. And so he left.

When finally Dad and Josephine arrived, we shared such a special time all together. They were enraptured with Luke, and I was just so happy to be able to share this most incredible moment in my life with them. It was probably the closest we have ever been as a family. I felt the loneliness drop away, and a surge of empowerment came just from their presence. I was part of a family that, for all its idiosyncrasies, was underpinned by love and loyalty. The thousands of miles that separated me from it on a daily basis made it hard to feel the love and support most of the time – but here was evidence that it existed.

I made a point of not speaking about Greg during Dad and Josephine's visit but, of course, his presence still loomed large. He was the father of my child, and my parents were naturally interested to know what role – if any – he was going to play in the raising of their grandchild. Too exhausted by new motherhood to pretend otherwise, I let it be known – in that subtle, unspoken way daughters do to their dads – that things were less than perfect on the Greg front. Dad – or Josephine – must have been intuitive enough to put two and two together and deduce that I was feeling anxious, and so they convened a meeting at the local Legal Aid offices to see about my rights.

Going home to England had always hovered as a possibility at the back of my mind. Ever since arriving in Australia and setting up a life here, England had always been there as my back-up plan. If it all gets too hard, I would tell myself, I'll go home. England was where my family was, where the farm was, that symbolic patch of land on the River Trent to which I always knew I could retreat. The farm, the place where I grew up, the place where my forebears had worked the land, the place where that stout, draughty old farmhouse sat as it had done for over a century, was my safety net.

Keenly aware that all was not right in my world, but unable to give expression to his unease, my dad had made noises about me bringing Luke back to England to live. The intimation was that he'd help set me up in the village and lend a hand where he could raising his grandson. And it was an attractive offer. Even entertaining the idea of a life without Greg in it made my heart soar a little bit. The very idea that for the first time in a long time, I wouldn't be doing everything on my own – that I could lean on others without feeling like a burden – was enough to make me cry with relief.

And so we sat together in the Legal Aid office and laid out my predicament. The Legal Aid officer was polite and listened indulgently as I enumerated all the reasons why going home to England might actually be the best option for both me and Luke.

When I'd finished, the Legal Aid Officer pointed out that moving back to the UK would be easier said than done. This was because both Australia and the UK were signatories to the Hague Convention, she explained. From what she said, I came to understand that if a child was taken from one country to the other without the express permission of both parents, the parent left behind could apply for the child to be returned to its country of origin.

I only heard half of what she was saying, because suddenly my mind was consumed with one thought only: *I'm trapped*.

'But what about access?' my father enquired. 'He makes no contribution whatsoever to the raising of the boy, he has no job nor any prospect of one. Surely that limits the access he can have to the boy?'

Unfortunately, the Legal Aid officer explained, the size or quality of the contribution a parent makes to the rearing of a child has no bearing on rights to access. Greg didn't have to contribute a cent in child support, and his right to see and spend time with Luke was unaffected.

Leaving the Legal Aid office, a pall descended on me. I came away believing that I could never return to England while Luke was a child. It would all depend on Greg's determination to bring us back and, knowing Greg, he would never willingly let us go. Only much much later did I learn that we may well have been able to return to the UK. If only I'd known.

Mindful that Dad and Josephine were only here for ten days, I put on a brave face and determined that we would spend what little time we had together basking in the reflected glow of the newest arrival to our clan.

But just as I had become used to having them around to help, they had to leave. I remember the taxi coming to collect them from my house to take them to the airport, and I stood on the doorstep with Luke in my arms, quietly sobbing.

As the car disappeared from the driveway, I felt suddenly very alone. It was just me again, with no one to rely on but myself. And now I had a little human life depending on me too.

9

Red Flag

from Luke's Baby Book

[in Rosie's handwriting]

6 April 2003

I've just put you to bed, little Luke, and you were so tired you fell asleep while drinking your milk from me. We had a lovely day together, playing with toys, crawling around (and you're now getting around so well), playing in your little farmyard and bouncing in your 'Jolly Jumper'. Each new day brings even more joy into my life and a sense of fulfilment I never believed possible.

I knew I would love you but I didn't realise it was possible to love you this much.

Sometimes I worry in case something happens to me and I can't be with you to watch you grow and develop. I lost my mum when I was six years old and I dread the same thing happening to you.

You have crèche tomorrow and you love the girls there. You are always happy to be dropped off and seem to have a great time playing. You now recognise me when I come to collect you and your face bursts into smiles and chuckles when you see me. If I don't pick you up straight away, you get very upset. I wish I didn't have to go to work but I know you're happy in crèche and I know you're safe so I don't need to worry.

Your dad came here for the day yesterday and you had a great day together. He loves you very much and I know he wishes he could be with you all the time. I worry about how well you may get on with each other as you get older, but for now, you're his little boy and he loves you.

I still worry that your dad and I haven't been able to settle our differences and create a family environment for you, but I'm trying hard to be friends so that we can enjoy time with you together and you don't miss out on spending time with your dad.

We both love you very much, no matter what.

Mum

xx

From Luke's Baby Book

[in Greg's handwriting]

4 April 2003

Saw you crawl for the first time last week. Look out world, you're on the move. Today you've eaten more than I have, and so solid and strong I think I should wrestle you now while I can still win. You are a joy and pleasure to have as a son.

I look back on the experience of Luke being a vulnerable, dependent baby and I realise it fulfilled every need I'd ever had. I had never thought I was the maternal type until I had Luke: and then I couldn't imagine my life without him.

I became a breastfeeding queen – and relished the experience. I couldn't imagine how anyone could not like breastfeeding. A lot of my friends found it hard work, but I just loved having the ability to meet Luke's needs. Together, Luke and I had quickly developed a routine, which as a baby, he seemed to really thrive on. I took great pride in preparing really nutritious food. Because I was going to be doing it all on my own, I had read all the books and listened to all the advice. I took motherhood very seriously and was studious when it came to being the best mum I could be.

As he developed and I went back to work, things changed slightly. Our routine was thrown, and more and more people became involved in our lives. It was easy to lose confidence. Everyone has their opinions of what you should be doing, and so I learned quickly to listen politely, try not to take their opinion as criticism but ultimately to trust that my own intuition was the best guide.

I suppose the thing that surprised me the most was that by virtue of giving birth, fellow mothers – whose connection to me was otherwise vague to non-existent – would confide the most personal things to me. We were all on this journey together, the same mad collection of hormones coursing through our veins, the same heady mix of joy and exhaustion dominating our days and nights. I felt I belonged to something big and fundamental, and it felt nice.

When Luke was first born, I was astounded that people came from far and wide to admire him. The hospital ward was filled with flowers and cards, and friends came from everywhere. In the street, complete strangers – old and young – would approach and stare adoringly at my baby. And I was so very proud of him. He was a thriving baby who met all the development milestones. He was beautiful, with rosy cheeks and big blue eyes.

*

The semi-rural idyll of Menzies Creek was both my comfort and my oppressor. The silence of those golden mornings in the bush, the light playing on the ferns, the sun-dappled gums were a daily joy. To wake with my little boy, wander out into the backyard and soak in the first of the morning's rays were moments of bliss. And yet, by lunchtime, the silence that had been so golden became oppressive, and I began to crave adult company.

Greg, to his credit, was incredibly hands-on with Luke in those early months. He would want to bathe him, change his nappy, burp him, feed him or take him for a walk. But because Greg hadn't read any of the parenting books or spoken to other mums, as I had spent the better part of the last six months doing, he didn't always do things properly. He always did things with the utmost affection and the best of intentions, but never quite right. And so a level of contention started to develop between us. It all came to a head over Luke's sleeping routines. I had read that when a baby stirs they need to learn to settle themselves, and so I began to make a conscious effort not to run to Luke and pick him up every time he cried. Moreover, I started to become stricter about instilling a routine in Luke's life – when he would wake, feed and sleep.

On one occasion, when Luke was about three months old, Greg was visiting, and I was so tired I could barely keep my eyes open. After Luke had been fed, burped and put to bed, I took the opportunity to have a nap too. I made a point of telling Greg that if he heard Luke stir he was to leave him in his cot and I would get him up.

A few hours later, I woke up in a daze. I walked into the living room and there was Luke in his bouncinette, perched precariously on a pile of books and folders on the kitchen table. 'What are you doing?' I yelled, as I scooped the bouncinette up into my arms. 'Why is he awake? Why is he on the table? Why can't you just do as I tell you?'

Momentarily taken aback, Greg was silent for a moment, then began to seethe. He looked me straight in the eye, rage bubbling away inside him. 'Woman follows man, man follows God. If man follows woman, it leads him to the devil,' he said evenly.

I looked at him puzzled, my head still fuzzy from having just woken up. 'What?' I couldn't get my head around it. 'What do you mean?' I continued, incredulous. 'As a woman I cannot have a direct link to God?'

There was a flicker of hesitation from Greg, but then a lifting of his head, as if in defiance.

'This is my house, Greg. I provide everything. But you're saying I am not good enough to have a relationship with God?' Why I felt the need to enter into a philosophical discussion, I'm not sure. Normally, he would spout nonsense like this and I would ignore it. But this time, I'd had enough.

'No,' Greg continued. 'Because you are a woman.'

I stared at him in disbelief. 'Just get out,' I said. 'Just leave now.'

And so here we were again, on that now familiar roundabout of Greg inveigling himself into my life, behaving perfectly normally for a period of time, helping me out with Luke and around the house – encouraging me to drop my guard – before hitting me with another doozy.

Here was a grown man who apparently thought it was perfectly okay to sleep under my roof, eat my food and drive my car, but still believed that I was the lesser person. It defied explanation. I was once again astounded by his sense of superiority, delusion and entitlement. Looking back, it's obvious to me now that all of that was a manifestation of something much more sinister: born of his deep-seated (but never acknowledged) inferiority complex. In his heart of hearts, he knew he was a failure as a father, a partner and a provider – and so he resorted to intimidation.

Greg had a funny relationship with religion. It was the haven to which he retreated when confronted with a world he couldn't navigate. He would cite entire passages of the Bible, reeling them off by rote, using them to make a point, but completely missing the bigger picture: that Christianity was a religion based in compassion, generosity and kindness to your fellow human being.

As the months progressed and winter turned to spring, I started to make the most of my surroundings. I loved being outdoors with Luke and my dogs. I would strap him into the Baby Bjorn and march all over Menzies Creek. The dogs tolerated Luke well. They had been my children before Luke was born, but they seemed to take their relegation to second division with good humour. The only trouble the dogs caused was between Greg and me. We would argue all the time about whether they ought to be indoors or outdoors. He wanted the dogs outside, where Luke wouldn't be exposed to their germs. But I argued they were family: that I'd had them five years, and they had lived with me all that time inside the house. It would be unfair to suddenly banish them.

Greg had these funny ideas about animal energy. He believed that exposure to animals somehow lowered your spirit – and so he became contemptuous of the dogs. As the years progressed, he would make comments about smelling the dogs on Luke and how Luke was being brought down by them.

In many respects, Greg was very over-protective of Luke – to the point of obsessiveness. Which is why, I suppose, I always trusted him with Luke. He didn't like strangers looking at Luke, and he certainly couldn't abide people in the street coming up and touching him. He tolerated my friends touching him, but only those who had children. His possessiveness towards Luke was sometimes overbearing.

One weekend, I consented to take Luke to visit Greg's parents. They lived in country Victoria, about two hours' drive north of Melbourne. I'd met them once or twice before and they were lovely people. But as I had never wanted to give them – or Greg – the wrong impression about our relationship, I had always steadfastly refused to visit them. I didn't see the point. But now with Luke in the picture – and with Greg so clearly proud to show off his son to them – I agreed to a day in the country. They were, after all, Luke's grandparents. They were the only family Luke had here in Australia. I figured I owed it to him to at least create a path for there to be a relationship between them further down the track.

Greg's parents were perfectly lovely – excited to meet Luke and very kind with me. Greg could not have been more proud – he just wanted their unconditional approval. But while he now had a son and they were inextricably linked to this baby, so fluid were the relations between Greg and his mother and father, they seemed unsure about exactly how much they would let themselves become attached. Of course, Greg was oblivious to all of this. To his mind, the visit was an important step in the recasting of our relationship. He took the visit to mean I was ready, finally, to be the family Greg always believed we ought to have been. The truth couldn't have been more different.

*

When Luke was four months old, I sent him to crèche. It almost killed me – but what choice did I have? With a mortgage to pay and no income to pay it, I had to return to work. I remember the morning I dropped Luke off for his first day of crèche. He cried as I left, and I sobbed in the car all the way into town. I felt like the worst mother in the world. Not even the fact that I had spent months beforehand expressing milk in preparation could extinguish the thought that I was abandoning my little boy.

I returned to my old job at the telecommunications company – and after two hours back at my desk, it felt like I had never left. The only change was I was now answering to a new manager, a young bloke who was very career focused. He had been sent from head office to whip our sales team into shape, and he relished the chance to throw his weight around. Crucially for me, he had no children. I could feel my heart sink by the day.

And so, I was thrust straight back into the ruthless world of sales, trying to juggle the increasingly impossible demands of a new boss desperate to impress head office with the daily (and nightly) requirements of being a mum. Most mornings I would struggle into work exhausted from the night before. But I felt I couldn't say to anyone at work that I'd had a sleepless night or that I was struggling. As a working mum, you have to be seen to be not compromising your role in any way. I was a wreck.

I would wake every morning around 6 am, express a day's worth of milk for Luke, get myself dressed, feed the animals and get Luke ready for crèche, where I would drop him at 7 am. Then I would battle peak-hour traffic to see clients all over metropolitan Melbourne or to attend the weekly sales meeting, which I would sit through with my mind racing, full of all the things I had to squeeze into the working day ahead, so that I could leave in time to make the mad dash back to crèche to collect Luke. I was always the first to drop my child off at crèche and invariably the last to pick him up. The childcare workers could not have been more pleasant, and they loved Luke like one of their own. But I couldn't help but feel judged as I swung wildly into the driveway each night and ran inside to collect my little boy.

Once home, the juggle began: feed Luke, bathe Luke, change Luke, whip up something vaguely nutritious for my own dinner and try to get Luke down, whereupon I would turn on the computer and do all the work I had missed because I was scrambling to collect and care for my son. I was asleep most nights at 9 pm, curled up next to Luke in my bed. I knew the books all counselled against co-sleeping, but I felt so bad as a mother, denying my baby the intimacy he craved by being at work all day, I wanted to make up for it as he slept.

And so the routine developed. On more than one occasion, I would be halfway into work, speeding along the motorway or stuck in traffic, and the phone would ring.

'Rosie, it's the childcare centre here,' would come the voice down the phone. 'Luke's running a really high temperature. You're going to have to come and collect him.'

When I was really stuck, I had no choice but to ring Greg. And he would make his way to Menzies Creek and collect Luke and take him home.

I was run ragged. That Christmas, intensely homesick for my family, I booked tickets for Luke and me to go to England. I was desperate for my family to meet Luke: and so we set off together on a six-week visit. From the moment I stepped off the plane, I felt like a weight had been lifted. Josephine came to collect us at the airport, and almost immediately, I relaxed.

I took Luke to meet his great-grandmother Nanna Atkin. There was no other family member to whom I felt closer. And so introducing her to Luke was one of my proudest moments as a mother. I still remember that day: the look of glee on Nanna Atkin's face. It meant the world to her. She had just turned one hundred – and while the body was failing, the mind was sharp. She told me she had been staying alive to meet Luke, and now that she had met him and seen how content I was, she could die a happy woman. To have been able to share time with Luke and her – it was so special.

The visit home was instrumental in reminding me the importance of family. For years now I had lived on the other side of the earth, building a surrogate family from friends, but this was the real deal. This hoary collection of misfits, in all their eccentric glory, were the people who would always be there for me. They were obliged to be by dint of being family.

We even brought Aunty Dorothy to visit Nanna Atkin. Aunty Dorothy had only recently had her leg amputated and was keen to show everyone her stump. And so, at various intervals during our visit, she would haul up her skirt and show it off.

'Keep your pants on, Aunty Dot!' came the cry from all assembled. She had no idea, of course. We were all in tears of laughter.

I came back to Australia with mixed emotions. Keen to get back and get on with my life, but sorry to have left the bosom of my family and painfully aware I might never see Nanna Atkin again.

Greg had been living at my property while I was away: feeding the goats and dogs, maintaining the yard. In return, he had a roof over his head and the use of my car. He had missed Luke terribly and wasn't in a great hurry to leave when we got back. I was okay with him having a day or two with us – it was nice to have a bit of help with Luke as I adjusted to the time change.

One afternoon I asked him to go to Bunnings to change something I had bought or, if not change it, try to get a credit note. He left, making all the right noises about doing what I had asked him, but returned an hour or so later having completely ignored my request. Annoyed that he had clearly decided my wishes were to be dismissed, I made some comment, reprimanding him. It was no big deal, to my mind, but my sense of exasperation was enough to trigger his anger.

I was sitting on the lounge room floor, spoon-feeding Luke in his bouncy chair, when suddenly Greg picked up a large clay urn, lifted it over his head and made to throw it at me. The next thing I knew, he was standing in front of me, enraged. He aimed a kick at my head. I closed my eyes, anticipating contact, but he pulled the kick back just in time.

I was in shock. Shaken and scared, I dared not move from the lounge, but sat, terrified he'd return. That was his first really aggressive gesture towards me. There was no physical violence per se – inasmuch as he didn't make physical contact – but the suggestion of violence was clear. He wanted to hurt me and had only just held himself back from doing so. I sat there shaking, doing my best not to lose it completely for fear it would upset Luke. And so began a cycle of threats and fear that would continue until the day Greg died.

10

Escalation

Luke was a contented baby. He slept and ate well, he loved the undivided attention I was able to heap on him when it was just the two of us and he'd grown to love crèche, where the staff lavished him with affection.

Luke was pretty easygoing as a toddler, too. I remember him having his first tantrum – if you could call it that – on his first birthday, just as he was learning to walk. My brother Terry took Luke's balloon off him and he burst into tears. It seemed that, as he learned to walk, he also learned how to have a meltdown to get his own way. It was a lesson he took to heart and would employ regularly in the ensuing years. In other words, he was just a normal kid.

*

After Greg's recent display of aggression, I started devising strategies for managing his exposure to Luke and me, believing that if I just managed to make clear the boundaries in terms of acceptable behaviour, he would adhere to them and I could manage to continue my daily juggle. All the while, without my really realising it, Greg's attitude towards me was hardening and his violent tendencies towards me, both psychologically and physically, were escalating.

Vital to his continued intimidation of me was the fact that I felt isolated from family and friends. Because I had always prided myself on my self-sufficiency, and because I lived so very far from any of my friends who also had children, I was loath to ask them for help with Luke. My parents' old friends Vi and Ray would help out wherever they could. They had moved to Australia from New Zealand and their children had all grown up and moved on. Vi was so good with Luke, and he loved her. But, for the most part, I had to lean on Greg, because he was unemployed, available and willing. After all, as Luke's father, I felt he bore no small amount of responsibility to help raise his son.

And so I battled on, trying to be a super-mother to Luke and feeling like I was drowning in the process. Whether or not Greg consciously thought it, or innately sensed it, I was weak and vulnerable and easy prey for his psychological stalking.

Previous to Luke's and my visit to England, Greg had made noises about having another child with me. And I had told him in no uncertain terms that I was repulsed at the idea of him coming anywhere near me. He still harboured these delusions that we were going to create a family together. What was really sad for me was that I would have loved another child. Until I had Luke I'd had no idea that being a mother could fulfil every need I had – that it completed me.

*

The phone rang in the middle of the night. It's never good news for a phone to ring in the middle of the night. I reached over Luke, who was asleep next to me, and put the receiver to my ear.

'Rosie,' came a familiar voice down the line. 'It's your dad. Sorry to call you so late, but I thought you should know Nanna Atkin has died.'

Half-asleep and groggy, it took a moment for the news to sink in.

'Are you there, Rosie?' continued my father. 'Can you hear me? Is everything all right?'

'Yes, Dad,' I finally managed to reply. 'I'm here.' And then the tears welled.

She had reached one hundred, she had packed four lifetimes into one, she had lived, laughed and loved with the best of them. But now she was gone, and I was devastated. The closest thing I'd had to a mum had passed away, and I had been 16,000 kilometres away when it happened. I felt sad, I felt guilty – I was bereft. I hung up the phone, rolled over and cried silently in the darkness.

Living away from home had been, for the most part, a grand adventure. Building a life on the other side of the world to all I had known as a girl was equal parts liberating and exhausting. For the most part, I didn't pine for my family. I missed them, to be sure, and wished on many occasions they were only 16 kilometres away – not 16,000. But usually I was too busy getting on with my life to sit around moping for them. In moments like this, though, you really felt the distance. I wanted more than anything to be home, to be comforted by loved ones and to offer comfort to those who needed it.

Moments like these make you stop and take stock. Was this my lot, then? Far from family for the momentous events? Dad and Josephine weren't getting any younger. Who was going to take care of them in their old age? As the only daughter, the task would traditionally have fallen to me. But stranded as I was in Australia – tied inexorably to this country by my son – any thought of repatriating was out of the question.

*

As 2003 progressed, I did my best to set parameters around my life, and Luke's life, which I hoped Greg would come to respect. Greg would always ask me to lend him money, which I usually did out of a mixture of pity and obligation. I felt that he had helped me out a lot around the property before Luke was born and stepped in to look after Luke whenever I needed him. So in an attempt to keep the ledger even, and not have Greg assuming the role of an intimate or equal partner in my life, I felt it was better to see the money I gave him as payment for services rendered.

Every now and then Greg would disappear to the Russian Orthodox monastery. He would usually go there for three months at a time, a period of relative peace in my life. From what they later told reporters, the monks seemed to see it as Greg taking refuge there whenever things got too complicated in his life.

He'd do the same things for them that he did for me: offer his services around the monastery and help out with physical labour in return for bed and board. And of course he would take part in their daily religious rituals – praying and attending services. I think he derived a sense of comfort from the monastic routine, plus he liked to associate with the sort of people he considered religiously pure and somehow morally superior.

One afternoon in the second half of the year, Greg called me when he arrived at Belgrave station out of the blue. He had no money and nowhere to live, but he knew full well that I would

90

take him in – which I did. I didn't know how else to handle it. When people were in need, I didn't like turning them away. When I have an emotional link with someone and they are at a low point in their lives, I can't turn my back. Perhaps I'm too soft-hearted, too forgiving.

I took Greg in with the caveat that he had to move out at the end of that month. And so a routine began to develop. I would go out to work each morning, dropping Luke at crèche on the way, and then return home to find Greg on the couch, watching TV. It started to infuriate me. He was leading the life I wanted to live. I wanted to be the one pottering about the house with my son, staying at home and rearing my child as a full-time mum while my partner went out and made the money to pay the bills. And I began to understand that this was a perfectly acceptable – if not desirable – arrangement from Greg's point of view. I started to resent his presence, and relations once again became tense.

At night, and perhaps sensing my disdain, he would borrow my computer and sit up into the small hours of the morning firing off job applications. He would come into my room, wake me up and tell me all about the general manager's role he had just applied for with its $150,000 pay packet. And I would lie there staring at him, amazed that he could be so delusional. In all the years I had known him, he hadn't managed to hold down a job for more than a couple of months, and even then they were pretty lowly positions. I couldn't understand what made him think he would have even the slightest chance of landing a senior management role for which he had no demonstrable experience. But such was his sense of entitlement.

At the same time, he worked hard to make sure I understood how inferior I was to him in every way. Nothing I ever did with Luke was right. I was, to his eyes, barely fit to call myself a mother, and with every day that passed, Luke was sliding backwards developmentally simply from being exposed to me. I used to brush it off as more ranting from a madman – but I was tired, I was alone and I was vulnerable. Like every new mother who had ever gone before me and would follow, I didn't need convincing that I was not much good at this motherhood thing. No matter how hard I tried or how much I worked, I only ever felt like I was barely keeping my head above water.

One afternoon, a friend of mine was having a party that I was determined to attend. Greg and I had been painting the bathroom together. As I left for the party, I told him to down tools, as I wanted to finish it in a certain way. Of course, when I returned, it was to discover he had ignored me and gone ahead and done it the way he thought it ought to be done. I was so angry, I grabbed a paint stirring stick and whacked him with it on his leg.

Both of us were in shock. It wasn't an especially hard whack, but I had been angry enough that it was done with real intent. I immediately started to apologise profusely, offering to take myself off to the police station to report the incident and admit fault. I was instinctively scared of how he might react: worried that he would retaliate with a show of force. But I was also terrified that he was going to use the incident against me. I wanted to neutralise its effect by owning it. I wanted, most of all, for it to never have happened.

Greg looked at me with a malevolent smile and said that there was no point going to the police. Feigning magnanimity, he told me to forget about it.

By the end of the month, the air was thick with tension. One morning he woke up in a really agitated state. I could hear him in his bedroom, muttering to himself. Suddenly, I heard a loud thud and shattering of glass. He had taken a framed photo of Luke and smashed it on the floor.

I kept my distance, scared of further provoking him. I ventured out into the kitchen, trying hard not to make any noise. Greg came bursting out of his room. He bowled up to me in the kitchen and stood over me. I recoiled, drawing myself away, terrified at the sight of this enormous man bearing down on me. His face was red with rage, his eyes wild. He aimed six punches at my head – drawing his fist back at the last moment each time, before it made contact. I flinched in anticipation of a beating – whimpering in fear and confusion. With a groan of exasperation, he turned on his heel and stormed out of the kitchen.

Sobbing, I raced into my bedroom, collected Luke and jumped straight into the car. Negotiating the road through a torrent of tears, I dropped Luke off at crèche before pulling up at the local shopping centre. For an hour, I wandered aimlessly about the shops, my mind racing. All I could think about was Ingrid Poulson, the woman who had been in the news recently after her estranged husband had murdered her two children and her father in the driveway of her home. Was that me? But Greg hadn't physically assaulted me – or Luke, for that matter. Surely he never would? The thought of it alone was too chilling to dwell on.

After what I felt had been plenty of time for Greg to have either cooled down or left, I returned home. As I approached the house, it became obvious Greg was still there, and I felt ill. I was returning to my home, my haven, which was inhabited by someone I didn't want to be there but whom I didn't know how to get rid of. I felt sickened and defeated at the realisation that Greg was becoming that presence in my life. He had just aimed six punches at my head for reasons I didn't understand, and now I didn't know what I was walking back into.

I stepped across the threshold tentatively, listening out for any sound of Greg. I heard his voice coming from the living room. He was on the phone and I heard him tell the person at the other end of the line that I was an unfit mother and he was concerned for his son's safety.

Enraged, I burst in and demanded to know who he was talking to.

'I'm talking to the police, Rosie,' he said calmly, staring at me with indifference.

I stormed across the room and grabbed the phone off him.

'Who is this?' I barked down the line.

The constable on the other end of the phone identified himself.

I looked at Greg, who was watching me with a self-satisfied grin. Whatever reaction he'd gotten from the policeman appeared to have emboldened him. I was suddenly scared again. I gripped the phone tightly, hanging on to it as if it were a lifeline.

The policeman asked me to put Greg back on the phone.

'Whether you think she is a fit mother or not, she sounds really scared of you,' I heard him tell Greg. 'I need you to pack your things and go.'

It seemed to placate Greg for some reason, and he hung up the phone and made for his room, where he started packing his things. I immediately phoned my neighbour, Adrian, and asked him to pretend to call in, which he did. Greg wasn't buying that for a second. He made some sneering comment about what a coincidence it was that Adrian had dropped by and walked casually out the door.

As soon as he had gone, I knew that I was at a crisis point. I picked up the phone and called Relationships Australia. They had a counsellor available, so I hopped in the car and went straight away.

My counsellor's name was Nick, and he was gentle and kind. He listened politely as I recounted the morning's events, then proceeded to contextualise them with accounts of previous instances of Greg's threatening behaviour. I remember him asking if Greg was violent to me. I said, 'Well, I don't think so. I mean, he hasn't actually hit me.'

As I spoke, and as Nick sat and listened, punctuating my narrative with expert questions at crucial junctures, it began to dawn on me: maybe there was a name for what Greg had been subjecting me to. Maybe, moreover, I wasn't alone. Maybe it fit a pattern and that pattern of abuse had been experienced by other women. And there was, oddly enough, a certain comfort in that. A kind of validation in the fact this was not a series of isolated incidents, but part of a wider whole – one part of a bigger picture of a problem that bedevilled society at large, not just my little corner of Menzies Creek.

And gradually, as our meeting went on and my testimony became more frank, Nick started to slide a series of pamphlets across the table to me. Each flyer contained a description of the many forms domestic violence can take – physical, emotional, financial. A checklist of the ways men intimidate and control women. And as I read the list and performed a mental checklist, it was like a light going on: I was a victim of family violence. I was the one in three.

As I walked out of Nick's office, I felt at once empowered and overwhelmed. By coming to understand that Greg's behaviour towards me constituted violence, I felt immediately stronger, as if by giving it a name I might better be able to manage it. But at the same time, I felt scared. If this was now my path, and that path had an already well-defined trajectory, did this mean I was destined to never escape the torment of Greg? Was my journey now to be that of every other woman debilitated by domestic violence? The thought was too depressing to dwell on.

That day marked the beginning of the rebuilding of my self-esteem. It's an important marker in the life of anyone who has suffered family violence to have someone explain the different types of violence that exist, for the terror you've suffered to be given a name, and to be assured, most importantly, that none of it is your fault. Family violence is a pernicious spiral. Because of the constant verbal abuse, you get worn down and become totally confused – your sense of self is completely eroded. And it takes a third party with experience in these matters to hold up a mirror and encourage you to look into it. I began to understand that it was no accident that Greg had come into my life – that he had targeted me precisely because I was physically isolated from friends and family and vulnerable because of it. Like a lion separating its prey from a fleeing herd, an abuser picks you off, isolates you from the safety of the group and moves in for the kill.

A new cautiousness crept into my dealings with Greg. Through the prism of family violence, so much about the way he treated me became clearer. There was a pattern to his behaviour, a perverse method to it that I had written off as his idiosyncratic madness.

Perhaps sensing my newfound determination – or perhaps out of dumb luck – Greg suddenly landed a job in sales with a transport company. It was enough of a steady income that he could also afford his own room in a furnished hostel in Caulfield. It was, he would casually tell me whenever he visited, the start of him rebuilding his life.

After six months or so, it certainly seemed as if he had turned a corner. He remained employed – a feat in and of itself – and moved into his own apartment and bought a car. He even started to save money. I could well have done with some of it, but never dared ask, not wishing to rock the boat or place any undue pressure on him while he was re-establishing himself. It was the sleeping-dogs-lie principle. As long as he was preoccupied with getting his life back on track, he wasn't crowding out mine — and that was good enough for me.

Greg began to make noises about wanting to have Luke stay overnight with him. But Luke was not yet two years old and I wasn't ready to be separated from him. I went to see a solicitor about my rights as a single mother. It transpired I didn't really have any. As Luke's father, I was told, Greg had every right to see his son. And until such time as I took my case to the Family Court, I had no legal right to deny him access. I resolved to try to sit down with Greg and a lawyer and mediate a more structured agreement, but in what would become a pattern, he did everything he could to avoid formalising an arrangement between us. It suited him for things to be fluid — that way he could come and go as he pleased, and I was just expected to accommodate him.

One night, when Greg arrived back from crèche with Luke in his arms, I noticed Luke wasn't wearing the jacket he'd been in when I sent him off to daycare. It was winter and already freezing.

'Where's his jacket?' I asked Greg, mildly irritated. 'I dropped him off in one this morning.'

He ignored me as he walked into the house and deposited Luke in front of the television. The Wiggles were playing — Luke's favourite show.

'I'm serious, Greg,' I repeated as he walked back towards the door. 'Where's Luke's jacket? It's too cold for him to be getting about without one.'

Out of nowhere, Greg's temper flared. He bent down and picked up Luke's diecast ride-on car: a heavy play-vehicle weighing a good 20 kilos. I winced, unsure of where – or on whom – he was intending to bring it down. With a howl of frustration, he smashed it down on the stair railing with an almighty crash. Luke looked up from the television, his face frozen in horror. I rushed to his side instinctively, placing myself between him and Greg. Luke started to wail as his father fumed at the doorway.

Greg strode across the floor and into the living room and grabbed me by the hair. He forced my head down, then pulled it back so I was brought face to face with him. Red-faced and raging, he leaned into my face and practically spat out the words, 'If you ever stop me from seeing Luke, I will kill you and kill your animals.' He pushed me down onto the ground, where I lay whimpering, then he stormed out the door. Next to me, Luke was wailing, his little face twisted in fear, tears streaming down his cheeks.

The following morning I went straight to Dandenong Court House to apply for an intervention order (IVO). On the spot, the magistrate issued an interim order prohibiting Greg from coming near me. A court date was set for me to stand before a magistrate and explain why I needed a more permanent order.

It was, in many respects, a watershed moment in my life. Raised in a household where encounters with the law – be it the police or courts – were rare to non-existent, it was a massive step for me to involve the police and justice system in what I had previously believed to be my little problem to manage. I had never been in court before; I had never been in trouble with the law. The workings of a police station and a courtroom were foreign to me. And I approached both institutions with a degree of humility, as if my problem would be a waste of their precious time.

A week or two later, there was a knock on my door. I had friends over and opened the door to see a policeman standing there in full uniform. He explained Greg had taken out an IVO on me, and that he was here to serve the papers. I was dumbstruck. I went to court weeks later to discover Greg was planning to testify to a judge that I was the violent one and he needed protection from me. I couldn't believe he would be so bold as to waste the court's time like this. The magistrate set a date several months hence for Greg's case to be heard, knowing full well that there was no evidence against me, that this was a nuisance claim and Greg would lose interest in pursuing it by the time the court date rolled around.

I was eventually granted a one-year IVO by a magistrate at Dandenong Court. I stood before him, nervous as you like, and explained why I feared for my safety. The whole process took no more than ten minutes. The order prevented Greg from coming in or near me or my home. He still had access rights, as Luke's father – for to change that meant a whole different process before the Family Court – but he would no longer be allowed to show up at my place unannounced. And because Greg had never shown even the vaguest of violent tendencies towards Luke, the IVO only named me as a protected person.

It was, I foolishly thought, an important first step in finally establishing the long-overdue boundaries between Greg and me. No longer was I going to allow him to co-parent Luke as he had been doing. New babysitting arrangements would henceforth be launched, with Vi – who couldn't have been more obliging – stepping in to pick up the slack left by Greg's absence.

It was a development that sent Greg apoplectic. He didn't like people as a general rule, but he reserved special disdain for people who busied themselves with the care of his son. He hated the idea that anyone other than him would be looking after Luke – bringing influence to bear on the way he was reared and the prism through which he saw the world.

Greg phoned one night – in breach of the IVO – to berate me about the new babysitting arrangement. I was at the crèche, helping to prepare for an upcoming fête, and Vi answered the phone. Greg proceeded to abuse her, calling her names and accusing her of unspeakable crimes against his son. She called me, and I phoned the police, who promptly reminded Greg he was in breach of the IVO. Not that he would have cared.

After an access visit a week later, Greg phoned me to say that after he had collected Luke, he had noticed an 'offensive smell' about him, and demanded to know whether Vi had looked after him the previous night.

Not long after, I received an official notice to submit to a paternity test. Greg had initiated the test to seek confirmation that Luke was in fact his son. It was another power game, another attempt to belittle and embarrass me. Another method by which to manipulate me, waste my time and exert control over me. But I was nothing if not resilient, and figured if the only way to mollify Greg was to wear him down with acquiescence, then that's what I would do.

So I freely gave of my blood and offered up Luke for testing too. The results came back indicating there was a 99.99 percent chance that Luke was Greg's child. Of course, the great irony is that I would have given the world for it to be otherwise.

11

The Cycle

With Greg working and living in Caulfield, things between us began to calm down. But for the occasional abusive text or phone call, he honoured the terms of the IVO and kept his distance. He was still seeing Luke every weekend, collecting him on a Saturday morning and returning him on a Sunday afternoon.

My grandmother had left a small amount of money for me in her estate, a modest financial windfall that I immediately invested in a state-of-the-art chicken coop. My country roots would flare every now and then, and I would be gripped by a new determination to reassert my farming credentials on the outskirts of suburban Melbourne, no matter how absurd that seemed.

At least one person in the neighbourhood seemed to understand. He had been a farmer all his life and had that salt-of-the-earth quality that reminded me of the farmers I had grown up with in Laneham. He was really good with animals and was only too happy to share his skills with an amateur farmer like me, so he helped me build my chicken coop. He was really passionate about sustainable farming, a subject that interested me greatly.

He was, to a large extent, an enlightened version of my dad, and I enjoyed his company enormously.

As we spent more time together as friends, it became clear that a mutual interest was developing. I had more free time as Luke grew, and with Greg on something of an even keel, I wasn't consumed with the task of managing him or otherwise remaining on permanent tenterhooks in anticipation of his next outburst. And so we began dating. It was nothing serious at first – my full-time job and parenting duties took up most of my waking hours. But when we were together it was easy, and I was reminded that relationships didn't need to be hard.

I didn't mention my new friend to Greg, knowing it would only cause unnecessary stress in my life. It's funny now that I think of it – it never occurred to me that Greg might be seeing someone else. Not that I would have cared. In fact, I would have welcomed someone else distracting him from harassing me. But I think, on reflection, I knew him well enough to know that he had devolved mentally to such a state of paranoia and introspection, there was no way he would trust someone enough to enter into a relationship with them. Which was, of course, to completely ignore the bigger elephant in Greg's room, namely, that no woman in her right mind would go within ten feet of him.

Even though I worked assiduously to ensure that Greg knew nothing, he nevertheless began to sense that I was seeing someone. Whether it was a change in my demeanour, or a sense that I had become that little bit more indifferent to his manipulation of me, he began to pepper me with questions via text, which I studiously ignored. The more I ignored him, the more abusive the text messages would become, accusing me of all sorts of depravity and alleging that I was purposefully exposing Luke to immoral behaviour of a most crude kind.

It was a window into how dark his soul was. That a mind was able to conjure such sick flights of fancy spoke volumes for how disturbed it was. But as long as Greg was otherwise adhering to the terms of the IVO, and collecting Luke and dropping him home at the agreed times, I was prepared to simply ignore it.

Perhaps feeling me slip from his grip, Greg resorted to the only control he had over me. It was crude, but effective. During a brief conversation one Sunday afternoon during the handover of Luke, I mentioned to Greg in passing that the time I had each weekend without having to take care of Luke was a godsend in many ways – time for me to get my life back. It was an epiphany for Greg. For six months, he had faithfully shown up to collect Luke and take him overnight, partly because he was his father and he relished the opportunity to spend time with him, but partly also because he believed it was in some way an annoyance to me. Greg lived to make my life miserable.

To discover that a gesture he had hoped was causing me no end of heartache was, in fact, helping me out threw him completely. And so it was time to move the goalposts. Suddenly, Greg started returning with Luke to Menzies Creek hours earlier than he was supposed to. I suspect he was hoping to catch me in the company of someone, which he never did – or at least impact on any arrangements I might otherwise have had. At first, I was happy enough for Luke to be brought home earlier. He was my life, after all, and I missed him terribly on the nights he was away. But after a while, I started to become annoyed with Greg arriving unannounced at my house.

After a month or so of this cat-and-mouse game, Greg finally asked me if I could meet with him for a coffee. We arranged to meet in a café in Knox, not far from Menzies Creek. We sipped our coffees and made awkward small talk until Greg finally got to the point. He told me he had been working hard for the past year, holding down a job, looking after Luke, buying him clothes and toys, because he had been trying to win my approval. Trying to prove to me that he could be a responsible provider and head of a household. I was astounded. All this time I had thought we were comfortably growing apart and developing lives independent of one another, he had been working to try and re-establish our relationship.

He told me he had been headhunted for a job – a promotion from his current role to work with a rival company. He told me all this with an air of anticipation, clearly seeking my praise. But I was too dumbstruck to say anything. Greg had twice been physically violent towards me, had once threatened to kill me and spent part of every day composing vile texts or emails to me. I couldn't fathom in which universe he thought it might be possible that we would get back together and play happy families.

'I'm sorry, Greg, but it's not going to happen,' I eventually managed to say, careful to deliver the news gently, lest he flare up.

He seemed genuinely deflated by my refusal – deflated and confused. In the recesses of that mind, he had us married off, raising kids and living some sort of suburban idyll. The only thing that stymied his fantasy was the cold-hearted English bitch who couldn't see what was good for her.

I left my coffee half-finished, made my excuses and beat a hasty retreat, wondering if I had imagined that entire conversation with Greg.

I got home from work that night to discover everything that Greg had bought for Luke in the past ten months in a pile on our doorstep: a car seat, a collection of toys and clothes. It was deliberately provocative, an act infused with such passive aggression that it was terrifying. It was, on his part, a declaration of war. If the past ten months had been relatively calm in terms of tension and hostilities between us, it appeared that the truce had been called off. And so I steeled myself. As it turned out, Greg didn't see Luke again for eight months or so. He didn't make contact and travelled overseas.

Luke turned three on 20 June 2005, and I remember the day well. I woke with him next to me in bed. He looked so peaceful – cherubic face, flawless skin, rosebud lips. If there is any experience more wondrous for a parent to watch over their child as he or she sleeps, I don't know what it might be. In the pre-dawn light, our lives together seemed pretty perfect. Certainly, work was unnecessarily stressful and Greg was a constant thorn in my side, but before sunrise – before any of that workaday messiness began to invade our space – it was just me and my perfect little boy. A special kind of happiness.

Not long after Luke's third birthday, I received a phone call from Dad in England to tell me he had decided to sell the family farm. I was blindsided by the news. The farm had been in our family for generations and, in a childhood marked by uncertainty, it had been the one constant in my life. The spectre of losing it made me realise just how important an anchor it was. It was my last remaining link to Laneham, and the touchstone of my childhood. It was the house in which all my memories of Mum – such as they were – were contained. It was the house in which I had mourned, grieved and celebrated all of the milestones in my young life.

My grandfather had pioneered the farm. It had been my dad's entire life. The expectation had always been that it would be passed down the generations. To say that my dad's decision to sell the farm took me by surprise would be an understatement.

Psychologically, the effect of the news was profound. And when it came to the question of staying in Australia or moving back to the UK, it all but sealed the deal.

Until this point, I had kept my options open and a foot in both camps. In fact, when I'd turned forty, a few months before Luke was conceived, I had thought about going back to the UK for good. Everyone close to me was busy raising kids and seemed to be going their separate ways. I had friends here – good friends – but the emotional pull of home had grown stronger and more undeniable with every passing year. I'd been homesick.

And then I'd become pregnant with Luke and something shifted. Suddenly the most important focus in my life lay not in what was behind me but in what was in front of me. What was in front of *us*. Luke's arrival had given me a sense of belonging in Australia that I had never previously had. He was my family here and we would build a life here together. We were the two-person Battys-from-Laneham diaspora, the colonial outpost of that proud, little-known farming dynasty from a bend on the River Trent.

After Luke was born, I had never seriously considered going home to England. And, anyway, as I understood it I wasn't able to go without Greg's permission. I couldn't just up and leave – Greg had rights, whether I liked it or not. It was something very few people understood. Often over the years friends would learn of my situation with Greg and with the best of intentions naïvely ask: 'Why don't you just move home?' If only it had been that simple.

When Dad rang to tell me he was selling the farm, he also informed me that I'd receive money from the sale. It was something I had never expected. If there was to be any financial benefit derived from that property, I had always assumed it would go to my brothers and not to me. My three brothers, Robert, James and Terry, had been encouraged to consider their futures as mapped out on the farm. Dad – and indeed my brothers – assumed they would all work on the farm and that a home would be provided to them. As the girl of the family, it was always made clear that was never going to happen to me.

And so, all of a sudden, I had a large sum of money coming my way that would make a huge difference to our lives. But for reasons I couldn't understand, I was utterly depressed about it. In the fullness of time, I would come to realise that my reaction was perfectly natural – grief in the face of loss. It was a severing of a tie to my past, an irrevocable cutting of the cord.

I must not have been able to hide my shock, because, when Greg next came to collect Luke, he asked me why I was moping – a rare moment of empathy from him. Without thinking, I told him about Dad's decision to sell the farm, how he had tried to offset the sting by reminding me how much money I stood to gain from it, but overall how much it had thrown me. I didn't notice it at the time, but it would become obvious in my subsequent dealings with Greg that the news must have marked him. What he took away was not that I was upset, but that I would soon be in possession of much more disposable income.

As the weeks went by, Greg became more and more convinced that I was seeing someone. I eventually confessed, hopeful that it might encourage him to back off – but it only provoked a new barrage of vile text messages and derogatory comments. The texts were a mixture of contempt and sick imaginings: Greg would delight in accusing me of the most perverted sexual antics, always in lurid detail. He accused me of somehow involving Luke or otherwise exposing him to these antics. It was another insight into his own twisted sexual depravity.

At first the text messages and accusations got me down. I felt dirty and debased. And for the longest time, I engaged with him, trying to reason or argue with him or otherwise defend myself. But responding to the slander only encouraged him, and so I learned to ignore it. Abuse from Greg simply became the wallpaper of my life. Eventually I became desensitised to it, unmoved by even the most outrageous slander on my character. And so the cycle continued.

12

Empowerment

It was 2005, and in a fit of pique one day Greg announced that he had no intention of being a part-time father. He said he never wanted to see Luke again. At first I was distressed – as he knew I would be. Luke loved the time he spent with his father, and, for better or for worse, Greg was his dad so I wanted to facilitate a relationship between them.

Not long after, Greg lost his job. He moved out of his apartment, sold his car and went to stay at the Russian Orthodox monastery for a period. The next contact I had from Greg was a message to inform me that he was heading overseas on some sort of pilgrimage. Israel, Egypt, Peru – it was a typically confused grab bag of destinations, all of which Greg intended to visit to answer a conflicting series of perceived religious callings. I know he funded most of the trip with credit cards, because for months after his return, I had debt collectors calling me asking if I knew of his whereabouts. Midway through his trip, he called me to tell me he had run out of money and would I transfer $2000 into his bank account. Even though I wanted Greg to have a relationship with Luke, I was also keen –

for my sanity's sake – for him to stay away as long as possible, and maybe even never come back. I transferred the money.

By the time Greg returned, eight months later, I had made the decision to leave Menzies Creek. My share from the sale of the family farm meant Luke and I were in a position to move up in the world, to purchase a place where we could settle and I could watch him grow.

After a month or so of searching, I settled on a property in Tyabb, on the Mornington Peninsula. It was, once again, a semi-rural pocket of Victoria, a beautiful patch of the world wedged between Port Phillip Bay and the Western Port. From the property, you could look out across the nearby waters of Western Port to French Island, beyond which lay Phillip Island. Tyabb was close to the townships of Mornington, Somerville and Hastings, both of which boasted all the shops and amenities we could need. It was ten minutes on the freeway from Frankston and fifty minutes – on a good run – on the freeway to the Melbourne CBD.

The house was a 1990s build. Brown brick, two storey, high ceilings, open and light. There was a pool off the back patio, a beautiful garden full of gums and natives, and a large paddock that stretched down a gentle slope. It was perfect. Close by was Tyabb Public School and down the road was Flinders Christian Community College. The moment I saw it, I knew Luke and I would be happy there. And so I made an offer on the house.

Because the IVO had expired, Greg was no longer restricted from coming near me or my property. Aware that I was keen to maintain the barriers the IVO had established, Greg promptly set about testing them, increasing the frequency of his unannounced visits, always picking up and dropping off Luke in hours outside those we had agreed, always hoping to catch me with another man. And each time, there was the confusing combination of abuse and overture. If he wasn't calling me a slut, he was inviting me to join him for a drink. His behaviour – slander one minute, seduction the next – was too erratic for me to take seriously. I explained patiently each time he invited me that I was not interested, to which he would invariably respond that I was a 'fucking moron'.

For his birthday in November I sent Greg an email, purportedly from Luke, wishing him a happy birthday. I attached a photo of Greg and Luke together.

Four days later, I received the following response:

I'm disappointed in you Luke. You have become too feminine since I have been overseas … Your mother's inheritance and since I have known her, continually calling her father for money and that fool giving it, supporting her in her folly rather than relying on your true father. Now with you moving to Tyabb to an overpriced property not even large enough to support a horse is another indication of thoughtlessness and ignorance itself. How I am expected to be more than a two hour amusement once a week only an idiot can explain (ask your mother). To think in the last five months you are now scared of the pool which you weren't and can still only ride your bike as skilled as I taught you, this shows the manly neglect you have suffered. Your present path you will probably become a homosexual and your mother doesn't have the right spirit to be concerned of this. There is a lesson to know Luke, no man gets into the bath for amusement with other people's sons, and when asked to wash your bottom only an idiot wouldn't be able to see through it. As for this loser [your mother has been seeing], he as a male after two marriages must be proud to disturb others' lives. If there was an ounce of truth coming from your mother's mouth she has not shared it with me, the foolish arse blower. Satan's tricks, and by the look of Vi learnt from her. The violence to your Grandfather would have manifested from Vi, distracting him with violence so not to be able to preserve her truly. Your spirit Luke has a dark hood on your head. It did come off when I saw you but five months away and evil has its glue in your mother's life. The pleasure your mother got from hearing I had not attended the Mormon Church was an obvious indication of her following an unrighteous path. Your baptism in England was to ensure your mother got some money, it was no indication of her faith. 2 hours once a week Dad.

It is telling how immune I had become to his ramblings that this email didn't strike me as even remotely unusual. Disturbing and deeply offensive, yes, but unusual, no. Take the tone and nonsensical, abusive content of the above email and multiply it into hundreds of text messages and phone calls, and you start to get a sense of what I was dealing with.

About a week later, and perhaps triggered by the email, I became very depressed. I was midway through the process of selling my property at Menzies Creek and settling on the house at Tyabb. Work was stressful, juggling Luke was exhausting and Greg was constantly abusing me. So when he called one night to launch into a new tirade, I broke down. The thought of him haunting my every waking moment was too much to bear. He had worn me down and I cracked.

'Enough, Greg, it's enough,' I sobbed. 'I can't do this anymore. I can't take it. Just have Luke. Take him. He's all yours. You can have custody of Luke. I can't fight anymore.'

There was silence on the other end of the line for a moment.

'Now, now, Rosie,' he began. 'There's no need to be like that. I'm sorry if you feel that way. And of course I don't want full custody of Luke. That's not what I want at all.'

Only years afterwards was I able to understand that full custody of Luke was most definitely not what Greg wanted. He wanted to torture and torment me – and that could only be done if he could use Luke as a pawn.

A month later, and on the eve of our move to Tyabb, I contacted Child Support to cancel Greg's payment obligations and waive the debts he had accrued. I had never actually received any payments from him for Luke, but I reasoned that relieving him of the obligation to make payments might possibly reduce the level of stress Greg was under, and hopefully reduce the tension that existed between us. It was to be another example of my complete naïveté when it came to Greg.

I had now been working for the telecommunications company for five years, and each year it had only become more stressful. By the time I made the move to Tyabb – significantly further away from my workplace than Menzies Creek had been – I was holding on by a thread to my job, worn down by the physical and emotional toll it had taken. The job I had been doing was coming to a natural end, and the only jobs available in the company involved a lot of travel and even more pressure. I couldn't have taken them even if I wanted them. Being a single mum in Tyabb with a toddler and working in the CBD were never going to be happy bedfellows. And if I am honest, I made the move there as a way of gently making it impossible for me to continue working in the corporate rat race. I was done.

The inheritance from the farm had given me a small financial cushion, so I used the time to set up Luke's and my new home.

Now that I had acreage in my life, I immediately wanted to fill it with the farm animals that had been such an important part of my own childhood growing up. And so to the goats, chickens and dogs I already had, I added a horse for good measure. My menagerie was complete.

Soon enough, a looming cash-flow crisis forced me to look for work again. With a toddler at home or in local daycare, my options were relatively limited. So I accepted a job doing telemarketing sales in nearby Mornington. On the plus side, it was nine to five, a ten-minute drive from home and required a bare minimum of brain power. On the down side, it was soul-destroying work and I hated it. With my self-esteem still under almost daily assault from Greg, this was just the professional diversion I didn't need. My career – which had once informed so much of my sense of identity – had stalled completely. I was showing up to work each morning in a light industrial complex on the fringes of a sleepy seaside town in Victoria's south – and it was killing me.

Into this mix, I still had to factor regular exposure to Greg, whose access visits to Luke continued. He would come to collect Luke and take him back to St Kilda where he was living. Sometimes he would bring Luke back to Tyabb the following day, sometimes he would not. If it had been a casual lack of organisation on his part, I wouldn't have minded as much the two-hour return journey in the car to collect Luke from St Kilda. But it was always done with malice and intent.

On one occasion, when I was five minutes late to an agreed handover meeting at Chadstone Shopping Centre, Greg bundled Luke into his car and told me I had missed the window and would have to drive to St Kilda to collect Luke. On another occasion, during a handover at Frankston McDonald's, he started to insist all pick-ups now needed to take place in St Kilda. I dissolved into tears on the spot, unable to take any more of Greg's controlling behaviour.

As Greg trailed me with Luke in his arms, I ran towards my car in the car park and fell to my knees, sobbing uncontrollably. 'Keep him! Just fucking keep him! I can't do this anymore!' I cried.

Greg tried to calm me down, but I got into my car and drove off.

'You fucking bitch!' he screamed after me. 'You drive out of this car park and I swear you will never see your son again!'

Three kilometres down the road, Greg found me pulled onto the shoulder, slumped over the steering wheel, crying. He pulled over and wordlessly buckled Luke in the child safety seat in the back of my car before driving off.

Greg understood that by changing his plans or failing to honour an agreement we had reached about returning Luke to me at Tyabb, he would be able to cause maximum disturbance to my life. The more time he could tie me up in time-wasting effort to accommodate his whims, the less time I had to get on with a life of my own.

I can hardly bear to recall this incident now, but I was so desperate and emotionally frayed I felt like I couldn't take it anymore. Of course, I would never have willingly given up Luke to Greg, but I was at the end of my tether.

Initially, I'd turned to friends to vent my frustration. And initially, they were very understanding and sympathetic. But, after a while, their patience for my predicament waned and, invariably, they would become frustrated – often with me. 'Why don't you call the police? Why don't you get the courts involved? Why don't you fight back? Why don't you move home to England?' But legally I had no options. The courts had made it quite clear that Greg had a right to see his son, and I felt that his harassment was just something I was going to have to manage.

Eventually, I'd run out of friends I felt I could burden with my troubles, and so I looked to see what services existed for women in my predicament. The act of taking the step to call a crisis line is a massive one. It's an acknowledgement that things have spiralled out of your control. It's putting your hand up and admitting yourself to a club you never wanted to belong to.

I dialled the number for the crisis line. Though the conversation was brief, it was revelatory. Not only was there someone who was willing to listen, they didn't feel the need to try and offer a solution or, worse, pass judgement. They spoke with a calmness and an authority in which I found enormous comfort. Importantly, they seemed to know my story before I even had time to tell it to them. Not the specifics, because they were unique to me, but the signposts, the triggers, the hallmarks of the violence I had suffered – they were all hauntingly familiar to the crisis line counsellor. They told me of a 'Women in Relationships' course that was being run in Rosebud, down on the Mornington Peninsula. Emboldened by this first venture into the realm of domestic violence services, I resolved to go along.

The meeting was held in a stark room in a nondescript community centre. I sat and listened. With every minute that passed and every second of testimony I heard from the other women in the group, I felt a quickening of my heart. They were speaking my story, giving voice to my pain and my fear. They were strangers, but each one of them could have been me.

I specifically remember one woman who had been stalked by her ex-partner for the past thirteen years. For thirteen years he had called her, texted her, lain in wait outside her house, followed her home from work. She lived in constant fear of him. Her every waking moment was consumed with thoughts of him. He wasn't technically in her life anymore, yet he controlled almost every aspect of it. And I was gripped by a dread that she was my future, that I was destined to forever be haunted by Greg and his increasingly irrational behaviour.

The course ran over several weeks, and it gave me the tools to properly quantify just how completely my own life was being affected by Greg. Surrounded by fellow victims of family violence, I felt empowered for the first time in years. I also took up riding lessons around this time, pouring my energy into my horse and focusing on something that gave me confidence rather than someone who undermined me. Little by little, I felt my self-confidence start to creep back.

At the end of the course I was so energised, I didn't want it to end. It felt almost as if we had formed a little family who were all now expected to go our separate ways. I was going to miss them all, and I was going to miss the intellectual stimulation of examining family violence as a social and psychological ill. For the first time since I had left school, I felt inspired by a subject and desperate to learn more.

I asked the woman who was running the course how she had come into her line of work, and she told me she had studied a Diploma of Community Welfare. I was convinced I had just found my new calling. I went home immediately and researched the course. Reading the synopsis was like reading a road map for how I wanted the rest of my life to play out. For years I had worked in the corporate space – not out of any real design, but simply because I had fallen into a job and, like so many others, ricocheted from one role to another without ever really questioning if it was what I really wanted to do.

Here was a vocation that would bring together my interest in social justice, my passion for making a difference to the lives of those less fortunate and my firsthand experience as a victim of family violence. The only catch? I still had bills to pay and a child to raise. So the belt was tightened a little at home, a line of credit was sought and I visited Centrelink for the first time in my life to tide me over while I studied. I was going to go into debt to complete the diploma, and there was no guarantee of a job at the end even if I did complete it. But I was determined to do it – for the benefit of my own, severely dented self-esteem as much as anything else.

When finally I started the course, being back in a classroom environment just felt so stimulating. I was your classic mature-age student – so grateful for the opportunity to even be sitting in a classroom that I threw myself into the course with gusto. I was eager to make the most of every second of the learning experience, which was compounded by the fact that, as a single mum, I only had a certain number of hours every day in which to study.

We were a mixed bunch of students. Some had spent years working in the welfare sector or on the fringes of it, dealing with families in poverty, families facing long-term unemployment and homes racked by domestic violence. But I had *lived* it, and I was vocal when it came to expressing my opinions. Sometimes, unless you've lived through something, you don't quite understand.

13

I'm in a classroom at Flinders Christian Community College with a group of other parents. Usually I'm too busy with work to collect Luke from school, but today the school has organised a talk for parents about the Life Education van that's about to visit the school. One of the teachers earnestly outlines the sorts of things they'll be discussing with the kids. Frankly, it all sounds a bit lame. I have to disguise a smirk, imagining Luke's reaction when some well-meaning educator tries to lecture him and his classmates about smoking and drugs. They're only eleven but they're already so worldly. I don't for a second think Luke or his friends are smoking drugs, but it's a new, internet-enabled generation. There's not much you can teach them that they haven't already discovered for themselves online. And so I start texting on my phone.

As it gets closer to 3 pm, I get up and make for the door. I'm not usually rude like this, but I want to make sure I don't miss Luke when he comes out of class. I want to surprise him with a lift home. He doesn't much like having to walk home from school, which is crazy, because it's just up the hill and he needs to become independent, not least because I'm always being told I'm too soft with him, that I indulge him too much.

But I figure he's still only eleven. There's plenty of time for him to find out how hard the world can be. And besides, I'm living on borrowed time. Before I know it, he'll be a teenager and then a young man making his way in the world. Much better to suffocate him with affection now, while he's still inclined to accept it.

Not that the pre-teen rot hasn't set in already. Here he comes now, pretending he hasn't seen me as he heads out of the school gates with his mate Jaxon. He's part-joking, part-serious, because he's reaching that age where it's dead uncool to be seen with your mum. It's even more uncool to show her any physical affection. So, as a joke, I run up behind the pair of them and go to give Luke an exaggerated hug.

'And this,' I cackle, 'is what happens to little boys who ignore their mothers.'

Luke's in a good mood and laughs as he pushes me away.

He and Jaxon talk about football and whether or not Luke will play up a year this year and join the under thirteens. Luke's not sure.

I watch him with maternal pride. He and Jaxon say their farewells and Luke clambers into the car.

On the way home we joke about embarrassing mums. I think how nice it is for us to spend time like this together. It's a good feeling. A good day.

14

Access

It's a funny thing being the mother of a small child. You develop a love–hate relationship with the strangest things. Take, for example, the Wiggles. Luke became a Wiggles fan almost by accident. It all started when he'd fallen sick with one of those twenty-four-hour viruses, the sort of illness that hits little kids like a tonne of bricks and knocks the stuffing out of them but is gone the next day. Someone had given me a DVD of the Wiggles and, out of desperation, I put it on. Luke was enthralled. He watched it back to back for the rest of the day.

To my mind, the Wiggles were a bunch of grown men in skivvies singing mindless tunes, but to Luke, they were demigods. He knew every song and every dance, and would bug me to put on the DVD every time we walked in the door. The songs did my head in, but I came to develop a grudging respect for the Wiggles: anyone who can capture and hold the attention of a child is truly talented. And anyone who can afford a single mother thirty minutes respite in any given day similarly deserves a medal.

I took Luke to see the Wiggles in concert several times. He absolutely loved it. There's something magical about taking a child to the theatre or a stage show for the first time: the look of wonder on their faces as they try to take in this fantastic world where relative strangers don brightly coloured costumes and dance and sing under lights for the amusement of a crowd. It was a dynamic that Luke adored, and a world that he really connected with. There was something of the natural showman in Luke. He was cheeky and funny. Even as a tiny boy he understood what it was to entertain and to make people laugh.

The last time we went to see the Wiggles together, the yellow Wiggle, Greg, had to bow out mid-tour because of illness. He had been diagnosed with orthostatic intolerance, a circulatory system disorder that affects blood flow. The announcement came over the PA before the show that Greg would not be performing. A video of Greg appeared on the big screen, explaining that he was not well and wouldn't be able to be with all the boys and girls. And most kids stared at it, took it in and got on with their dancing and singing. My little boy, who up until that point had been standing excitedly in anticipation of the concert beginning, crawled onto my lap and sat there for the rest of the show. He was devastated.

In the car on the way home, he asked me if Greg Wiggle was going to die. He felt things deeply and was easily moved to tears.

Which is not to say that he was soft. When the occasion demanded, Luke could be the bravest little boy around. Like any kid, Luke suffered the usual ailments and injuries as a boy. There was the broken wrist following a fall off the monkey bars, an accident that required emergency surgery, which he took utterly in his stride. Me, not so much – but Luke was calm throughout.

There was the broken collarbone when at the age of three he fell out of his bed. Once again, he was stoic in the face of what must have been acute pain. He needed grommets put in to address what doctors were convinced was a partial hearing problem in his left ear (an operation to which Greg was vehemently opposed, convinced any stay in hospital was simply an opportunity for doctors to ply you with medicines that were part of some grand government conspiracy). And once again, Luke never raised a complaint.

Luke also underwent several lengthy and painful dental procedures after it was deemed the enamel hadn't formed properly on his back teeth. The dentist remarked on how brave he was, and how most children his age would have required general anaesthetic.

So he was brave. But the soft centre was what defined him. One evening we sat down to watch the movie *Marley & Me*. Friends had recommended it, knowing how much Luke and I loved dogs. At one point I got up to go the kitchen, only to find Luke sobbing when I returned. The bloody dog had gone and died.

That was the kind of little boy he was – and it made me really proud. In a society in which men too often are raised to distance themselves from their emotions, my little boy was very much in touch with his. And while it meant he was occasionally prone to melodrama, and on more than one occasion would be in a flood of tears following some small occurrence, for the most part it was a sensitivity I wanted to nurture. It would stand him in good stead, I reasoned, when he grew up and was left to negotiate the world on his own.

*

It was 2006 and armed with a renewed sense of empowerment – and midway through my studies for my Diploma of Community Welfare – I decided it was time to put some legal parameters in place around Greg's access to Luke. My previous strategy of preferring to keep the Family Court at bay, and instead work out a flexible arrangement, had been an abject failure. And so I looked to the Family Court to be my salvation, to consider the facts of my case and soberly inform Greg that his access to Luke would necessarily need to be more predictable.

I remember the day in court clearly. I had spent weeks beforehand working with my solicitor, preparing documents to present to the court, outlining Greg's history of violence and unpredictability. At the time, I even felt bad for collating a dossier whose only objective was to put rules and restrictions around the one thing in Greg's life that appeared to truly mean anything to him: time spent with his son.

And so we both fronted up to the Family Court in Dandenong for mediation before the court's sitting registrar. I had instructed my solicitor to apply for Greg's access to be restricted to alternate weekends only. I was, after all, the primary carer – and the sole provider. The constant to-ing and fro-ing from Tyabb to St Kilda was not only inconvenient but hugely disruptive to Luke's life.

Greg acquitted himself with typical arrogance, intimidating my solicitor and the registrar to the point where the registrar had to reprimand him for being a bully and completely out of line. I sat there feeling quietly vindicated. At last, a third party – and someone of influence – was seeing Greg for the bully he was. Someone who could make a difference was being treated firsthand to a tiny sample of the extreme abuse I had gone to great lengths (with no small amount of trepidation) to document in my court submission.

But as the mediation went on, it became increasingly obvious that my request for alternate weekend access for Greg would be roundly ignored in favour of Greg's preference to see Luke at least once a week. Agitated, I began to speak up, interrupting the registrar, making sure he was aware of my displeasure and frustration. Fearing I was about to be reprimanded, my solicitor quickly intervened and took me outside the room, telling me to calm down and advising me it was better to go along with the court decision rather than antagonise the registrar.

I felt cheated. I felt betrayed. I felt confused. Why had I spent weeks compiling a dossier with my solicitor if that dossier was not even referenced during the mediation? Why was I the one walking out of the court feeling like I had done wrong for daring to suggest Greg's access to Luke be more predictable – alternate weekends would have been more sustainable due to the travelling distances?

As she shepherded me out, my solicitor made an attempt to explain why the arrangement was for the best. But none of it made sense. Not least the fact that I had forked out a considerable amount of money I really couldn't afford on legal representation that I felt had acted more in Greg's interest than my own or Luke's.

How differently it could all have turned out if I had been referred to the help I so desperately needed, instead of being sent home with a court order I knew was going to play directly into Greg's hands and an immediate future that made my stomach churn with anxiety. I now had orders in place from the Family Court permitting Greg have access to Luke every weekend. In the event he contravened those orders and kept Luke longer, or attempted to take him earlier than set out, there was no point my calling the local police, because only the Australian Federal

Police could enforce Family Court orders – and only once the court had ordered them to do so.

And so I came to understand that, while magistrates in criminal courts could issue IVOs restricting Greg from coming anywhere near me, a Family Law court order granting him access to Luke would almost always override the IVO, except in exceptional circumstances when magistrates suspended family court orders for short periods of time. All of which meant I simply felt more vulnerable.

It was a vulnerability that Greg seemed to sense – and exploit. After several weeks of adhering to the new court orders and picking up and dropping off Luke at the times the Family Court had deemed suitable, Greg disappeared on one of his regular visits to the Russian monastery.

The timings are not clear – because I wasn't there and I've never had contact with the monks that live there – but it was later reported that on a visit to the monastery around this time, Greg was experiencing paranoid delusions.

During dinner one night in the monastery, he leaned across to Father Alexis, the spiritual father, and said, 'Can you see them?'

Not understanding what Greg was talking about, Father Alexis replied, 'See what?'

Greg responded: 'There are worms coming out of the liver of the man sitting next to me and they are attacking me. I have to move away.' Father Alexis would later tell *Four Corners* investigative journalist Geoff Thompson that Greg had confided in him that he was a diagnosed and medicated schizophrenic – something I was unaware of at the time – who had smoked too much marijuana.

When Greg returned to Melbourne from the monastery, he was homeless. He arrived at Dandenong station one evening at

7 pm and called me, saying he had no bed for the night and asking if he could stay with me and Luke. It was a tactic he had used before: showing up as darkness fell and banking on my better nature to admit him into the house. And so I found myself once again in a familiar bind: did I turn him away and incur the wrath of my son, who was genuinely excited to see his father, and possibly trigger more violence from Greg? Or did I show him yet another kindness, in the vain hope it may mollify him? I didn't have the energy for another fight and, anyway, it felt like no matter what I did – whether I tried to accommodate Greg or tried to fight him at every turn – it made not a scrap of difference in the end. And so, reluctantly, I agreed to let him stay in the spare room for the weekend. His adherence to the court orders had been to the letter and he clearly had nowhere else to go. But the pattern was repeating again.

The following afternoon, we were all outside feeding the goats and putting the chickens into their coop for the night when Greg's mood suddenly darkened. It was terrifying how quickly it could happen – like a shadow passing over him. Apparently he had seen a new chicken egg incubator in the coop and suspected it had been put there by one of the fictional men he believed I was secretly dating. He flew into a rage, storming back into the house, ordering Luke to collect his things, declaring he was leaving and taking Luke with him. Luke, who had only just turned four, stood rooted to the spot in the living room.

I tried to calm Greg down, telling him to stop being ridiculous: reminding him he had no house, no car and nowhere to go. 'You're not taking Luke anywhere,' I said, picking up the phone. 'And if you don't calm down, I'm calling the police.'

Launching himself at me, he began to wrestle the phone off me, grunting loudly as Luke looked on in terror. Greg threw me against the wall and held me there by my neck. Then he hurled me to the floor and kneeled over me, holding his fist to my face. 'I'd like to knock you into next week,' he spat.

Terrified, I managed to squirm from his grip and run from the house. The cold air hit my face. Tears streaming down my face and my heart racing, I tore up the driveway and onto the street. I looked frantically over my shoulder to make sure he wasn't following me, then ran to my neighbours' house, banging loudly on their front door. Rhys and Penny took me in and attempted to calm me down, urging me to phone the police.

I made the call. 'He's still in there. Luke's there too,' I said in a panic. The police told me to remain calm, to keep away from the house and to wait for the patrol car that had been dispatched.

Waiting for the police to arrive felt like an eternity – in reality it was probably more like a couple of minutes. I paced the living room at Rhys and Penny's house, desperate to rush back across the road and rescue my boy. But it was me Greg wanted to hurt, not Luke. I was the one in danger.

When the police turned up, they offered to escort me back to my house. As we walked in, I looked into the living room to see Luke sitting calmly in front of the television while Greg cooked his dinner in the kitchen as if nothing had happened.

He looked up to see the police, registered their presence, then turned back to his cooking, apparently unmoved.

I glanced nervously at the police, who were exchanging looks. Mortified that they thought I was making it all up – like some melodramatic woman with a talent for overreaction – I felt a wave of embarrassment.

'Mr Anderson, you're going to have to leave with us,' one of the young constables finally said.

Greg looked up from what he was doing with an air of studied indifference. For a moment it appeared as though he was going to ignore them. Then, finally, he moved away from the stove top, coolly collected his things and walked out into the night, flanked by the police officers.

Two hours later, the phone rang. It was Greg, asking if I could come down to Frankston train station to collect him.

No charges had been laid. With no obvious signs of me having been physically attacked, it was my word against his. And the police, having defused the situation by removing Greg, had done what they could. It was, after all, just another domestic.

Greg's expectation that I would come down and pick him up as if nothing had happened completely threw me. How dare he? After everything he'd put me through! I put down the phone and this time I held firm. I didn't feel responsible for him and I would not pick him up. Where he slept that night was not my concern.

*

I had reached the point where every decision in my life was made according to what would least likely provoke Greg. I was living in fear of him. Which, of course, was exactly what he wanted.

Having been subjected to his rage once more and having glimpsed how tenuous his grip was becoming on whatever self-control he had left, I resolved to get my affairs in order. I had studied family violence and I was aware of the statistics. One woman a week was killed at the hands of a current or former partner. My experience with the police and court system had led me to believe that they were ultimately unable to protect me. I had watched Greg's steady mental deterioration, and I knew how much anger and paranoia simmered away inside him. He was a time bomb waiting to go off, even if no one else could see it. The possibility that I would become a statistic at his hand was, to my mind, very real.

From the moment Luke was born, I had lived daily with the possibility that I would not live to see him grow into a man. This was not because I truly feared that Greg would kill me but because I had lost my mother at such a young age. As Luke approached the age I was when Mum died, I think I relived the fear I felt at the time (in the same way someone may worry when they reach the age at which their parent died). And that bothered me, not so much for myself but for Luke – that he could go through life without a mother. That, after all, had been my experience.

And so I sat down to write a will.

Important Information to Accompany the Will and Testament of Rosemary Ann Batty

I make this record to clarify the exact relationship that I have with Mr Anderson. He is in NO way my partner and I am definitely in NO kind of relationship with him. He is the father of my son, Luke, and to that end I endeavour to maintain a healthy, amicable relationship with him with Luke's best interest ALWAYS in mind.

He has never contributed financially to my property, but has often assisted me with maintenance, cutting grass, repairs around the home, gardening and generally assisting where he can when requested.

I believe Greg suffers from a mental imbalance but to my knowledge, this has never been medically diagnosed and I am not aware that he has taken any prescribed medication to assist with his behaviour.

He has admitted that he hears voices and I have witnessed frequent bouts of paranoia and delusion. In the fifteen years that I have known Greg, his behaviour has deteriorated and his frustration and anger have intensified. Without question, he has become more religious and seeks the comfort and surrounds of religious environments and religious people. He has no commitment to a particular religion and, since I've known him, has been involved with the Mormon Church, Hare Krishna, Russian Orthodox and, on occasion, Jehovah's Witness and Seventh Day Adventist churches.

His family have remained extremely important to him but I don't know how much they are aware of his erratic behaviour. He eventually alienates himself from any friendship that he makes – particularly people he lives with as he becomes increasingly paranoid under pressure. His previous flatmate, Darren, in St Kilda, frequently spoke to me about Greg's unreasonable behaviour but was too intimidated by him to confront him about it. To my knowledge, at each address where Greg has lived, he has been asked to leave because of inappropriate behaviour. His family relationships are the only ones I have known him to be able to maintain and this, I believe, is because they don't see him often and he doesn't live close to any of them.

I know that Greg loves Luke and I have done everything to encourage his role as Luke's father even when put under pressure to refuse him contact with Luke. I have never felt that this was the correct approach. Luke, without reservation, loves Greg and I believe that Greg is good with him. He has always spent time playing with him, teaching him things and introducing him to Christian beliefs. I have no doubt that he does his best by Luke. However, Greg is incapable of accepting any responsibility for himself. He is unable to hold down regular and reliable employment, maintain a fixed address and certainly not able to maintain healthy relations whether with work colleagues, friends or acquaintances. His controlling, deluded and paranoid tendencies eventually surface.

To date Greg is approaching forty-seven years old. He is living in shared accommodation that is partly furnished. It is shabby but obviously all he can afford on unemployment benefits. He has no savings, no car, no furniture or possessions other than basic clothing. I worry about what will happen to him in the future and definitely have concerns about his ability to have Luke to stay with him in a suitable environment.

I am not trying to defame Greg because he can be a caring and fun-loving person. I care for and have cared for him deeply, but have had to accept that is it impossible to maintain a healthy relationship with him. For my own wellbeing over the years I have had to distance myself from contact with him but this has proved difficult as I have enjoyed his company and sincerely hoped that we could resolve our differences. I know now, and accept, that this is impossible. I also have no doubt that he loves me and his behaviour towards me is out of hurt and frustration, not understanding why I continue to push him away. He has never demonstrated any remorse or regret for his actions or acknowledgement that his behaviour has ever been unacceptable. I believe he sees me as the person with all the problems and is in denial regarding his actions towards me. It has always been impossible to discuss issues of any kind with him.

I make these points to demonstrate that, although Greg loves Luke as much as any father, he is not the person that should care for Luke as his sole guardian should anything happen to me in the future. As Luke's mother, I want the best for my son and that is why I am taking the time now to document my wishes – at the same time sincerely hoping that this will never happen. I need to feel that if Luke is to find himself without me in the future, that I have done what I can to take care of his best interests and wellbeing, both financially and emotionally. I believe that I know what is best for Luke and I hope that this is taken into account if anything should happen to me.

My Wishes
Guardianship: As per my Will, I have chosen Mark and Sharon. They are the best parents that I know and have the best family structure that I know. I have deliberately nurtured our friendship ensuring that Luke feels comfortable with and close to both their sons. He knows them better than anyone else. Sharon attended his birth and has felt a special connection towards him since then. They also know how important I believe Greg's presence in Luke's life is, and they have been friends I have turned to in times of stress regarding both Greg and my role as Luke's mother. They also know my family in England and would encourage Luke to keep this important link. Should my family live here in Australia, then my choice of guardians may well be different, but I feel like Luke should remain in Australia to be close to Greg and what feels familiar and safe to him, i.e., crèche/school and his friends, swimming classes etc. Mark and Sharon live in a lovely open farm-

like setting and Luke would love having the opportunity to grow up in this environment.

My Family: I would love my Estate to pay for frequent trips for Luke to the UK to see my relatives, particularly his grandparents and my brothers. I also hope that they will take the time to visit Luke in Australia when possible so that he never forgets me and our English heritage. I welcome both my parents and brothers to take any of my personal possessions that they feel would be important to them if this should help them remember me. I owe my parents so much for everything they have done for me and wouldn't have the home or any of the lovely items within it without their help. I hope they understand the choices I have made and want them to know how much they mean to me. Even though I have chosen to remain in Australia, not a day goes by that I don't miss my family and wish they lived close by, particularly in regards to Luke as he would have benefited greatly in having his uncles around as good male role models.

Greg: Over the years I have tried to place healthy boundaries between us. This has been difficult as I have seen the pain it causes Greg. I don't think Greg realises how much I have cared for him and these actions are to protect us from hurting each other further and displaying inappropriate behaviour for Luke to witness. I have wanted to assist Greg wherever and whenever I could but understand that this would not be helpful in the long term, and Greg has to take responsibility for the decisions he takes, both financially and emotionally. I would like my Estate to purchase a unit, or similar dwelling, as an investment for Greg to live in. Also, a suitable car for Greg to drive. Both purchases should be bought and maintained by my Estate and not put in Greg's name. This way he would have the benefit of having them but unable to sell them or dispose of them. He would then have a suitable place to live where Luke could stay comfortably when visiting overnight and a car to collect Luke whenever his access visits are scheduled. Once Luke has reached the age where he can drive his own car, then Greg would be expected to take over the car and maintenance costs himself and it could be put into his own name and given to him. No further assistance would need to be given as Luke would be independent enough to visit his father utilising a car of his own. Greg would be able to stay at the unit as long as he wishes, but it is to remain in Luke's name as an investment property for him, as our existing house in Tyabb would be considered his possible home when mature enough to live there.

I would be happy for Greg to have any sentimental possession of mine should he wish to take anything to remember me by. I would also be happy for my Estate to pay for an annual holiday for Luke and Greg to go somewhere in Australia/New Zealand together. This could be camping, skiing or something of that nature. Nothing too extravagant – but somewhere they both would like to go and stay in comfortable accommodation with sufficient spending money to enjoy the trip. I hope that Greg respects my decision that Luke should live with Mark and Sharon and continue access/custody arrangements as per decided by the Magistrates Court. I sincerely hope also that by including Greg in this way that he understands how much I want him to continue to be a good father to Luke and how I have tried to recommend these arrangements with this in mind. Should Greg counteract my guardianship recommendations and insist that Luke live with him then I hope Mark and Sharon will take the matter to court in an attempt to have this arrangement enforced. All costs to be met by my Estate. Should the judge decide in favour of Luke living with Greg then I retract the above and offer no assistance to Greg for both accommodation or transport. I would expect him to take full financial responsibility for Luke and to be in a position to provide a suitable place to live. All of my assets and money in my Estate would be managed by my Executors in trust for Luke until he reaches twenty-five years of age and I have complete faith that they would handle my affairs fairly and in Luke's best interest.

Mark and Sharon: I know they would treat Luke equally as if he were their own son and this is why I have chosen them to be both Executors and Guardians. I would love Luke to grow up learning the importance of saving and respect for financial affairs – mainly so that he will act responsibly when he finally inherits my Estate and also so that he won't feel obliged to give money to his father to bail him out or enter into any enterprise that Greg may introduce him to where he could squander his inheritance. I trust their judgement completely. Perhaps they have a better perspective on some decisions where firmness is required! I hope they encourage Luke to pursue University, TAFE or an apprenticeship of some kind. Anything where he shows passion and spontaneous ability. I trust them to utilise funds from my Estate to ensure Luke is given the same opportunities that their boys receive and the same appreciation for possessions/gifts and having to save for things that are important to them will therefore teach him the value of things. I hope to improve on this with Luke over the next few years myself and I know Mark and Sharon have a firmness that I lack that Luke will respect.

Funeral: What a topic! My favourite songs/hymns of all time are:

'What A Wonderful World' (Louis Armstrong)

'Imagine' (John Lennon)

'Amazing Grace'

'Morning Has Broken'

I probably prefer to be cremated and my ashes returned to England where they can be thrown into the River Trent from the flood bank in the field at the rear of our farmhouse. I always loved looking at the river from my bedroom window and somehow or another that view is most prominent in my mind whenever I think of home. I would like something to be engraved on my mum's gravestone in remembrance so that Luke always has a place to visit and reflect on my memory. I have always returned to my mum's grave when I've wanted to talk to her and tell her things that were troubling me. It's important to have somewhere to go even if it may be on the other side of the world. As much as I love living in Australia I am so torn about my heritage and was devastated when Dad sold the farm. I know that the scattering of my ashes would involve all my closest friends and family – and would like my Estate to pay the expenses for Mark and Sharon and their family to accompany Luke over to England for the occasion so that they can remember me and have a good holiday together to enjoy a lifetime trip that Luke will always remember with some happiness mixed with obvious sadness.

I know that my true friends will pull together and provide the love and assurance that Luke will need – but I intend to stick around and hope that these wishes and requests never have to be put into effect.

Thanks to you all and, if the worst should happen, ENJOY! Enjoy my memory and laugh at my silly insecurities and shortcomings. Maximise whatever wealth can be taken from my Estate without leaving Luke short. I would be ecstatic if all friends and family could get together either annually or biennially and have a BBQ in my memory. An occasion to bring everyone that was important to me together to help Luke keep his connection with me and all that I have tried to stand for. Sincerity, generosity and integrity in regards to both friendship and family. I have sometimes fallen short in these areas but I have always attempted to be the best I can be. I hope Luke can continue to improve on them for me. Please include Greg as best you can and as much as he allows. I know how troubled he continues to be and hope one day that he may find the peace that he seeks.

Signed, Rosemary Ann Batty
Dated: Saturday, 19 August 2006

15

David

England for me was a refuge, a place where everything was frozen in time and where I was permanently in my carefree early twenties. It was the place to which I could retreat whenever my alternate universe in Australia was spiralling out of control.

It was also my 'get-out' clause, the back-up life I had in reserve, to be invoked whenever the Australian experiment fell in a heap – even if the romantic notions I had of my homeland rarely stood up to scrutiny.

So, determined to give myself a break after a rubbish couple of months, I bundled Luke onto a plane and headed home for Christmas in 2006. The plan was to relax in the bosom of family, take stock of my life and regroup. More than that, it would be a chance to celebrate that most family-oriented of holidays with the people in the world who meant the most to me.

On the flight over, I whipped myself into a state of anticipation: Christmas with my family and a chance for Luke to better get to know his English relatives. I couldn't have been more excited.

Of course, the reality didn't quite match the fantasy. We arrived to leaden skies and a cold that seemed to permeate every layer of clothing we owned, such a contrast to the summer we'd left behind. Far from home, removed from his routine and at an awkward age, Luke clung to me like a limpet. My parents made an effort to draw him out, but it only served to push him further into his shell. Not surprisingly, there seemed to be a chasm between both parties that neither knew how to broach – leaving me with the job of mediator.

In my romantic imagination, Luke would have had the same close relationship with Dad and Josephine that I'd had with Nanna Atkin. I wanted him to enjoy the same easy intimacy with his grandparents as I had seen other kids his age back in Australia enjoy with their grandparents. Of course, the crucial element to those other relationships was that all parties were in Australia. They weren't separated by 16,000 kilometres.

Naturally, the distance that separated us also had an impact on the bond between my parents and me. I hadn't told Dad and Josephine about the finer details of my relationship with Greg – they knew many things but not everything. They knew, in a vague sense, that Greg and I were estranged and that things were complicated between us, but they had no sense of the extent of his violence towards me. I just didn't think there was anything to be gained by upsetting them with details about a situation I felt they could do nothing about. I was too far away for them to be of any practical use, and I suppose I was too proud to admit I wasn't able to handle it on my own.

If I am honest, there was also an element of embarrassment that I had gotten myself into this situation. While it was not my fault that Greg had mental issues, I could almost hear the approbation that would be forthcoming from a father or stepmother extremely concerned that the state of my domestic affairs had gotten so dire, and frustrated that they were not in a position to do anything about it.

The England of my imagination was a familial paradise that would solve all my problems. But the reality was something different. Now I had to banish that fantasy and readjust my expectations. I felt very alone on the plane trip home to Australia.

*

In January 2007, Luke bounded off to his first day of school. Tyabb Public School is a lowset collection of buildings nestled in a grove of gum trees on the main Mornington–Tyabb Road. Typical of primary schools in semi-rural areas, its students come from a broad cross-section of the local community. In the area live young families, retirees and professionals who either make the daily commute into Melbourne or Frankston or are among the growing ranks of telecommuters: people who had moved into the area for a tree change, thanks to technology allowing them to largely work from home.

I had always been hyper-aware that I was raising an only child and went out of my way to ensure Luke was at least as socialised as any other kid his age. My friend Leonie had two boys who thought of him as a younger brother and would co-opt him into whatever rough and tumble they were up to whenever we visited them in Adelaide. I would watch on tentatively with a mixture of concern and relief as he was initiated into the rough play that young boys love so much. There were often tears – and they were most commonly Luke's – but to my mind it was important that he learn what it was like to have to hold his own in a big family dynamic.

It was a desire only underscored by the fact that I knew I spoiled him. Mothers – or at least most of them – are always feeling guilty, convinced they are doing something to stuff up the development of their children. I was all but certain that I was not nearly disciplined enough with him – letting him sleep in my bed, perhaps not being as strict with bedtimes and diet and routine as I ought to have been. I always figured it was better to be raising a happy child than a harangued one. And I was a great believer in picking my battles. There were some things – such as politeness to adults, basic social skills, using manners and knowing wrong from right – that were fundamental. These were things we drilled all the time, and I was always proud of the way Luke conducted himself in the company of adults. The other things, I figured, we would work out as we went along. There were only so many hours in the day, and I only had the energy for so much push-back and nagging in any given twenty-four hours. Like every other mother, all I could do for the most part was muddle through and hope for the best.

On that first day of school, I was a basket case of mixed emotions, like every mother on that day. There was relief that I had managed to get him safely to the point where he would be making his schoolyard debut. Somehow we had navigated the myriad health crises and other pitfalls that are a hallmark of every toddlers' years, and here I was about to launch on the world a little human being. There was also sadness at that early period of our lives being over. On some level I had known for years that I was not going to have any more children, but sending Luke to school seemed to close that door with a thud – and it hit me hard. And, of course, there was anxiousness. Would he be okay? Would he find the toilets? Would he have a nice teacher? And – crucially – would he be quick to make friends?

I remember watching him walk into his classroom, his spindly legs barely able to hold up his oversized backpack, and I wanted to bundle him up, take him home and put off this big-wide-world stuff for another year.

As it happened, Luke thrived at school. Having been exposed for so many years to the childcare environment, he didn't appear to suffer from the separation anxiety experienced by many other kids starting school, and soon he'd made a tight-knit group of friends.

*

Since we'd come home from England, visitors had been scarce. I began to reflect on how difficult it can be, sometimes, for a single parent to insert themselves into the life of a community. Quite apart from the fact you have no one to share parenting duties with, you're rarely at the top of barbecue or dinner party invitation lists because, well, a single parent can make for a vaguely awkward social dynamic. Being a single working mum meant there was precious little time for me to forge friendships at the daycare drop-off or, later, at the school gates. It also meant friendships that might have been forged while studying for my diploma at college had to be abandoned before they'd even had a chance to develop. There was no time for coffee after class or a meet-up for a cheeky Thai when a child was waiting to be collected and whisked home for dinner, bath and bed.

One morning I was out in the back paddock shovelling poo, thinking how my old world didn't have a place for me, and my new world didn't have a place for me either. I figured I could either let this sense of vulnerability overwhelm me or I could do something about it. So I resolved to sort out my life. And the first thing I needed to get me out of my slump was someone to ease my loneliness.

I put hours into the creation of my profile on the dating website RSVP. I had heard the horror stories, how it was a hunting ground for middle-aged Lotharios and, worse, confidence tricksters determined to prey on lonely women and fleece them of their life savings. It's safe to say I dipped my toe very tentatively into the online dating scene, zealously screening any overtures that were made and only responding to those who met strict criteria.

David was one of the men who made contact with me early on in and, initially, I was careful about giving anything of myself away. We met for coffee half a dozen times before we went on a proper date. He lived in Mornington – which was only a twenty-minute drive from Tyabb – so I would squeeze in our rendezvous for the afternoons and evenings when Greg had Luke.

David was really respectful, very well-presented and a great conversationalist. We had lots in common, sharing views and values. I saw him with his children and liked how he was with both them and his ex-partner. He was an excellent cook who loved food and wine. In many respects, I had never had a partner who was so compatible. I was in my mid-forties, and I was learning for the first time how companionable someone could be.

And so I eased myself into a relationship with David, always convinced at the back of my mind that it would never last. While David was all about making plans for our future together, I found it hard to plan for anything further away than a month, because I feared that he was too good for me. He was good-looking, kind and funny and had a good job. He was everything I had ever wanted in a partner, but surely I didn't deserve that. Did I?

I worried that, once the first flush of a new relationship had worn off, he would get to know me better and become bored. It never once occurred to me that he was lucky to be with me. It was simply a question of what I felt I deserved, and what I had come to expect from life. The dark cloud of Greg had hovered above me for so long, and his relentless chipping away at my self-esteem had done its work. Thanks to Greg, I felt worthless and incapable of being interesting to someone like David.

I didn't explain to David the full extent of the Greg story, fearing it would be enough to turn him off me. I also did my best to shield him from Greg. As night followed day, I knew what Greg's reaction was going to be when he discovered I was seeing someone new. Sure enough, the first time David stayed at my place in Tyabb, Greg brought Luke home earlier than we had agreed upon. I did my best to keep Greg at the front door and take Luke into the house, but he soon twigged that I had company. And the obscenities started to flow.

'You open your legs to anyone!' he shouted. 'You're a whore! Where's your self-respect?'

I just wanted him to go away. I wasn't in the mood for a stand-up fight so I simply bore the brunt of the abuse, tried to calm him and sent him on his way.

Returning to the house, I was certain I would find David packing his bags and making to leave. He was shocked, but wasn't about to abandon me.

Later, after the dust had settled and he'd had time to process it all, he said, 'I can't believe you let him speak to you like that.'

'What did you want me to do?' I replied defensively. Despite being the victim, I was once again being made to feel I was to blame. 'I just wanted him to go.'

Months passed, and despite the spectre of Greg hanging over us, David stayed – and stayed. With each week that passed, I felt less like I was going to be abandoned, and so I allowed myself to feel vulnerable with him. It was such an enormous relief to be with someone and not feel I had to be on my guard every moment we were together. I felt safe in David's presence. Safe and nurtured. I felt for the first time in a long time that I could breathe.

David and Luke got on well too – at least, as well as a five-year-old and a fifty-year-old man who was not his father could get on. They were never going to be best mates, but David never sought to parent Luke and, as a result, Luke was happy to take him on his own terms. Besides, Luke was an intuitive kid. If he saw that David made me happy, that was enough for him.

And so began roughly five years of relative calm in my life. As contemptuous as Greg was of David, he tended to keep his distance. His visits to collect Luke for the weekend never faltered and for a period it seemed a routine was working. Greg was living in Caulfield in a hostel, but with his own space. He was living on Centrelink benefits, unable to find or hold down a steady job.

Because I had David in my life, and was no longer isolated and vulnerable, the harassment just about stopped. The vile text messages reduced to a dribble, the threatening phone calls all but ceased and Greg's tendency to show up and invite himself onto my property abated. The only real control he was able to exert over me was the extent to which he made my life difficult when it came to managing our respective time with Luke.

Greg knew, as he had known for years, that the easiest way to screw up my life was to tinker with the arrangements we had in place over the shared custody of Luke. A little shift in plans here, a little adjustment of agreed procedure there, always subtle but executed with laser-like focus. It was the old unilateral shifting of goalposts because he knew how much it could impact on me. Except now, with David in the frame, it wasn't just me who was affected.

'Why do you let him do that?' David would demand to know with increasing levels of frustration. 'He's doing it to mess with you, you know that?'

Of course I knew that. But what would he have me do?

One day, David and I had tickets to go and see St Kilda play footy. The plan was to drop Luke at Caulfield on our way to the game. Greg knew we had football tickets and were on a timetable. Which was just perfect as far as he was concerned.

I made sure that we arrived at Caulfield at the agreed time because Greg had zero tolerance for me being late for a drop-off or pick-up. He had been known to leave a pre-arranged meeting point in a fit of pique if I was even a minute late, requiring me to go out of my way to find him and Luke. As a result, I was always five minutes early for our rendezvous. And if I was going to be late, I would always phone ahead. It was a complete double standard, and yet more evidence of his obsession with exerting power and control over me.

But when we arrived at Greg's place, he wasn't home. He wasn't picking up his phone. And the clock was ticking. As David became more and more agitated, I became more and more stressed – stuck in the middle again and trying to accommodate everyone. We eventually took Luke to a nearby park and waited. Some time later, Greg came sauntering around the corner. As he appeared, I could immediately feel David's hackles rise. Greg feigned surprise to see us, made no mention of being late and put on a show of over-the-top friendliness towards David, which only provoked him more.

In a state of high frustration, David pushed Greg. Greg pushed back. I shouted at them both to knock it off. David pushed again, then Greg grabbed David and put him in a headlock. The pair of them scuffled as I screamed for them to break it up, and Luke started to become really upset. Both of them lost their glasses at some point, leaving them to grapple blind. Two grown men wrestling with one another in broad daylight, neither of them able to properly see the other one – if it wasn't so stressful it would have been comical. Finally I managed to pry them apart. Luckily nothing other than pride had been hurt.

It set the tone for their relationship going forward. They both did their level best to avoid one another, and did their utmost to talk down the other to me. I knew Greg was a disruptive, potentially violent influence in my life – I didn't need David reminding me. He was a problem to which there was no obvious solution – and no amount of complaining about him to me was going to change that simple fact.

When my brother Terry married, I took David back to England to meet my family. We had a wonderful time. Luke was that little bit older, meaning he was better able to connect with my parents and brothers. I felt really close to David and was proud to introduce him to my family, all of whom loved him and loved seeing me so happy.

The wedding itself was lovely. It was just so nice to be there with a date – to have someone by my side to dance with and drink with. A photograph taken at the wedding captured a real intimacy between us – it was a golden moment for us as a couple.

The only jarring note was when, with the best of intentions, my brother took David aside during the wedding reception. 'Mate, it's so great you're in my sister's life. Since you've arrived she's happier and Luke is a much better behaved kid.'

I felt sad about how little my family understood about my life in Australia. They didn't realise or understand the amount of strain that Greg's abuse put me under as a single mother. They didn't know about my life, and I didn't feel that I was able to explain.

When we got back from England, David proposed to me and gave me the most beautiful ring. I couldn't have been happier. I'd long ago given up on the idea that I'd ever be married, and here I was engaged. It felt really nice. I'd never been the girliest of girls – not one of those women to fantasise about a white wedding. And yet there was something undeniably special about someone wanting to commit to spending the rest of their life with you. I floated happily along in a bliss bubble for a while.

But before we'd had a chance to discuss dates, venues and timings of our nuptials, David lost his job. He was eminently employable, so it wasn't a disaster. But, because of his age, it took a little longer than he would have liked to find gainful employment commensurate with his level of skill and experience.

Soon after David lost his job, he moved in with me and Luke at Tyabb. In stark contrast to Greg, David conducted himself admirably during that time, getting up to go to the gym every morning, applying for jobs every afternoon.

Not long after he moved in, David began agitating to bring forward the wedding ceremony. But I wasn't in the mood for rushing it. I hadn't been married before. If, as seemed likely, I was only going to get one shot at having a wedding, I wanted to do it right. I wanted friends and family to attend from England, I wanted a lovely venue and a degree of planning. I wanted it to be special, not something you squeezed into the next available weekend, which caused tension between us.

In the meantime, things began to subtly change between us. In so many respects, David was an excellent influence on Luke and on me, teaching Luke about discipline and teaching me about the importance of creating boundaries. But it seemed that the more David was exposed to Luke, the more his tolerance for him waned. Perhaps David felt on the outer of the tight-knit two-person world that Luke and I had come to function in. I respected David's right to discipline Luke whenever it was appropriate, but often there was implied criticism of my mothering skills in his behaviour, which only served to drive a wedge between us.

In the end, I simply didn't see David wanting to be a father to Luke, which was more than fair enough. He had his own children, and Luke technically already had a father – which was no small part of the problem.

Greg put an enormous strain on David's and my relationship. He was the unwelcome, overbearing third person in what should have been a couple. And as he had done in so many other parts of my life, he eventually managed to sabotage my relationship with David and destroy my chance at finally getting married.

David and I broke up a few months later and I handed the engagement ring back. I was devastated. I kept thinking that perhaps we would work out our differences. But all my attempts to contact him were more or less rebuffed. Reluctantly, I convinced myself to move on.

My life returned to its pre-David rhythm. I worked, Luke went to school and Greg dipped in and out of our lives. But for a few notable incidents, Greg had demonstrated his ability to adhere to our custody-sharing arrangements while largely leaving me alone during my relationship with David. With David gone, however, I was once again isolated. Experience alone should have told me it would only be a matter of time before Greg started circling again.

16
Risk

When Luke was in Year 3, I decided to move him to Flinders Christian Community College, which was across the road from Tyabb Public School and at the end of our street. One of those modern private schools that have popped up on the periphery of major cities, the college boasted a state-of-the-art campus and a reputation for strong academic results.

Luke's first few months there were tough going – as is often the case with kids moving to a new school – but he soon started to forge his way. He developed a reputation for being the kid who would always be ready to entertain the class with a quip or a joke. He enjoyed attention and had the mildest streak of exhibitionism. You only had to watch one of the many home videos he recorded of himself to see a performance gene lurking in there somewhere. My son the ham.

Around the same time, I enrolled Luke in weekend sailing lessons down at Mornington. On his very first morning, I dropped him down at the yacht club where Greg had come to watch. I stayed for a while to make sure Luke was having fun, and then went off shopping, expecting Greg to return Luke home after the lesson.

I arrived home to a series of garbled messages on my answering machine from people I didn't know at the yacht club. They said something about an ambulance having been called and someone having been taken to hospital. I flew into a panic, thinking something had happened to Luke.

As it turned out, it was Greg. The weather had taken a turn and the waters had become choppy. The children were all corralled inside, and a couple of the dads went down to the water's edge to secure the sailboats. While Greg watched on, a cleat broke off from one of the boats and flew several metres, smashing into Greg's wrist. If it had hit him in the head, he would have been killed.

Relieved that Luke was okay, I rushed to the hospital to find Greg in a state of high agitation – clearly in a large amount of pain, but more distressed about being detained in hospital than anything else. The doctors and nurses didn't know what to make of him. His wrist had been tended to, he had been made as comfortable as possible, and yet he kept railing against being held in hospital. He point-blank refused to let Luke in to see him, saying that he didn't want his son to see him in that state.

Greg was refusing to receive visitors, but I contacted his brother, whose number I still had in my address book. I felt sorry that Greg was badly injured and I did what I would do for anyone in that situation and visited him in hospital. I found him lying prostrate on the bed, utterly deflated. He had clearly been crying. I had brought him fruit to eat, because I knew, given his paranoia, he would hate being in hospital. Sure enough, he was convinced they were putting poisons into him and that ASIO were monitoring his hospital stay.

He remained in hospital for a couple of weeks and it almost broke him. His family came to visit at some point. They hadn't seen Greg for a few years and were shocked to see him so vulnerable.

One afternoon, the director of nursing took me to a side room and told me they'd had to restrain Greg. He had wanted to close the curtains between the nurse station and his bed, so convinced was he that he was being spied on. But the hospital staff wouldn't let him, fearing that he was suicidal. His anger flaring, he had picked up and thrown a water jug at the window and started abusing the staff. It took several people to sedate and wrestle him back into bed.

I was certain they would not discharge him without giving him a psychiatric assessment. There was no way, I reasoned, that trained medical professionals could be exposed on a daily basis to Greg and his manic behaviour and not conclude that he had undiagnosed mental health issues. But while I wasn't entitled to know what medical assessments were done it seemed to me that he left without any kind of psychiatric check.

With nowhere to live and a wrist to rest, he retreated to his parents' home an hour north of Melbourne, where he took up residence in a bungalow at a nearby property. The compensation from the yacht club had started to dribble in, which gave him enough of a financial cushion that he didn't feel the need to harass me. And so, for another ten months or so, I was insulated from Greg, only briefly crossing paths with him when we met for the Luke handover. For the first time in a long while, I felt vaguely confident about the quality of the accommodation that Luke was staying in when he spent the night with his dad. But Greg eventually tired of living so far away from Luke and decided he wanted to move closer again.

I promise to love and keep safe ♡ xoxox ♡

Luke's petition to get a parakeet for 'his next pet'

I'm not being pushy but for are next pet I think I want a ~~xxxx~~ Paaraket.
I will try my hardest to feed/her/him and promise to keep away from the cats 24/7 and will pay for his food. I don't mind what bird it is but after all those storys you told me about you and your budge and I want to hand train him and everything!
I promise to keep him ~~xxxx~~ safe and love him.
♡ xoxoxoxoxox ♡

He started taking Luke camping during his access visits. He had a tent and other camping equipment but it was more often than not an activity born of necessity, because he didn't always have a home. Then I became aware that on some overnight access visits Luke had slept in Greg's car, and I was very concerned. But Greg had put the fear of God into me and had threatened to kill me if I prevented him from spending time with his son.

Before long, Greg stopped keeping Luke overnight, much to my relief, preferring to return him to me at Tyabb then drive down to the water's edge at Hastings to sleep in his car.

Since the hostel in which he had been staying in Caulfield had been demolished, its tenants had been left to fend for themselves. For a brief period afterwards, Greg had once again worked the Hare Krishna and Mormon Church circuit in St Kilda. But this time, he wore out his welcome with remarkable speed. And so he'd become a vagrant, sleeping in his car and using the showers at the public swimming pool.

I often paid for tickets for Greg and Luke to do things so they could have some quality father and son time together. Of course, there was never any acknowledgement from Greg of my financial outlay: it would have been too much of a concession of failure on his part.

With David no longer in the house, Greg started encroaching on our lives again. Many was the morning that I would wake up to find his car parked outside on the nature strip. As we ate breakfast, he would let himself onto the property and come around the back of the house.

It was around this time that I bought a mobile teddy-bear-making business, and my garage became a warehouse for bear 'skins' and stuffing. Luke was about to turn ten, which meant I had more time in any given day to dedicate to my new business venture. Ten-year-olds, I was fast discovering, have far less need for their mothers than younger children. Luke had grown into a remarkably mature boy for his age. I don't know whether it was because he was so often in the exclusive company of adults, or whether it was because of his atypical home life, but he had a wisdom about him. And yet, in so many other ways, he was still a little boy. He would never let me tell me anyone, but he had recently resumed the habit of creeping into my bed at night and sleeping next to me. And always, he needed to have his feet touching mine.

He was a funny kid, too. It seemed with every year that passed the ham in him only grew in stature and eccentricity. He had taken to filming himself and uploading the videos on YouTube. Nothing especially noteworthy, just a young kid mucking around, mostly talking gibberish. I was proud of the independent, kind, good-looking young man he had become. He was my companion: the one constant in my life. And I lived for him.

It was mid-May when I took delivery of a huge order of teddy bears and was completely overwhelmed. Greg dropped Luke off one afternoon and, seeing me struggling with boxes and shelves, asked if I needed some help. Without waiting for my response, he started putting up shelves and unpacking the boxes. It was a pattern I was smart enough to recognise: I needed help, I was vulnerable and Greg saw it as an opportunity to turn on the kindness and inveigle himself further into my life.

One afternoon not long after, I was working the franchise in Narre Warren and got stuck in traffic on the way home. Greg was due to collect Luke that evening, so I phoned to ask if he could come to Tyabb earlier and pick up Luke from school. He made it halfway there before his car broke down. He walked the rest of the way to Luke's school and collected him, as promised. I phoned ahead and asked my friend to take them both to footy training.

By the time they returned, I was at the stove cooking dinner. In a fit of ten-year-old pique, Luke took one look at the meal I was preparing and said he didn't like it and had no intention of eating it. I had worked all day, had the looming presence of Greg in my house and wasn't much in the mood for a critique of my cooking skills. And so I started to become snarky with Luke. I then asked Greg where he was planning to sleep that night, since his car had broken down. He became agitated, intimating that my innocent enquiry was somehow a slight on his homelessness: a subject about which he was very touchy.

'You can sleep here tonight if you need,' I heard myself say. The thought of him walking back to wherever his car had broken down, or worse still, me dropping him off to his car in the dark for him to crawl into and sleep, seemed too cruel. The bleeding heart in me had won again.

'You can sleep in Luke's bed if you like, and he can sleep with me,' I said.

It was as if a switch had been flicked. He looked at me threateningly. 'Is Luke sleeping in your bed?' he said accusingly, his tone rising to one of indignation. 'Is he sleeping with you again?' It was one of Greg's bugbears. He was convinced I was somehow making his son soft.

'Oh Greg, just drop it,' I said. 'Forget about it. It's probably best if you just leave. I want you out of my house now.'

He stared at me for a moment and there was silence. Luke hung his head. I could feel the tension rising in the room. Then, fulminating and muttering to himself, Greg collected his things and stormed out the front door.

'What did you go and do that for?' Luke said, clearly annoyed with me.

'Oh seriously, Luke? Not you too? I was not going to be spoken to like that by your father.'

'No!' Luke replied petulantly. 'Why did you tell him I'd been sleeping with you?' He was embarrassed that he was still afraid of the dark and crept into my bed every night. He was angry that he would now be forced to explain to his father why he slept with his mother. He was mad, moreover, that I had somehow provoked such an extreme reaction in his dad.

Before either of us knew what was happening, Greg burst back in the front door and came flying towards Luke in the living room.

'Greg!' I shouted. 'What are you doing? Get out of my house! Leave him alone!'

He bore down on Luke, who was sitting on the lounge, and in a rage, started yelling at him. 'How long has this been going on?' Luke cowered in front of him, clearly terrified.

Instinctively, I leaped across the living room to stand between them to protect my little boy.

Greg turned his rage towards me. I saw that manic look in his eyes – a look I knew so well – and took flight. Greg started chasing me though the house – past the kitchen, through the living room, around the dining table. At some point, he picked up a glass vase and started coming at me, the vase raised threateningly above his head.

I grabbed the phone and frantically dialled triple zero. Luke was crying on the lounge, begging his father to stop. I shouted my address into the receiver as I continued to evade Greg's grasp. He chased me into a corner and started grappling with me for the phone. I began to scream.

Ripping the phone from my grasp, Greg grabbed me by the hair and pulled me to the ground. The pain was intense as he yanked at my hair, but the fear was greater. He lifted the vase above his shoulder and held it close to my face. I raised my hands to cover my head, bracing for the blow. I begged him to let me go, to leave Luke alone. 'Leave! Just leave us alone!'

Luke begged his father to stop. 'Get off her! Leave her alone!' he was crying. 'Call the police, Mum! Call the police!'

Greg aimed his boot at my thigh and kicked me.

Then there was silence. I opened my eyes. Greg had gone. The only sound was Luke's whimpering and my own laboured breathing.

I pulled myself up off the floor, comforted Luke then called my neighbour, Chris, who sat with us as we waited for the police to arrive. I remember straightening my hair and trying to look respectable for the police's arrival. Luke sat silently in the living room, tears streaming down his face as Chris comforted him.

When finally the police showed up, they stood on the doorstep as I relayed what had happened. They asked me to come directly to the police station to report the assault, took a description of Greg and set off to find him. I drove down to Hastings Police Station and filed a report. I was told to attend Frankston Magistrates Court the following morning to seek a family violence intervention order.

Meanwhile, the constables who had come to the door were scouring the neighbourhood for Greg. They found him walking along the road not far from my house, the glass vase still in his hand. According to police reports of the arrest, at first Greg ignored them, refusing to acknowledge their entreaties to stop and speak to them. As they proceeded to arrest him, he became abusive, ranting and raving and calling them names.

The arresting officers took him to Hastings Police Station, where he continued to be aggressive, refusing to cooperate, refusing to answer questions, responding to their every enquiry with a torrent of abuse. He was taken to a holding room as the constables called in their supervisor. Police notes from the night indicate the supervisor decided Greg was prone to 'mood swings' and, as a result, he was sent in an ambulance to Frankston Hospital for a psychiatric assessment.

The ambulance and Frankston Hospital emergency room notes from that evening record that Greg complained about sore wrists, but upon arriving at the hospital for psychiatric assessment he was 'calm, rational, articulate and completely normal'. Privacy laws prevented me from ever being told the outcome of Greg's psychiatric assessment.

The police charged Greg with 'unlawful assault', 'assault by kicking' and 'assault with a weapon'. He was told to front up to Frankston Magistrates Court the following day, where a family violence intervention order would be served.

The police entered details of the assault into their internal database, called the LEAP system. But their records would later indicate they left the 'Assessment of Future Risk' box blank and failed also to tick the box indicating that a child had been present during the assault. Luke was listed as a secondary victim of the assault.

As per protocol, the incident was referred by police to the Child Protection Service, a division of the Department of Human Services, and a local family violence service, and a file was automatically generated recommending counselling for both Luke and myself. The family violence service notes from that day indicate that only the first page of the police report from that night was ever received. It further notes that as per standard procedure at no point was a copy of the file passed onto me.

The following day, I fronted up to Frankston Magistrates Court. I walked into the foyer, where respondents for the day's proceedings were all milling about, and was shocked when I saw Greg standing there too.

Without a clue as to where I should be or to whom I should speak, I stood on the spot, assuming at any moment someone would be along to explain what I was expected to do. I hadn't been referred to Legal Aid – all I had were instructions to be at court at nine-thirty that morning. I didn't even really understand what I was there to do.

I tried to avoid Greg, but he eventually saw me and sauntered over. 'You need the police prosecutor,' he said, clearly amused at the level of discomfort his presence was causing me. 'They're over there.'

Without answering, I made my way through the crowd to the small office out of which the police prosecutor operated. He was so rushed, trying to make sense of the briefs he had only received that morning that he barely acknowledged me.

'I'm just not sure what I am supposed to do,' I ventured, as he hurriedly swept up an armload of files and made for the courtroom.

'IVO application,' was the only reply I got as he bustled into the courtroom.

Until my case was called and the magistrate kicked off proceedings, I hadn't even understood that the police had taken out a family violence safety notice on my behalf. But – as I would learn in the months to come – it didn't have the restrictions on it that I required, meaning that I would be forced to go back to try to have it tightened. At the time, and in the confusion of the

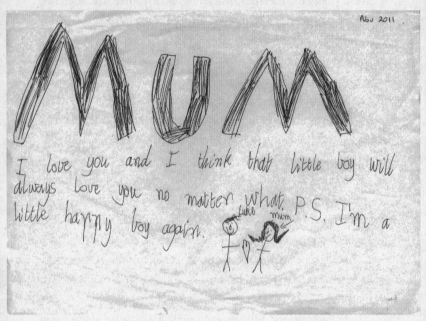

A note from Luke to me, written in November 2011

moment, I was just swept along in the proceedings. It was all over before I even understood what was going on.

Greg was served with an interim IVO in which Luke and I were listed as protected persons. Under the terms of the order, he was not allowed to commit family violence against us or damage my property, and he was told he needed to seek counselling from the Men's Referral Service.

As for the assault charges, they were to be heard at a later date, and this would keep happening. The assault took place on 16 May 2012, but it wouldn't be until 8 January 2013 that the matter was to be heard in court.

The next day, I received a phone call from the family violence service. I told them I wished to change the access Greg had to Luke but was worried that it would only provoke him to further violence. They recommended I seek a change to the access arrangements with the Family Court, which would mean engaging a lawyer and going through the time-consuming and expensive process all over again. In the meantime, they suggested, it would be best if Greg's access visits to Luke were 'supervised'.

Some days later, Child Protection contacted me to say they had assessed me and deemed me to be a responsible parent and therefore the best placed adult in Luke's life to provide that supervision. I did point out that I was also the person that Greg had threatened to kill. But they explained that their remit was simply to protect the child. The courts, they informed me, had the responsibility to protect me and they had done that with the issue of the IVO.

I pointed out that, in their wisdom and despite a serious assault charge, the courts had also let Greg walk free from the court on bail, and that previous experience had taught me Greg didn't much care a jot about orders written down on pieces of

In May 2012 Like wrote me this note, suggesting I 'laugh out loud' and 'take a break'.

paper. They told me to call the police in the event he breached the IVO.

I was still a relative novice when it came to dealing with these sorts of bureaucracies and institutions. I had enormous respect for the legal system. I had been raised to pay every parking fine I ever received. I believed that if a court deemed something to be so, it would be so. And if an institution called Child Protection said it would protect my son, I took them at their word.

The authorities were involved now, I told myself. The courts, Child Protection: they have this situation in hand. All I needed to do was continue to do everything by the book – follow their advice and trust in their processes – and everything would be okay.

A week or so later, the family violence service sent Luke to a counsellor. The psychologist gave Luke something to play with to distract him and began asking him questions about how he felt when he saw his father attacking his mother. By all accounts, Luke was a model patient: speaking openly about Greg's assault, and referring without any real sign of distress to multiple other examples of his father's extreme behaviour. If the psychologist had probed longer and deeper – and he did see Luke two or three times – he might have concluded that a ten-year-old for whom violent, religious-themed outbursts from his father were so commonplace they barely raised an eyebrow was a child who needed some careful attention. But he didn't.

The one comment that Luke made to the psychologist that did resonate was his regret at not having been able to protect me from Greg's rage. 'I tried to stop him,' Luke said of Greg. 'I tried to pull him off Mum, but I was too little.' When the psychologist told me, it nearly broke my heart.

Two weeks later, I received a letter from the Department of Human Services advising me that Child Protection had completed their investigation into Luke and concluded he was not at significant risk and, therefore, his file had been closed.

And so, I had once again been cast adrift. The very people I had believed were now going to come to my rescue and do everything in their power to protect us from Greg had finally deemed we were safe.

Perhaps, in retrospect, we presented as too capable: intelligent, composed individuals who could take care of themselves – and Child Protection simply had more pressing cases of children in danger. Nevertheless, I felt abandoned.

17

Anxiety

When you write down, one after the other, all the incidents in which Greg sought to harass, harangue and assault me, it's easy to get the impression my life was one great big misery: that I lived in a state of constant fear. But in actual fact, I didn't. Greg definitely cast a long shadow over my life for a long period of time, but there were also many happy times.

Luke and I mostly had a ball. He was becoming better – and funnier – company with every year that passed. We had developed a rhythm, a happy sort of co-dependency. We fought and bickered as all mothers do with their children. He muttered angrily under his breath at me whenever he didn't get his own way, and as he lurched towards adolescence he began to ever so subtly push me away, to assert his independence.

There was no doubt that, at ten years of age he increasingly began stepping up in his role of man about the house, and while I was sad my little boy was growing up, I was proud of the little man he was growing into.

I had always sought to ensure he had a childhood like any of the other boys in the neighbourhood, and had gone to exhausting lengths to organise birthday and pool parties to foster a social group for Luke – paranoid as I was that he didn't have brothers and sisters. But he was in my company most often – and as a result, I spoke to him like an adult. I never shied away from having the big conversations with him – especially if he initiated them. Religion and the Bible and God were obviously high on his conversational list, especially after weekends spent with his father. I always made a point of remaining as neutral as possible on the subject, wanting to encourage him to explore spirituality if that was something he wished to do when he got older.

Obviously, I was both suspicious and hyper-conscious that his dad's worldview – if indeed you could call it that – was likely to be having an effect on Luke. But while I disagreed with much of it, I strove to never criticise Greg in front of Luke. He was his father, after all. For all his many faults, he loved Luke unconditionally. And, for better or worse, I believed it was manifestly more important for Luke's emotional development that he knew the experience of having a father who loved him than not having a father at all.

Besides, Greg's violence, when it flared, had only ever been directed at me. In some respects, he verged on being a model father when it came to looking after Luke. He would spend hours with him at the basketball courts shooting hoops or hitting the tennis ball against the wall. He would take him to the library and they would while away the time poring over books together. He taught him to ride a bike and would happily play in the pool with Luke and his friends for hours on end.

When Greg was with Luke, he was 100 per cent with Luke. There was no attempt to juggle the care of Luke with other things he had to do or other people he wished to spend time with. In many respects, Luke was his whole world.

To Luke's credit, he hadn't faltered in his dedication to his father – even after all Greg had done to me and all Luke had seen. He remained loyal to his dad, faithfully trotting off with him every weekend to whichever sporting event he had on.

And Greg remained loyal to his son. He never missed a single session of Luke's weekend sport. He may have been mentally unstable, but his dedication to Luke seemed beyond question.

*

In the final months of 2012, life for Luke and I resumed a kind of routine. Greg would collect Luke every Saturday and take him off to his sporting fixture – leaving me to pursue the teddy-making business.

The police would occasionally call me asking if I knew Greg's whereabouts. Because the police had brought the assault charges against Greg, I was never aware exactly where the proceedings were in court. And it was not a subject I was especially keen to raise with Greg. Our interactions now were cursory at best, and communication was hampered by the fact he no longer had a mobile phone.

Meanwhile, a subtle shift had taken place in Luke. Where previously, his dad had been the slightly odd apple of his eye, a man who, despite a few idiosyncrasies, was his fun-loving, attentive father, Greg had become a tragic figure who Luke was starting to feel sorry for. And Luke, being a sensitive kid, was torn between the loyalty he knew he was supposed to feel and the growing sense of pity and distaste he actually felt for his dad. None of it was helped, of course, by the fact that, as Greg's mental deterioration continued, he was increasingly unfit for mixed company. Luke once came home from sport complaining that Greg had been earbashing the other kids and parents with tracts from the Bible. Luke was starting to become embarrassed by Greg. He was self-conscious about Greg's ratty old car, which by now Greg was living out of. And he told me he didn't want his dad collecting him from school anymore.

Bundled into all of this was Greg's physical appearance, which was declining by the month. Where previously he'd always been well groomed, no matter his housing circumstances, now he started to present as a homeless man. His clothes became shabbier and his personal hygiene declined. On more than one occasion, I had to tell him to buy some deodorant because his smell was offensive.

It never occurred to me that Greg's appearance or behaviour was starting to concern other parents, because none of them ever mentioned it to me. But, looking back, I am sure there was a growing sense of disquiet about Luke's odd dad.

The Christmas and New Year period came and went. As 2013 kicked off, I looked at my finances and decided I needed to alleviate the pressure on my outgoings. As it happened, a work colleague had recently split from his wife and needed somewhere to live. I had a big house with an empty room, and so invited him to live with Luke and me for a while. His weekly board would help with the bills, and his company around the house would also be welcome.

Lee moved in early in the new year, and while I was mindful that it would be a development that would not please Greg, I was determined to stop living my life in fear of him or making decisions about what would or would not please him. For too long I had second-guessed my every life decision based on how it would affect Greg. It was classic family violence, the subtle psychological pressure that the perpetrator manages to bring to bear on every aspect of your life, often without you even being aware of it. Besides, Lee was quite a few years older than me, and there had never been any suggestion of romance between us. I had hoped – naïvely as it turned out – that Greg would be untroubled by his presence.

The first interaction they had was one afternoon when Greg came by to collect Luke. The first words out of Greg's mouth as Lee introduced himself were, 'I don't like you.' Part of it was jealousy on Greg's part – because he wasn't able to be the only male influence in Luke's life. Part of it would have been motivated by some strange belief that Lee was leading the life he ought to be: living in the house he ought to be in.

And so I found myself at a familiar juncture with Greg. How was I supposed to react to his verbal abuse of Lee? Let it destroy me or dismiss it? I look back now and can see the cycle of violence quite clearly. You do get used to the abuse and you cope with it, and that's why the perpetrator has to dial up the violence, because they're no longer getting the reaction out of you that they used to. With hindsight, I can see that as Greg's life began to disintegrate his need to control and have power over me only increased.

One Thursday in January, Greg came over to collect Luke. I was hanging washing on the line and Lee was having breakfast in the backyard by the pool. Greg let himself onto the property and walked around the back, as had become his custom. As he passed Lee, he spat out, 'I don't like you. You're a parasite.'

I turned around from the washing line, surprised to see Greg standing there.

'Get Luke,' he said to me. 'Tell him I'm here.'

He was clearly in a bad mood. When he was in a mood like that, I knew not to provoke. As we walked around to the front yard and Luke climbed into Greg's car, Greg looked at me and said, 'I never liked David. I don't like Lee. You need to watch yourself.'

I didn't respond, figuring it was not worth my energy.

Greg took Luke out for the morning. I knew they would be back by lunchtime, because Greg never had any money to buy them lunch and had hence developed the habit of structuring his outings around lunch at my place. In their absence, I decided I wasn't going to take Greg's abuse anymore. I needed to make clear to him what was acceptable behaviour and what was not.

I heard the car pull up outside and went to the front gate to meet them. Luke ran inside and I closed the gate, keen as I was to make sure there was some sort of physical barrier between Greg and I.

'Greg, there are some things I need to discuss with you,' I started.

He cut me off, staring at me angrily. 'Right now, I would really like to kill you,' he said, seething with barely controlled rage. 'You think you are going to outlive me in this lifetime, but I can make you suffer. I will cut off your foot. I hope you have made a will.'

He climbed back into his car and drove off.

I stood rooted to the spot, shaking. I felt sick. I was used to Greg being nasty, and certainly he had said his fair share of hideous things to me in the past, but there was something about this threat that was chilling. Chopping off my foot was so specific – that comment especially troubled me. Why my foot? Was it something to do with the Bible? There was no real way of telling, such was Greg's muddled mental state.

I decided I had to go immediately to the police. The time had come to stop thinking I could contain this on my own and to get the police involved. Greg had crossed the Rubicon now. He had made it clear, as if it wasn't clear enough before, that he meant to do me harm. For my sake, and for Luke's, I had no choice but to take the fight to him.

I went inside to collect the car keys and drove straight to Hastings police station. I knew that Greg was due to come to my house the following day at 10 am to collect Luke, so while reporting his threat to kill me, I informed the police of as much. The initial reaction from the police officer on duty could not have been more comforting. The constable could see the state of distress I was in and assured me every measure would be taken to find and intercept Greg, and if he showed up in the meantime, I was to call triple zero immediately.

'We'll be on standby to come to your house tomorrow morning,' the constable said. 'Meanwhile, my suggestion would be that you make sure Luke isn't there in the morning, and we'll come out and arrest him.'

I had a sleepless night, worrying that Greg would steal onto the property under the cover of darkness and lie in wait until the morning. At daybreak, and after feeding Luke his breakfast, I dispatched him to the neighbours. True to confounding form, Greg appeared at my house at nine-thirty the following morning – half an hour early. Before I had a chance to call the police, he was on the doorstep. I started panicking, worrying what he would do to me, aware I was all alone.

I gathered myself and answered the door. 'You're early,' I said, feigning nonchalance. 'Luke's down at Josh's. He'll be back in thirty minutes.'

Greg glared at me menacingly. 'I'm going to get a coffee then,' he eventually said. 'I'll be back at ten.'

Watching his car pull out of the cul-de-sac, I leaped on the phone and called triple zero. The police arrived some ten minutes later. Two young constables got out of the police car and came to the front door. Visibly distressed, I explained they had just missed Greg, that he had gone for a coffee and said he would be back in twenty minutes. I felt comforted that they were there: at least I wouldn't have to face Greg alone.

'We can't wait, ma'am,' said one of the constables. 'If he comes back, just call triple zero again and a patrol car will return.'

I was incredulous. 'What?' I heard myself say. 'But you can't go! You can't leave me here! He threatened to kill me yesterday!'

The constables stood awkwardly looking at each other. 'We've had a call to attend another job, ma'am. We have to go.'

'But you can't leave me!' I was starting to become hysterical. 'I was in your station all afternoon yesterday and you told me to call triple zero, which I did, and now you're just going to drive off and abandon me? He'll be back here any minute. You have to stay and arrest him!'

'With respect, ma'am, you can't tell us how to do our job,' one of the policemen replied. I could tell they were starting to form a perception of me as an hysterical woman. Neither of them had been at the police station when I had arrived, in a state of high agitation, the previous afternoon. Neither of them properly understood the history between Greg and me. To them, I was just another complainant, a crank with her crazy ex-partner conspiracies who had phoned triple zero and now had to be indulged.

'Have you ever been threatened to be killed before?' I continued, my voice rising shrilly, tears streaming down my face. 'He's a six-foot man! I'm terrified!' All the emotion of the past fourteen hours came tumbling out.

They made to leave. Sobbing uncontrollably, I went back into the house and slammed the door, convinced I had once again been abandoned by the very people whose job I thought it was to protect me.

Luckily, the police had been sufficiently moved by my hysteria that they had radioed their inability to attend the other job and, instead, waited at the top of my cul-de-sac. When eventually Greg returned, they intercepted him, arrested him and put him in their car for transport to Hastings police station.

They came back to my door to apologise. One of them introduced himself as Constable Paul Topham. 'I just wanted to say sorry about the misunderstanding,' he said. 'He is a dangerous man. When we arrested him, he started ranting and raving and hurling abuse. We nearly had to use capsicum spray.'

I felt a massive surge of relief and felt validated. At last, people were seeing Greg for the mentally unstable, potentially violent offender I had known him to be for the past decade. Apparently, after shouting at the police all the way to the station – calling the two arresting officers 'faggots' and 'big girl's blouses' – Greg had continued to abuse them as they put him into a holding cell. While the officers started processing the paperwork that accompanies an arrest, Greg continued abusing them from the cell, continually pressing the duress button to force them to come to the cell, even though there was nothing wrong.

'You're the ones who are criminals!' Greg shouted at them repeatedly.

Later that day Greg was charged with threatening to kill me, threatening to inflict serious injury, contravention of an IVO and use of an unregistered vehicle. He was remanded in custody overnight and taken directly to Frankston Magistrates Court to answer the new batch of charges.

Police opposed bail, with the police prosecutor arguing that the combination of Greg's violation of the IVO, plus the seriousness of his threat and history of violence meant he should be held in custody until he faced trial later in the year. But for a variety of reasons, including that Greg had no previous convictions, he was subsequently released on bail and walked from the courtroom again a free man.

Constable Topham, who had attended the court as one of the arresting officers, took me aside and urged me to seek a variation of the IVO – he was concerned its terms didn't go far enough – but I told him I had no idea how to do that or even where to start. To date, I had simply been carried along by police processes, fronting up to court each time I was told to, blindly confident the system would take care of things. I was starting to suspect it was all a waste of time.

My experience had shown that reporting to police, making a statement and turning up to court only ended up with you leaving court dissatisfied, having stood by and watched as decisions were made on your behalf about points of law you didn't understand. And at the end of it all, nothing fundamentally changed.

'He's a real nasty piece of work,' Constable Topham said to me. 'Have you thought about going back to England?'

I smiled benignly and nodded. He didn't know the half of it.

I heard later the police were frustrated that Greg had been released on bail.

Coincidentally, just over a week later, another set of completely unrelated charges were laid against Greg, and a warrant issued for his arrest. From the Child Sex Offences unit headquarters in South Melbourne, Detective Senior Constable Andrew Cocking made email contact with Constable Topham, enquiring after Greg's whereabouts. Two months previously, on 17 November 2012, Greg had been caught accessing child pornography on a computer in the Emerald Hill public library. DSC Cocking was in charge of investigating the case. For a complicated set of reasons involving current privacy laws, I was never informed.

Yes, I was involved in a custody dispute with Greg. Yes, the authorities were acutely aware that despite Greg showing troubling behaviour, he still had court-authorised access to Luke on weekends. Yes, Greg was facing a series of charges (for which he never fronted up to court), among which were a threat to kill me. And yes, Child Protection had been called in to assess whether Luke was in danger and had deemed he wasn't. Yet no one was permitted to inform me that Greg had been arrested for accessing child porn on a computer. It would be months before I was to find out – and then, only by accident.

Of course, all of this – court proceedings being adjourned (because Greg failed to show) and a child sex offence investigation – was going on without my knowledge.

After Greg's latest threat to kill me by chopping off my foot, and after I had subsequently watched him be granted bail and go back to his life, I tried to get on with my own life. But nothing seemed to be gelling. The teddy-making business was not working out as I had hoped and I was in a permanent state of high anxiety. I would wake in the morning after a fitful sleep and spend the day rushing around at a million miles an hour, trying to do everything at once and, as a result, not achieving a single thing. I couldn't even sit still long enough to read an email. I had an overwhelming sense of not having enough time. I was incapable of prioritising – everything had a sense of heightened priority – and so very little got done.

A friend recognised my dilemma and started picking Luke up for school and bringing him home. It was simple, small acts of kindness like that which kept me from going completely off the rails.

I would start off the day feeling all right, but by mid-morning, I was having trouble breathing and feeling a tightness in my chest. I finally took myself to a doctor, and she explained I was suffering from anxiety brought on by post-traumatic stress. It made sense. She advised I undertake a course of medication, against which I immediately bridled. I had always felt like medicating yourself was a cop-out. But in the end I took her advice and felt better almost immediately. I am on the same anti-anxiety medication to this day.

My situation wasn't helped by the fact I had somehow fallen through the cracks in the system. I would come to learn later that usually a woman in my predicament would have been referred to family violence support services, that a case worker would typically have been assigned whose job it then was to hold my hand through the various legal processes that were unfolding around me. As it was, I was left to navigate it on my own.

At a court hearing in mid-February 2013 for the issuing of a final IVO (stemming from Greg's attack on me with the vase some nine months previously), the magistrate refused to issue a final order because Greg was not present and therefore unable to answer the claims being made against him. Greg was hardly ever present. He had come to understand that non-appearance in a courtroom was a sure-fire way to keep the system tying itself in knots, leaving him to walk the streets and do as he pleased. Another interim order was issued, with a return date of 17 May set for another mention.

I was confused again. And upset. I left the courtroom crying, feeling that the magistrate was somehow angry with me – and once again feeling as though I had been left in limbo.

18

Threat

While Luke made a good show at school of appearing like the happy-go-lucky, goofy kid, it masked a much more complicated little soul. There would often be moments in his last year of school when I would come across him morose, convinced he didn't have any friends. If you had pulled out a class photo and gone through it with him, of course you would have identified four or five boys he was close to. But any acts of carelessness on the part of his friends often knocked Luke's self-esteem for a six.

If you asked me what it was that set him apart from other kids his age, I would say it was his sensitivity. It wasn't just that he was the first kid in any group to be moved to tears – especially if he thought he had been the victim of some sort of injustice – but also that he was the kid that seemed so completely in tune with the moods and temperaments of those around him.

He really just wanted to please and fit in and, to a large extent, make those around him feel comfortable. I often wonder if perhaps he had been forced to grow up in that sense faster than other kids. Maybe kids who come from broken homes or have parents with dysfunctional relationships, as Luke did, become mediators between their warring elders, taking onto their little shoulders at an early age the responsibility to placate Mum and Dad. If that was what Luke felt compelled to do, it makes me sad. All I ever wanted to do was to give him as normal and happy an upbringing as possible.

*

As much as we were able, Luke and I resolved to get back to leading our lives as normally as possible in that first half of 2013. I felt like I was in court every other week, as the succession of charges against Greg were called for mention, then adjourned because he had failed to show. It was wearying in its predictability.

One afternoon in April 2013, I collected Luke from school as usual and drove him up the hill to home. He'd been unusually quiet in the preceding week. I did my best to shield him from the ongoing court processes, and was especially careful not to badmouth Greg in front of Luke, but I worried that he was being caught in the web of negativity nonetheless. It transpired that was the least of my concerns.

'Dad showed me a knife,' Luke said out of the blue as we drove up the hill.

I almost drove off the road. Determined not to show my shock and to encourage him to share, I feigned nonchalance. 'Oh really?' I replied, trying not to sound alarmed. Maybe it was one of those fruit knives he kept in the car, I told myself. Greg was always eating meals in his car. Perhaps it was an innocent gesture.

Luke was sitting in the front seat, staring out the window as I drove. It was a textbook case of a child using the safety of a car ride to divulge a confidence, knowing you are sufficiently distracted with the job at hand to not overreact.

'Why did he show you a knife?' I asked.

'We were in the car and I was playing on my iPad and he was praying, then he pulled out a knife and said, "It could all end with this. Cain has spoken."'

I felt like I was going to vomit. My heart sank as my mind began to race.

'He said he was tired of this life and wanted to go to the next life,' Luke continued. 'And he said he wanted me to go with him.'

Apart from feeling sick to my stomach, I felt so sorry that this ten-year-old boy – my baby – was having to carry all of this around. I felt sorry and guilty. But mostly I just felt terrified. Things had been serious before, and Greg had dialled up the intensity of his violence towards me, but this was something else. I felt Greg had gone to the next level – and it was clear I had to shut down any access he had to Luke.

As the full impact of Luke's revelation began to sink in, I started to reassess the one fundamental belief I'd had in Greg up until this point. I knew he would happily do me harm: that much had been proven. But Greg lived for Luke, literally. As the rest of his life continued on its downward spiral, the only good thing left in it was his son, and the joy he derived from watching him grow. Greg would have given Luke anything. He would go hungry for Luke. If Luke was ill, Greg had been known to spend his entire Centrelink benefit for a week taking Luke to a naturopath. There had never been any hint that he would harm Luke – until now. This was a game changer.

It still seemed unbelievable, and part of me wondered if Luke had heard correctly or if the conversation had been taken out of context or if I had misinterpreted it. In the recounting of the story, Luke hadn't seemed the least bit perturbed, but then, unusual was his normal, so who could tell?

The eldest of four, I was born and raised on a farm in Nottinghamshire, England, with fields for a backyard and farmyard animals for pets. LEFT: Nanna and Grandpa Atkin with me on the day of my christening in 1962.

BELOW: Mum and Dad with my little brother Robert (left) and me in the front garden of our farm cottage.

TOP: Pretending to play the piano with my brothers James (left) and Robert.

ABOVE LEFT: Mum on holiday at the beach. She died suddenly aged thirty-seven in 1968 when I was just six.

ABOVE RIGHT: Smiling for the camera, aged around four.

TOP LEFT: Me (second from right) with my friends at St Joseph's Convent in Lincoln, which I attended until I was sixteen.

TOP RIGHT: Working as a nanny in Austria (here aged twenty-one) gave me the travel bug, and a few years later I made the trip to Australia.

ABOVE: Soon after I arrived in Melbourne in the 1980s I met Leonie. We've been friends ever since. Here we are enjoying ourselves at a fancy-dress party.

TOP LEFT: On 20 June 2002 I gave birth to my beautiful boy, Luke Geoffrey Batty. Luke's dad, Greg Anderson (MIDDLE RIGHT), wasn't my partner at the time but he was always part of Luke's life.

TOP RIGHT: Luke with my darling Nanna Atkin just months before she died, aged 100.

ABOVE: Luke aged six months in a Liverpool United jersey, being initiated into family footy fandom – with my brothers Terry, Robert and James during a visit to the UK.

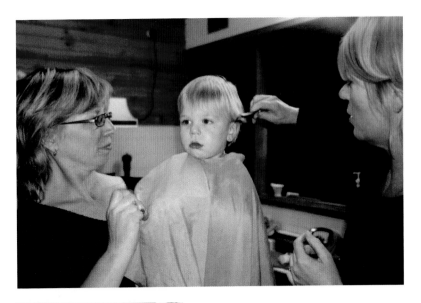

TOP: With Leonie, giving Luke his first haircut.

ABOVE LEFT: With Dorothy the goat – Luke loved animals as much as I do.

ABOVE RIGHT: Luke aged about four. He was a typical little boy – clever and brave on the outside with a soft, compassionate centre.

TOP: Aware that Luke was an only child, I made sure he spent plenty of time with other kids, and Leonie's boys, Daniel and James, were like big brothers to him: from left, Leonie, Daniel, James and Luke.

ABOVE LEFT: Luke enjoyed a laugh and was loved for his ability to entertain. Among his presents on Christmas day he received a stuffed toy of SpongeBob, one of his favourite characters.

RIGHT: Luke and my then partner David in Arguments Yard in Whitby, UK. David was an important person in Luke's life, but they did enjoy an argument.

TOP LEFT: Luke at a Flinders Christian College athletics carnival. He loved his sport.

TOP RIGHT: Luke hamming it up at his SpongeBob birthday party.

ABOVE: Luke and me with my parents when they visited Australia.

Luke Geoffrey Batty, 2002 – 2014

RIGHT: My son, Luke, was killed by his father on 12 February 2014. The next day I spoke to the media assembled at my front gate, the first of countless appearances I've made to discuss family violence. *Photo Nicole Garmston/Newspix*

BELOW: Two days after Luke died, students from his school, Flinders Christian College, paid tribute to him at Tyabb Cricket Ground. *Photo Alex Coppel/Newspix*

Luke's funeral was organised by Flinders Christian College, to which I am eternally grateful, especially principal Max Cudden. The whole community turned out to say goodbye to Luke on 21 February 2014. Luke's coffin was bright yellow, his favourite colour, and was decorated with his much-loved SpongeBob toy. Mourners wore a splash of yellow, which symbolised, for us, joy, intellect and energy.

All photos by Fiona McCoy

TOP: With the then Victorian Police Commissioner Ken Lay and other campaigners, including Fiona McCormack from Domestic Violence Victoria, on the 2014 Walk Against Family Violence in Melbourne. Two days after Luke died I had met with Commissioner Lay and he has since become a close ally in my campaign for change. *Photo David Caird/Newspix*

ABOVE: Speaking at a forum on family violence in Melbourne in September 2014, I urged people to consider it when they cast their vote in the forthcoming state election. *Photo Norm Oorloff/Newspix*

In October 2014 I was named the Victorian finalist for the 2015 Australian of the Year Awards (TOP – *photo National Australia Day Council*) just days after winning the Herald Sun Pride of Australia Courage medal (ABOVE LEFT – *photo David Caird/Newspix*). I wondered whether I was worthy but was determined to keep speaking out.

ABOVE RIGHT: At a National Museum exhibition in Canberra featuring a doll given to me by my godmother when I was little and dressed in clothes knitted by my Nanna Atkin. Each Australian of the Year finalist chose an object of special personal significance for the exhibition. *Photo Jason McCarthy, National Museum of Australia*

On 25 January 2015 I was named Australian of the Year at an awards ceremony at Parliament House. In my speech (TOP) I dedicated the award to Luke and made a commitment to educate the community and ensure family violence victims receive the respect, support and safety they deserve. *Photo National Australia Day Council*

ABOVE LEFT: With Prime Minister Tony Abbott and the other award winners, Drisana Levitzke-Gray, Jackie French and Juliette Wright. *Photo Stefan Postles/Getty Images*

ABOVE RIGHT: With National Australia Day Chairman Ben Roberts-Smith VC MG. *Photo National Australia Day Council*

TOP: Speaking at a candlelight vigil in Melbourne in memory of those who have died as a result of family violence and organised by Safe Steps Family Violence Response Centre. *Photo Amanda Summons Photography and Safe Steps*

ABOVE LEFT: With Police Commissioner Ken Lay in 2014. In early 2015 we were named chair and deputy chair of a national advisory panel on family violence. *Photo Tony Gough/Newspix*

ABOVE RIGHT: With artist Christopher Pyett and his portrait of me, which was entered in the Archibald Prize and hung in the Salon des Refusés. Christopher chose yellow for the background in honour of Luke and said that the portrait was the most moving and spiritual work he'd ever done. *Photo Barbara Pyett*

TOP: Speaking with author and Full Stop Foundation patron Tara Moss at the All About Women conference at the Sydney Opera House in March 2015. *Photo Prudence Upton*

ABOVE LEFT: *Herald Sun* cartoonist Mark Knight's October 2014 cartoon illustrates a powerful point, that family violence is a much greater threat to lives here at home than international terrorism. *Courtesy Mark Knight*

ABOVE RIGHT: *The Australian Women's Weekly* has been hugely supportive of my campaign against family violence, even featuring me on the cover. *Courtesy* The Australian Women's Weekly, *main cover image by Michelle Holden*

TOP: Discussing ways to inspire change at an Australian Human Rights Commission event attended by 2000 people, with fellow Australians of the Year Drisana Levitzke-Gray and Jackie French, Australian Local Hero Juliette Wright and MC Annabel Crabb in July 2015. *Photo Matthew Syres for the Australian Human Rights Commission*

ABOVE LEFT: In June 2015 a plaque was erected in Luke's memorial garden at Tyabb Cricket Club with the help of the local community, Tyabb Cricket Club and Mornington Shire Council.

ABOVE RIGHT: With a portrait of Luke by Jacqui Clark. It's a lasting reminder of Luke and is now a symbol for the Luke Batty Foundation, set up to help women and children affected by family violence. *Photo Robert Leeson/Newspix*

I was due in court a couple of days later, where Greg was supposed to face the various charges against him. On 22 April, I went to Frankston Magistrates Court, a place I was getting to know well. Constables Topham and Anderson were also there to speak to the criminal charges that Greg was facing, including the threats to kill and assault charges. Greg didn't show, meaning the matter was adjourned to the following day.

The next day, I went along again. Greg didn't show again. As he wasn't there to answer the charges, the matter was adjourned again. Each day was another day I wasn't working. Each day that Greg wasn't held accountable by a court of law or closer to being behind bars, my anxiety was reaching unprecedented levels.

I didn't know it was possible not to show up to court. That's how naïve I was. I attended each day on my own. Friends had offered to come along as a show of support, but I was determined to face Greg on my own, to show him I wasn't so afraid of him that I needed a posse. Besides, my closest friends were all engaged in the business of keeping my life afloat – picking up and dropping off Luke, being at home to receive deliveries for the business – while I sat for hours in the court foyer waiting for my case to be called.

I didn't have a lawyer because I couldn't afford one. The business had left me so financially stretched that my cash flow was negligible. But Legal Aid was means-tested, and because of the capital value I had in my property, I wasn't eligible. Ironically enough, Greg was eligible for Legal Aid. The legal system benefits those who are chronically poor or stinking rich. If you sit in the middle, you're on your own. Not that I was especially comfortable financially. It was a huge struggle to keep my home, and I would lie awake at night worried about how I was going to pay the bills and mortgage. I had a child for whom

I was solely responsible. The last thing I wanted to do was fall off the property ladder because it was nigh on impossible to get back onto it.

And so I fronted up to court alone. I figured if I spoke from the heart and explained the situation rationally, everything would be okay. I didn't realise that there are pre-conceived ideas about victims on the part of judiciary and police prosecutors – I just assumed they were all there to help me.

On day two, I sat with the police prosecutor Darren Cathie, and we used the time to prepare my evidence for the following day. I told him about the knife incident.

'He said what?' Darren asked me, incredulous. 'And you are sure about this?'

It was one of those moments where someone's reaction to a piece of news justifies your own rising sense of panic. So used to playing things down or having my concerns dismissed as melodrama, I was heartened – almost relieved – to find the news of the knife incident shocked the police prosecutor as much as it had me.

On 24 April, the third day of court, I did expect Greg to show up. The matter to be mentioned on this day was the variation of the IVO. If a matter involved his continued access to Luke, I reasoned, he would most definitely show up to contest it. But Greg didn't show up again. Darren Cathie called me to the witness stand nonetheless. The matter was being heard by Magistrate Goldsborough. Was it a coincidence that the first time my case was presided over by a woman was also the first time I felt like a judge actually listened to me and understood the danger Luke and I were in? I don't think so.

Darren Cathie prompted me to reveal to the magistrate the details of the knife incident.

'Luke told me Greg held up a knife, and I assume it to be a sharp knife, as his father would use to cut fruit or whatever. And he said, "It could all end with this. Cain has spoken …"'

The magistrate's demeanour, which had previously been all business, changed immediately. She looked up from her notes. 'He said that to you or he said that to Luke?' she asked.

'He said it to Luke,' I replied.

'How recently?' Magistrate Goldsborough asked.

'It would have been the Easter holidays, so that's in the last two weeks,' I replied. 'I think Greg has spoken to Luke about wanting to leave this world. I had always believed that his religious beliefs would prevent him from committing suicide. But now I am concerned for Luke. Even if I feel bad about betraying his confidence here today, because he will be upset that I have told anyone.'

And it was true: Luke's compulsion to tell me had been because he knew he could trust me. Of all the people in his little world, only I understood how complicated and complex his father was. Even at the age of ten, Luke knew that his dad was a person to be contained, managed and indulged. It was such a lot for a kid his age to be dealing with.

Magistrate Goldsborough had heard enough. She said my desire to want to foster a relationship between Luke and his father was commendable, but that things had clearly progressed beyond the point at which that was safe for Luke. Almost immediately, she tightened the IVO's parameters, including an order that Greg surrender any 'firearms or other weapons in his possession'. She also directed that he not be permitted to be anywhere near me or Luke.

Magistrate Goldsborough further recommended that Greg be automatically remanded in custody when arrested. Warrants were duly issued for Greg's arrest. Darren Cathie contacted Malvern Police Station immediately, advising them to arrest Greg when he fronted in five days as part of his bail requirements. I had long ago let go of the idea that an arrest warrant meant immediate action by the police. Like most law-abiding citizens, I had at first assumed that once an arrest warrant was issued, a crack force of detectives and police officers mobilised and scoured the countryside and did not rest until the perpetrator was apprehended. And certainly, in some cases, that is what happens. But when it is 'just another domestic', it doesn't become the force's top priority.

If I didn't exactly feel emboldened by my day in court, at least I felt for the first time that someone was taking seriously the threat that Greg posed. The authorities – or at least some of them – were gradually coming to the conclusion that I had reached long ago: Greg was a mentally unstable individual prone to outbursts of violence, and as long as he was allowed to roam the streets unchecked, our lives were in danger.

That same afternoon, I took Luke to football training to find Greg's car parked next to the oval. As we walked past, I saw him sitting in the passenger seat, chair reclined, with his feet up on the dashboard.

'Have a nice day in court?' he smiled.

I was furious, fuming inside. He was clearly pleased with himself, amused at the inconvenience he had caused me. Power and control. This was what he thought of the law. This was his attitude to the myriad legal processes swirling around him. He had learned that by making himself uncontactable and elusive, he could easily evade the law.

'You need to speak to the police, Greg,' I finally managed to reply. 'You're not meant to be here, you're in breach of bail conditions.'

'Not anymore,' he smirked.

And this was the thing about Greg. He knew from experience exactly what he could get away with. He understood that each of the various legal proceedings involving him existed in splendid isolation from the other, which led to the ridiculous situation where I was able to come directly from a courtroom where he had been recognised as a disturbed individual who should not come within 200 metres of Luke or me to find him parked at Luke's footy training. Because he hadn't been present at court that morning, and therefore hadn't been served with the new IVO, he was not beholden to it. Paperwork and flawed process: it was to become my enemy.

I thought for a moment of telling him about the day's court proceedings and the new directive forbidding any contact with Luke. But I was scared of his reaction. No, I thought, better that that comes from the police or the courts rather than me.

Even as I knew things were escalating, I was doing my best to rationalise and downplay the danger I felt both Luke and I were in. It was probably a coping mechanism on my part: as the machinery of the law increasingly proved itself incapable of helping me, the only way I could get through any given day was to tell myself it was all going to be okay. How else do you cope with that level of fear? But a few days later, I attended one of the victims support counselling sessions that had been organised as a result of a previous court hearing – it had taken a threat to Luke before I was recognised as being in need of help. I sat with a psychologist, Jan, and dissolved into tears. I was a wreck.

Because Greg was so religious, part of me believed he would never kill.

'Rosie, you cannot underestimate how dangerous this man is,' Jan said. Specifically, her concern was that Greg had

187

mentioned using a knife on two occasions. And it wasn't just the knife that was the problem, it was the fact that he had envisioned exactly what he would do with it. She told me she was really concerned for my safety.

It was nice to have an understanding ear, but I didn't know what to do with that information. Once again, I was not linked into domestic violence crisis services. I wasn't made aware, for example, that going into hiding in crisis accommodation was an option. In fact, it had never occurred to me. I guess I thought that crisis accommodation was a safe haven for family violence victims who had left their partner and home. I wasn't with Greg to start with, so it didn't seem relevant. I had been led to think that the law had it under control, that if I had faith that the wheels of justice would continue to turn, Greg would eventually be contained, and Luke and I would get on with our lives.

So it never occurred to me to go to a women's shelter. I had a house, it was mine, Greg didn't live there nor have any right now to come anywhere near it. I still felt that if I kept firm boundaries and made sure he kept to the terms of the IVO without allowing for any breaches, as I had done in the past, the law would catch up with Greg.

Oddly enough, I also felt really sorry for Greg. I felt strangely responsible for his feelings, aware of how devastated he would feel to not be able to see Luke anymore. At the end of the day he was homeless, he had no prospects, and he was about to be forcibly estranged from the one person in the world who made sense of his mess of a life. He was to be pitied.

Or maybe I was, for being too generous and forgiving. Greg knew that I was generous by nature and had taken advantage of that generosity for over a decade. Why would he stop now?

19

The heat from the day is still hanging in the air. There's a heaviness – it's one of those baking Victorian summer afternoons. I call out to Luke to get his things. We're running late, as usual, for cricket training.

'Do I have to go?' Luke asks me plaintively, from the couch where he is engrossed in the television.

'Yes, you have to go,' I reply wearily, trying to make it sound like I mean it. 'You're part of a team, you've made a commitment, you have to follow through on it.'

It feels like the responsible thing to say, alluring as the prospect is of not having to run him up the road and drop him off, then turn around and come home to snatch a precious forty-five minutes of extra work time, before rushing back up to the oval to collect him.

'But I don't feel like going,' Luke replies.

'Well, life is full of doing things we don't feel like doing,' I say, reaching for one of those platitudes that parents everywhere perfect without knowing how or why. 'Come on, grab your things.'

It's getting to the end of the cricket season. There's only one more match left to play. Following through on a commitment and being a part of a team: those are the lessons we will learn today. Even if I want nothing more than to close the door, curl up on the lounge and let the world pass us by.

As we pull out of the driveway and make our way down the street towards the Tyabb Cricket Club, I notice Luke is distracted. He's quieter than he usually is. There's something playing on his mind.

'Are you okay?' I ask.

'I'm fine,' Luke replies, looking distractedly out the car window.

'Are you a bit nervous about seeing your dad again?' I venture.

There is silence. Then Luke replies, 'Oh, a little bit.'

He's doing his best to sound nonchalant about it. I can't help but feel he's putting on a brave face, and most likely for my benefit – I feel a pang. My little boy. When did he become my protector?

'Do you want me to hang around?' I ask. 'Do you want me to stay?' I knew Luke wasn't frightened of his dad – otherwise I would never have left him with Greg. He might have feared his dad's anger but he didn't fear for his safety.

'No, Mum,' Luke replies. 'I'll be right.'

I know that there's been a shift in the way he looks at his dad. It was probably happening before we went to England, but it is more pronounced now we are back. Luke doesn't want to spend time with his dad anymore. He's embarrassed by him – embarrassed that he lives in his car. Luke is getting older, becoming his own young man – he is pulling away. Whether it's because he is growing up and becoming more mature or because Greg is sliding further into madness, I can't say. Most likely it's a combination of the two. Either way, Luke appears to have woken up to his dad. And the worst part is, Greg cannot have failed to notice it.

I pull into the driveway at the Tyabb Cricket Club, and we bump along the dirt access road. Past the tennis courts where kids are being coached, past the paddocks that surround the sporting grounds. The grass brown and brittle under the summer sun.

As I park the car between the clubhouse and the oval, I see Greg in the distance. He's sitting on the fence around the perimeter of the oval, a good 200 metres away, slightly separate from the other parents. It's daylight. There are kids and parents everywhere. I tell myself that, as long as there are people around, as long as Greg is not alone with Luke, things will be fine. As he clambers from the car, lugging his cricket gear, I tell Luke I will be back before training has finished.

Upon spying Luke getting out of the car, Greg stands up – I can just make out a big smile and a wave. Luke meets his dad with a smile and a hug before making a beeline for his teammates, gathering now just outside the cricket nets.

I drive home to finish off some emails and prepare a few things for dinner. I bustle about the house, but the whole time I watch the clock to make sure I am back at the oval in plenty of time before training finishes. I don't want Luke to be left there alone with Greg.

20

Meltdown

They say that if you put a frog in a pot of boiling water, it will hop out straight away. But if you place a frog in a pot of tepid water and gradually increase the heat, it will not move – but rather slowly boil to death.

For the past ten years, Greg had been gradually turning up the heat, and like a frog in a pot, I couldn't tell anymore how hot the water had become.

A week after I had been to court and Magistrate Goldsborough had altered the IVO to prevent Greg from having any contact with Luke, I drove Luke to his football match at Dromana to see Greg waiting there. I was alarmed, unable to understand why he hadn't been served with the new IVO – and, more importantly, why he hadn't been arrested.

Noting my distress, a friend took me aside and told me to call the police. So I dialled the number for Hastings police station and a young constable answered the phone. 'Look, I have just been in court, there's a warrant for the arrest for Greg Anderson and he is here now,' I said.

The constable asked me to hold while he checked the LEAP system. Before long he came back on the line. 'No, I'm sorry, ma'am, there's no warrant. I don't know what you are talking about.'

'But I have just been in court,' I retorted.

'There's no record in our system,' he replied. He looked further in the LEAP database. 'Oh hang on,' he said, after a while. 'Are you talking about the incident in January?'

'I don't know about that incident,' I answered, suddenly alarmed. 'I don't know what you are talking about.'

'Oh,' the constable said. 'Then I'm not at liberty to discuss it, ma'am.'

I was immediately alert. What incident in January? What more could Greg have done, and to whom? Suddenly it occurred to me that I had no idea what Greg was getting up to in the times he was not haranguing me. What more could the police possibly have to hang on him? And why hadn't it been done?

Greg stayed at the football match, careful to keep his distance on the other side of the oval. He watched Luke play, then at half-time, swept in to where the team were having their drinks, chatted with Luke and left. Whether he was aware of the new IVO, I didn't know. Until the papers were physically served on him, they were not legally binding. And how do you serve papers on a transient who lives out of his car? Greg knew that – and was quite happy to continue to exist in ignorance of the court orders.

When I got home that afternoon I again phoned Hastings Police Station and this time spoke to Constable Topham. 'I think your colleague maybe spoke out of school this morning,' I said. 'I think he may have made a mistake, but he alerted me to the fact there is some other investigation that involves Greg. What can you tell me about it?'

'Leave it with me, Rosie,' Constable Topham replied. 'I can't tell you but, if it were me, I'd want to know. Let me check with my superior.' A minute later he was back on the line explaining that for 'privacy reasons' he was not allowed to elaborate.

I assumed it was yet another incidence of violence, a petty altercation between Greg and someone else. Then I said to Constable Topham, 'I was in court the other day when warrants were issued for Greg's arrest. Why didn't your colleague know about these when I phoned this afternoon?'

Constable Topham went on to explain how there was a black hole in the police IT system meaning it sometimes took up to three weeks for a warrant issued in court to be entered into the LEAP database. As I understood it, the warrant would go to the issuing police officer (in this case, Constable Anderson) who would then seek to find the perpetrator and arrest them. If the arrest could not be made, the warrant papers were sent (sometimes even faxed) to a central office where someone had to manually enter the data into the LEAP system, whereupon it was accessible for every police officer in the force. It was not unusual for the whole process to take up to a month. If the issuing officer was on holidays, the whole thing was held up until they returned. If the perpetrator was elusive, the whole thing was held up again.

Meanwhile, the victim is left in no-man's-land, unprotected by the orders the court has made and unprotected by the police. I began, once again, to feel incredibly vulnerable. When you go to court, you have the support of the police officers on the day, and you feel emboldened. There are people in your corner. But once the matter has been heard, they dissipate. And with this dissolving of my 'team', the continuity of my story was shattered. My protectors were called to tend to myriad other victims and matters. I felt like I had been cast aside.

And then there was the horrible realisation that this course of action I had chosen might only serve to make things worse. I had gone to court and pressed my case because I felt that with the courts and police on my side, I could safely stand up to Greg, knowing that someone had my back. But now I was beginning to realise that I had poked an angry bear and turned to look at the army behind me, only to discover I was on my own.

I once again steeled myself: for the sake of Luke and for the sake of self-preservation. As macabre as it was, I came to accept that because Greg was a transient, Luke and I were the only constants in his life. We were the only honey trap to which he was vulnerable. If he was going to be arrested, we would necessarily be implicated.

On 7 May 2013, I received an email out of the blue from DSC Andrew Cocking, introducing himself and asking if I might know how to locate Greg. He didn't mention for which matter specifically he was pursuing Greg, saying only it was serious but he couldn't be more specific than that. I phoned him back and started sharing with him how he might locate Greg – places in St Kilda I knew he had frequented in the past: the Hare Krishna temple, the Mormon Church.

In the course of our conversation, DSC Cocking said he was someone I could trust. He made it clear that he was on my side, that he worked in the city and could be relied on. It also seemed to me that he was suggesting that the best way to draw Greg out was to use Luke as bait.

I hung up the phone feeling faintly reassured. The police in the big smoke were now involved and there would be an upping of the ante in terms of finding Greg and arresting him.

Constable Topham also phoned me. Upon establishing that I was expecting Greg to show up at Luke's footy training the following afternoon, instructed me to call triple zero the minute

I spotted him. I did not know, but multiple warrants were out for his arrest – including for threats to kill and child porn charges.

The following morning I received an email from DSC Cocking. 'I have informed all the police with an interest in your husband to get their paperwork ready in anticipation,' he wrote.

To which I fired back, *'Thanks Andrew, but he is NOT my husband.'* I added a smiley face emoticon.

A minute later, DSC Cocking replied, 'Appreciate that. That's what happens when you start typing too early in the morning.'

Around lunchtime, I sent another email to DSC Cocking. 'I would just LOVE to know what else he's done. Somehow it gives me comfort that it's not just myself that he has directed his anger toward.'

I didn't receive a reply.

That afternoon, feeling anxious and frightened, I bundled Luke into the car and headed to Tyabb oval for footy practice. I didn't let Luke know what I hoped would take place, nor had I spoken to any of the other parents. The only thing I wanted more fervently than to see Greg finally arrested was for it to be done discreetly – without other parents being implicated, if possible, and certainly without Luke having to bear witness to it. I didn't want him to see it, and I didn't want him to suffer the humiliation of his friends seeing it.

Many knew of the problems I had been having with Greg. Some of them knew the full extent of it, others knew enough to know that ours was a strained relationship and the police were involved.

The AFL oval is set back off the main road, 300 metres down a gravel drive, past a set of tennis courts. As we pulled into the car park next to the oval, sure enough, there was Greg: standing at the fence around the oval's perimeter, a little apart from the other parents, taking in the boys as they practised. I made a mental note of his outfit to pass on to police then had a quiet word with the manager of Luke's team, asking her to keep an eye on Luke while I called the police and retreated to the main road to wait for them to arrive.

As instructed, I called triple zero from the driveway entrance, explained who I was and why I was phoning, and was told the matter would be taken in hand. I stood on the roadside, expecting the police would be along at any moment. I watched the road anxiously, waiting for the sight of a police vehicle, nervously glancing back over my shoulder at regular intervals, fearing Greg would catch me in the act.

Thirty minutes later, I was still standing at the driveway, almost mad with panic. I rang triple zero a second time and explained all over again who I was and why I was phoning. My voice by now was shrill, my patience all but drained. Football training would soon be over, and Greg would disappear back into the ether. The whole enterprise would have been a stressful waste of time. All day and most of the previous night I had worked myself into a state anticipating this moment – and now it was not even happening.

'I just need to know if anyone is coming,' I pleaded with the triple-zero telephone operator on the end of the line. 'He is going to leave at any moment.'

The voice at the end of the phone line assured me everything was in hand.

After forty-five minutes, I was distraught. I rang Hastings Police Station directly and spoke to a police officer. He told me if I wanted him to help me, I needed to calm down.

'I have been stood here waiting for forty-five minutes,' I screamed down the line. 'My violent ex-partner who has threatened to kill me on several occasions is just metres away, he's threatened my son with a knife and you are telling me to calm down?'

'You just need to calm down, Rosie,' came the reply. 'We've had police there all night.'

'You what?' I couldn't believe what I was hearing. 'What do you mean you've had police here all night? I haven't seen a single police car.'

'They're undercover police,' the constable explained. 'They're in an unmarked car.'

I was incredulous. 'You mean to tell me there have been police here all this time, but they haven't made an attempt to arrest Greg?'

'Rosie, there's a problem,' the constable said. 'We can't do anything tonight because the paperwork hasn't arrived. We haven't received the warrants to arrest him.'

I thought I must have been hearing things. Nothing made sense. I was at once confused, scared and very, very angry.

'But I arranged all this with Detective Cocking this morning. He emailed me to tell me everything was in place for an arrest. I don't understand. Why would he say that? Why would he put me through all of this? Why are the police even here if they can't arrest Greg? I don't understand.' I was becoming hysterical. 'Why the fuck are they here!?'

There was a moment's silence, then the officer replied, 'To make sure you are okay.'

I hung up the phone, tears streaming down my face, and in a blind panic, I jumped into the car and sped down the dirt track back to the oval car park. Parents turned from watching the footy as I skidded to a halt on the gravel.

I leaped out of the car, crying uncontrollably, screaming for the police to reveal themselves. 'Where are you?' I yelled between sobs. 'Where are you?'

Overwhelmed, I collapsed on the grass, sobbing into the ground. I felt defeated, exhausted, beaten down. What did I have to do to get this man arrested? What was it going to take to get Greg out of my life? Why, when I had placed my faith in the police to follow through on a promise, had they let me down in the most spectacularly cruel fashion? My wails echoed out across the empty paddocks.

I must have lain there crying for a good three minutes before a car pulled up alongside me. A window was wound down and a man identified himself as a police officer. As I pulled myself up off the ground, still racking with sobs, the undercover policeman explained they had come with the intention of arresting Greg, but because the paperwork had not been received, they were powerless to do anything.

As they spoke, I watched helplessly – and with a rising sense of panic – as Greg walked calmly down the driveway before being swallowed up by the darkness.

The drive home with Luke that night was a blur. I was emotionally drained. I felt so embarrassed that I had made such a spectacle of myself in front of fellow parents. I was supposed to attend a football social club event that Saturday night, but my friend advised I shouldn't go. People had apparently been so appalled by my behaviour, it was better if I kept a low profile for a while. From that point on, I was never sure how welcome I was at the club, and so I distanced myself from them all, believing it was probably best if I simply withdrew.

I don't know how much Luke saw or heard. He knew afterwards that I was really upset with his dad, but I certainly didn't want him thinking that I was conspiring with police to get his dad arrested.

I rang the police station the following day, disturbed about the night before and keen to get some kind of explanation. It was only at the insistence of DSC Cocking, after all, that I had agreed to take part (and allow Luke to take part) in their scheme to finally arrest Greg. I wanted some explanation as to why it hadn't happened. I got the same policeman who had answered my call the night before. He wasn't able to explain what had gone wrong. He did add though – rather unhelpfully – that my getting upset 'didn't help matters'.

'Can I please speak to the person in charge?' I asked.

He wouldn't put me through to anyone. Tired of being stonewalled, I eventually hung up the phone.

I called back an hour or so later and got another policeman. He said he was familiar with the circumstances that had led to the previous night's debacle (my words, not his), and promptly went into an explanation of the delay that sometimes occurred in the reception of warrant papers.

If the trauma of the night itself hadn't been enough to destroy my faith in the police, their reactions the next day certainly did it. They also set the tone for the remainder of the year, tipping me into a heightened sense of anxiety from which I never really emerged. I lost all confidence in the system that night. It was clear that the people who were supposed to protect me weren't going to. If Greg was going to be stopped, I was quite clearly going to have to do it alone. The very thought exhausted me.

What the police could never begin to understand was how much fear and anxiety goes into having someone arrested. They didn't consider the impact it might have on Luke to see his father arrested. They didn't think of the sense of shame Luke would feel in front of his peers and I would feel in front of other parents. Not to mention the absolute fear I felt at having Greg arrested in public and provoking him in this way. I felt like the police were dismissing me as just another melodramatic victim of domestic violence. They had no idea of my history, no idea of the years of abuse. Because they dealt with so many people and so much drama on a daily basis, I was just another one to be appeased and humoured.

Three days later, I was summonsed back to Frankston Magistrates Court for yet another hearing on the variation of the IVO. Driving there, I felt increasingly anxious. My heart was racing, my emotions were swinging wildly between feeling desperately upset and extremely angry. When I arrived, police prosecutor Darren Cathie greeted me and apologised immediately, explaining that I didn't need to be in court after all. There had been a mistake: Greg still had not been served, so he was not present and therefore I wasn't required.

I lost it with him. 'What is the fucking point of all this? I mean, I jump through all these hoops and do everything the police and courts advise, and it doesn't make a scrap of fucking difference. I don't know why I even bother.'

Darren apologised as I stormed out to my car.

Here we all were again: me, Luke, the police and courts all being controlled and manipulated by a madman who knew how to play the system. I had finally decided to take the stand that friends, counsellors and authorities had been urging me to take for years – and this was the result. I'd attended court four times regarding varying the IVO and Greg hadn't attended once. I felt more vulnerable and exposed than ever. But it's not like there was any turning back. Once the process is in play, you are committed – the lines are drawn.

My decision to participate in Greg's arrest had set in train a course of events from which it was now impossible to withdraw.

I emailed DSC Cocking late in the evening of 21 May – thirteen days after the previous failed arrest attempt.

'I received a telephone message from Greg this evening to say he will be at Tyabb football ground tomorrow (Wednesday) evening to watch Luke training. He usually arrives around 4.30 pm and training concludes by 6 pm.'

The following morning, DSC Cocking emailed me back. 'I have emailed a request to Sergeant Ellams of Hastings Police Station to assign some members to attend the club tonight.'

And so I braced myself for round two. Arriving at the football oval, I noticed Greg straight away. I scanned the car park for any signs of a police car – marked or otherwise – but saw nothing to reassure me. I parked and watched nervously as Greg greeted Luke. In the time it took me to locate my phone in my handbag and pull it out to dial triple zero, Greg had disappeared. No doubt aware that the dragnet was closing around him, he opted to skip out. But he had made his point, flouting court orders, thumbing his nose at the police who had failed to arrest him to date. It was a typical act of bravado and arrogance from a man who thought he was above the law.

That evening, I emailed DSC Cocking.

'I arrived at footy at 4.39pm. Greg greeted his son for only a few minutes and then apparently left. He arrived on foot and was returning to St Kilda by public transport, I believe, from what Luke told me. I did not notice any police present and I'm not aware that they apprehended him unfortunately.'

The following morning, DSC Cocking replied.

'I was off yesterday so I arrived at work this morning and received an email reply from Sergeant Ellams that he was not able to attend to my request because his patrol units were tied up with an urgent matter elsewhere. Please contact Mornington Police with any further information as to Greg attending the footy and CC me in the future.'

I read his email at the end of my working day. I'd had enough of this tedious process. My frustration was palpable and I fired back a reply. 'Sure,' I wrote. 'I contacted them during the afternoon too but he'd disappeared before I called 000.

'He appears to be aware that they are likely to arrive so I don't have much faith next time. They have other priorities and my experience so far hasn't been great.

'He is not pressuring me to see his son or making unreasonable demands so until he does I shall accept the situation and hope that the next time I have to call them isn't because I am being threatened again with violent behaviour. Such is life.'

DSC Cocking responded, asking me if I might know places that Greg might frequent. To the best of my knowledge, the sum total of the investigation that had gone on to locate Greg between football training sessions was to ask me if had any leads and do a cursory check of the White Pages. If it wasn't so tragic, it would have been laughable.

And so, the following week at footy training, with a wearying predictability, Greg appeared again at the oval. Almost on autopilot, and this time with very little faith in there being a satisfactory outcome, I retreated to the main road as I had once before and called the police. Parents turning in to the oval who knew me were stopping to check if I was okay. I kept assuring them I was fine and urged them to drive on.

And then a police officer appeared. As he pulled into the driveway, I flagged him down and told him what Greg was wearing.

'Can you hop in the back and point him out to me?' the officer asked.

'No, I'm not really comfortable with that,' I replied, envisaging Greg's anger when he saw me colluding with the police. Just then, one of the mothers at training in whom I had confided the extent of my Greg troubles, called my mobile to tell me Greg was heading my way.

I leaped away from the police car, terrified, and hid in bushes near the tennis club. From behind the bushes, I watched as the police waited for and intercepted Greg. In what seemed like a very short amount of time – with what appeared to be an atypically small amount of fuss – Greg was handcuffed and put into the back of the van.

As the paddy wagon pulled out of the drive and onto the main road, I emerged from the bushes and watched it disappear from sight. Was that it? After all this time, could it really have unfolded in such an undramatic fashion? I had come so far and navigated such disappointment, I didn't dare to let myself believe it could all end so easily. Surely there was more drama to come.

Greg was taken to Hastings Police Station and transferred to an interview room. Whatever stores of composure he had called upon during the arrest had clearly dissipated during the short car trip to the police station. By the time he arrived, he was his usual belligerent self. He abused the arresting officers, calling them every name under the sun and telling them, 'God will get you!' He continually pressed the duress button and let rip with a torrent of obscenities every time a police officer attended to him. The arrest warrants were served, bail was opposed and it was deemed that he would be remanded in custody until his next court appearance, some ten days later.

A flurry of communication ensued between Darren Cathie, DSC Cocking, and Constables Anderson and Topham, sharing information and preparing for Greg's next day in court. The contention among them was unanimous: under no circumstances should bail be granted. Given the warrants already out for his arrest, his priors and his failure to attend any of the previous court appearances to which he had been party, it seemed impossible for there to be any other outcome.

But when Greg's lawyer (paid for by the Legal Aid that I was unable to access) applied for bail, the police prosecutor did not oppose it and Magistrate Franz Holzer granted it.

21

Supervision

On the night of 3 July 2013, there was a knock on the door. I almost jumped out of my skin – Luke had gone to bed and Lee had gone out, so it was just me and the dogs pottering about the house.

Heart racing, I crept to the door, planning in my head how, if it was Greg, I would run to Luke's bedroom with the phone and call the police.

There was no need. It was the police.

I flung open the door, incensed.

'Are you Rosemary Batty?' came the enquiry from one of the officers.

I was momentarily thrown. 'Yes,' I replied angrily. 'Why?'

'We're here to serve a court summons,' the officer explained.

I was confused. 'I don't understand,' I said, taking the envelope from the officer's outstretched hand and opening it.

Greg had been to court and made an application to have the IVO changed – requesting to have Luke's name removed from the order so that he could resume contact with him.

Before I had time to process the fact Greg had now started to try and use the courts against me, I rounded on the policemen standing on my doorstep. 'And you had to serve this now? Of all the times during the day, you thought this time of night was the best time to come and serve papers on a woman you know lives in fear of her life?'

The officers looked at me wide-eyed. Clearly, they either knew nothing of my situation, or if they did, it had never occurred to them that knocking on my door at night might not be the most appropriate thing to do.

And so Greg was taking me to court. On top of everything else I had to deal with, I now had to go into a courtroom and defend my attempts to protect my son. It was yet another burden that my already trembling shoulders would struggle to bear.

When I walked into the courthouse two weeks later, there was Greg, already waiting in the foyer, smiling at me, clearly very pleased with himself. I couldn't make eye contact – I was seething with anger. The fact that Magistrate Goldsborough was presiding that day made me feel marginally less furious. At least there was a chance Greg's idiocy would be seen for what it was. Greg had legal representation, but again, I couldn't afford it.

As we waited in the foyer for our case to be called, the police prosecutor who had been assigned to the case, Ross Treverton, approached me to go through proceedings. Noting that SC Kate Anderson opposed any variation to the IVO, he asked me what I wanted to do. I told him that I didn't want Luke removed as a protected person on the IVO, but nor was I opposed to Greg seeing Luke. I still wanted to foster a relationship between them – I knew Luke still wanted to see his dad. And the threat that Greg would kill me if I ever prevented him from seeing his son still echoed in my mind. We discussed the out-of-school activities at which I thought it appropriate for Greg to attend. Football, cricket and Little Athletics would be fine, I reasoned, because they took place in daylight and there were always lots of people around. But Scouts was not okay: it happened at night, the Scout Hall was in a dark grove, and the car park where kids were dropped off and picked up was not, to my mind, safe.

I was visibly distressed at having to be there at all – shaking and teary. I had so much pent-up frustration and anger. So much fear. All mixed in with an overwhelming exhaustion at still being involved in this two-person war of attrition. Finally our case was called and we entered the courtroom. If Magistrate Goldsborough remembered me or my case, she made no initial show of it. I took my place in the courtroom and sat quietly as the proceedings got going.

Greg's lawyer, a suited, middle-aged man from a local private law firm, went through his client's desire to have the IVO varied, and Prosecutor Treverton noted the opposition to it. Magistrate Goldsborough started querying Greg's lawyer about his client's long history of previous charges, including an outstanding matter that appeared not yet to have been heard by a court of law.

'Those would be the child pornography charges, Your Honour,' Greg's lawyer volunteered.

I gasped out loud – my head was suddenly spinning. I let out a whimper. My stomach lurched as once again my world was upended. The child pornography charges? What was he talking about? I looked across at Greg, who was unmoved, staring straight ahead. The magistrate and lawyer kept speaking, but I could only make out the odd word, the rest a blur. Prosecutor Treverton looked to me imploringly, but I shrugged my shoulders and shook my head, indicating I had no idea what they were talking about. I had broken into a cold sweat and felt the anxiety rise in me like a wave.

I was horrified. At the very mention of those two words – child pornography – my mind began racing, suddenly reassessing every interaction Greg had had with Luke since he was a little boy. The overnight stays, the camping trips, the pool parties. I felt nauseous. Was Greg grooming him? Had he been inappropriate with any of Luke's friends? Had he exposed Luke to things no child should ever be exposed to?

And suddenly cast in a new light were all the derogatory comments, overtly sexual comments by Greg about me and the men who had been in my life. The vile intimations about them sharing a bath with Luke, the hideous aspersions about sharing a bed: they all made sense now. They were simply a reflection of his own sick mind. His own dark inner thoughts.

I leaned forward and hissed at Prosecutor Treverton that I had changed my mind: in light of this new revelation, I wanted to withdraw any access Greg had to Luke.

Magistrate Goldsborough seemed to be shocked too. Suddenly, everyone in the courtroom, except for Greg and his lawyer, seemed to be performing mental gymnastics to recalibrate everything they understood this case to be about. A short adjournment was called so I could speak with Prosecutor Treverton. He took me to a private meeting room and closed the door.

'Did you know about this?' he asked, incredulous.

'No! I'm more shocked than anyone,' I said. 'I feel sick about it. Why didn't I know this? Why wasn't I told?'

'Well, it changes everything,' he continued. 'I'm going to press for no contact at all.'

Feeling a small ripple of validation, I agreed. I didn't want Greg to have direct contact now although I *would* be prepared to allow phone contact.

Back in court, the magistrate gave her ruling. The IVO was to be varied after all, giving Greg access to Luke at sporting events, 'such as cricket, Little Athletics and football' where he was permitted to 'speak to Luke in the company of others'. Telephone contact was not allowed.

Prosecutor Treverton saw me sitting defeated in the courtroom foyer afterwards and urged me to contact a law firm. He explained how, because the child pornography charges had not yet been heard by a court of law, Greg had to be considered innocent until proven otherwise. Magistrate Goldsborough had acted to the full extent the law allowed her to. It seemed to me that the law was there to protect everyone else but the likes of Luke.

He further explained that if I wanted permanent change to the custody and access arrangements for Luke, I would need to initiate Family Court proceedings.

In an email the following day to the psychologist who had been recommended to me, I wrote: 'It was a hideous day in court. Was there from 9.30 am until about 4.30 pm. I was emotional and angry at everyone and didn't handle myself well.'

For a week or so following the court appearance, I withheld from Luke the news that his father was facing child pornography charges. I didn't know how to tell him. I was also conscious that he was still angry with me for betraying his dad to the police in the first place. Finally, I figured it was better that he heard it from me than from someone else. Following my experience with my mother's death, I've always felt strongly that children needed to be kept informed.

'So Dad's a paedophile as well as everything else?' Luke responded with an air of defeat when finally I sat him down and told him. I was taken aback. I wasn't aware he even knew the meaning of the word. The news threw him into a funk.

A week or so later, he was still moping about. Normally happy-go-lucky (in spite of the turmoil that seemed constantly to surround him), he became sullen and detached. One evening he had returned from school particularly flat.

I asked him what was wrong, expecting to receive the standard response, 'Nothing.'

But instead, he slumped at the kitchen table and told me he 'hated' his life and didn't see the point of being alive. 'I might as well commit suicide,' he said.

His words cut me to the quick. I was thrown into a blind panic. How did he even know about suicide? Where had he come across it as a concept? And how bad did an eleven-year-old's life need to be for him to consider it? It broke my heart.

Several days later, I took Luke to the first of his art therapy sessions. They had been recommended as the best way to determine how much he was being affected by traumatic events in his life, because he might express in drawings things he was unable to otherwise find voice for. Luke was initially reluctant to attend, but dutifully trotted off into the therapist's private office once we arrived.

I wasn't informed at the time, because what happened in the sessions was private between Luke and his therapist, but I would learn later that Luke's ideations of suicide – as immature and undeveloped as they were – were symptomatic of a wider malaise. He had been carrying so much for so long, it was bound to have an effect on him.

He sat and scribbled as the therapist gently asked him about his life. He said he was worried about me: about the stress I was under, trying to pay the bills, trying to manage his father, trying to keep up a brave face for his sake. He said he was embarrassed by his father, aware of his mental health issues, and he fretted about the effect they had on his friends. He wasn't able to share any of his worries with his mates because he worried they would judge him for it.

He told the art therapist that he felt 'responsible' for his father's wellbeing, adding, 'I think I am the only thing he is living for.' He said he worried that his father might have to go to jail, because he had hurt people in the past, including me. And Luke said that he had witnessed some of that violence. He said he wasn't scared that his father would hurt him: he had never felt in danger. But, chillingly, he was worried that I was going to be hurt, and possibly killed.

When I later heard about it, it struck me what a burden that had been for a little boy. And also how emotionally mature my son had been. Only eleven and able to give expression to these most profound, disturbing truths. My heart ached.

Even my strategy of keeping Greg engaged with Luke's sporting activities was backfiring. I had naïvely believed if Greg could interact with Luke and the other parents in his various sporting clubs, it would force him to behave normally in the company of others, and show Luke what it meant to have a normal father.

But Greg's mental state was deteriorating, and on a couple of occasions he quoted passages from the Bible to other dads. Luke was mortified. Increasingly, too, parents of other children became aware of the IVOs out against Greg and my ongoing court battle to restrict his access to Luke. Understandably, they were none too excited that this man who had been arrested multiple times for assault was a semi-permanent presence in their own children's lives. Most parents were supportive of me, but unsurprisingly, they began to ostracise Greg and alienate him from club activities.

It all reached a climax without me even knowing.

Around this time, the mother of a boy on Luke's footy team approached me while the boys were playing, annoyed that I hadn't told her that Greg had threatened the coach with a knife.

'He did what?' I replied, astounded. 'But I had no idea! Nobody told me!'

It turned out that the coach had wanted Luke to play ruck, but Luke didn't want to play ruck. Greg had stepped in and told the coach under no circumstances was Luke going to play ruck – to which the coach quite rightly replied something to the effect of, 'Mate, I'm the coach, I'll play Luke wherever I think is best.'

Greg's response had been to stare down the coach before saying something along the lines of, 'I have a knife with your name on it,' and stalking back to his car.

I confronted the coach about it. 'You have to tell me when these things happen,' I implored. 'I need to know these things so I can protect myself and my son. You might not think it important, but that sort of thing needs to be reported to the police.'

Of course, it was exactly the kind of information I should have a right to know. The child porn charges were another case in point. DSC Andrew Cocking had known about the charges but had acted to the letter of the law by respecting Greg's privacy. However, surely in circumstances such as mine, there are mitigating factors that should be taken into account. Clearly DSC Cocking felt constrained by Victoria's privacy laws.

Why, I wondered, did the law regard my right as a mother determined to protect her son as less important than Greg's right to privacy? If it were the child of a police officer or politician, for example, would he or she have thought it acceptable for authorities to withhold that sort of information?

Now that the child porn charges were out in the open, the law firm that Prosecutor Treverton recommended suggested I contact Child Protection and inform them of the latest developments. Child Protection agreed that Luke's file ought to be reopened (but only at my suggestion – at no point did there appear to be any official passing of information or referral of a possible child sex offence to Child Protection, oddly enough).

While they arranged for further investigation, they visited me at home and asked me to sign a written undertaking that I would ensure Luke was protected at all times. I knew that if I could not guarantee Luke's safety, they would be within their rights to remove him from my care.

'I will not allow Luke to have any unsupervised access with Greg,' the document read. 'I understand that supervision means that Luke will be in my line of sight at any time. I will not allow Greg to take photographs of Luke. If I become aware of Greg taking photographs of any child, I will notify Child Protection and/or the police.'

A second meeting was then scheduled, again at our house. Child Protection had already been in contact with DSC Cocking, requesting further information, specifically the nature of the porn (it was images of young girls) and whether its possession ought to be cause for concern. On the morning of 5 September 2013, Child Protection officer Tracie Portelli and DSC Deborah Charteris from the Sexual Offences and Child Abuse Investigation Team of the Victorian Police arrived on my doorstep. It was just after breakfast, so Luke was taking the morning off school. Not wanting to be the helicopter mother sitting there prompting him throughout his interview, I left the three of them at the kitchen table and retired to the home office space nearby, where I pretended to be working. I nevertheless listened proudly as Luke as summoned all his maturity to speak to the adults as equals.

He was trying to be mature in his little way, by holding himself upright in his chair, using language beyond his years and displaying overt politeness towards the strangers, bless him.

'Do you know what Child Protection is? What kind of work we do?' came the first question.

'Your job is to make sure that kids are safe,' Luke replied.

'That's right. And do you know why we are here to speak to you?'

'Dad.'

'Yes, that's right. What about Mum. Tell me about Mum?'

'She's mostly good. Though she can have anxiety attacks.'

'Tell me about that.'

'I don't like it when Mum gets sad,' Luke said. I felt a pang.

'What causes this?'

'When she thinks too much. Like, how are we going to pay our taxes, how are we going to care for the animals.'

'How does this make you feel?'

'I want to help Mum. I am okay if we need to move house.'

'What caused Mum to feel this way?'

'Dad hit Mum. Probably this. Then Mum moved jobs. It's hard and there's not enough money.'

'Tell me about Dad.'

'I was age three, Dad wanted to take me away from Mum. Dad put me in a room. I peered around the corner. Dad slammed Mum's head on the wall. Mum ran to the neighbour's house. I remember all of this.'

'What happened next?'

'I don't remember. Mum then got scared, we got anxious around Dad. If we ever saw him again, I worried that he could hit Mum. There are two sides to Dad, he can be nice and then angry.'

There was silence as the officers took notes. And then, as if to ensure they were not getting the wrong idea, Luke said: 'Dad is good. He always has a smile on his face.' Before adding, with what I am sure was a despondent tone: 'I am the only thing that is good for Dad.'

'Tell me about Dad getting angry,' said one of the women.

'He makes his own cigarettes, then he starts praying. He is Christian and he acts a bit different. He would see stuff. He does not talk to me. He just prays really. When he is praying, in his head he is okay.'

There was silence again, and then I could hear Luke choking back tears. I wanted to run to him, to comfort him, but fought the urge.

'How do you feel about Dad?' Tracie asked.

'I love him to bits,' Luke said through tears.

'Are there bits about Dad that are not so good?'

'He acts different, he starts praying and walks off. I get a bit embarrassed about Dad.'

One of the officers asked if he ever felt scared of his dad. Luke said he had never been frightened of Greg.

'Have you ever felt uncomfortable around your dad?' came the question from one of the women.

'There was this one time,' Luke began, describing the scene in the car when Greg produced the knife. 'Dad picked up a knife and said, "It could all end with this."'

'Tell me about this.'

'We were in Mornington, next to the beach in the parking area. He lost himself. He didn't know what he was doing, really.'

'Tell me about this.'

'Dad used to be a carpenter. He has tools in his car. He uses the knife to open stuff, like, he will buy me Lego. He cuts up apples with the knife. Dad was praying. I was on my iPad. He didn't ask for a turn for a bit, then he said, "It could all end with this. Cain has spoken." I felt that he was going to kill me.'

I felt sick and relieved all at the same time. Finally, someone other than me was being made aware of the danger my little boy and I were in.

The officers asked why Luke felt he might be killed.

'Oh, I don't know,' he replied, starting to go cool on the idea of betraying his father to these two strangers. 'I have heard some stuff. Friends watched some things on TV like *Nightmare on Elm Street* – that sort of stuff.'

DSC Charteris pressed Luke, asking him if he thought Greg would hurt him.

'I felt he was going to hurt himself, not me,' Luke replied.

I came out from where I was sitting, unable to remain quiet any longer. 'But that's not the only thing he said, is it Luke?' I ventured, trying to sound as nonchalant as possible. 'Your dad also mentioned going to another world together, didn't he?'

At this Luke became suddenly upset. 'Mum!' he said, raising his voice and making me jump. 'Why do you have to say these things? He didn't say that.' He glared at me. 'I can't remember anything else.'

And with that, he shut down. I had betrayed a confidence – crossed an invisible line. For whatever reason, whether he thought my interjection was somehow an affront to his own powers of recollection or whether out of loyalty to his father, Luke had put me back in my place.

I understood from the stares of both Portelli and Charteris that I wasn't helping matters, and so I retreated again, to let the interview conclude without me. It was just that the thought of Child Protection once again leaving with the impression that all was actually well in our world, and that Greg was not the clear and present danger I had been making him out to be, was too horrible to contemplate. We needed help. We couldn't fight this man on our own. What was it going to take for someone to take our cries for help seriously?

I would later learn that they did take Luke at his word, concluding in their case notes that he was not in any danger from his father.

In the days after her meeting with Luke, DSC Charteris had a meeting with her superior, Detective Sergeant Peter Drake. Luke was not, according to DSC Charteris, in any grave danger. There was no evidence of any offence or a threat to kill having been committed by Greg, and Luke did not appear to live in fear of his father. They substantiated that Luke had been harmed by family violence but, because I was a protective parent who had agreed to a plan, they took no further action to protect Luke, and never participated to support my efforts to strengthen protections for Luke and myself. They never interviewed Greg, and in October 2013, the case was closed.

Four days after Luke's interview, I was back at Frankston Magistrates Court to seek a variation on the IVO. I wanted it tightened, to limit Luke's exposure to Greg to football and cricket. Greg had been exploiting the fuzzy language of the existing IVO, showing up to Luke's Scout Hall, hanging around as he came and went from Scouts in the dark. I wanted to bring an end to it.

I arrived at the court to two pieces of bad news. The first was that the presiding magistrate was going to be Magistrate Holzer – *not* Magistrate Goldsborough. The second was that upon learning that I was planning to ask for a change in the wording, limiting him to attend football and cricket only, Greg had shouted abuse at the police prosecutor, Diana Davidson, and stormed out of the courthouse.

Magistrate Holzer called my case and, once again, I was in a courtroom, feeling sheepish and apologetic. Clearly annoyed that Greg had not fronted for the hearing, Holzer indicated he was inclined to adjourn the hearing until such time as Greg was present. I felt the panic rising in me. Greg was playing the system to maximum effect and each time I was being left vulnerable. I refused to be stymied once again by ridiculous court process.

As Prosecutor Davidson explained my desire to change the IVO to exclude Scouts, Magistrate Holzer spoke of his own experience of Scouts and the level of adult supervision that was provided. I felt that the inference from the judge was that if Greg could attend cricket and football matches to see his son, he couldn't see why he should not also attend Scouts.

I began fidgeting in my seat. As he continued to spar with the police prosecutor, I got the impression that he considered me a troublemaker, that I was some kind of harridan determined to prevent the father of my child from enjoying his God-given rights to see his son.

And this was the problem with the court system. There was no continuity. Magistrate Holzer may not have known the particulars of Greg's violence towards me and Luke because he had not been presiding on the previous occasions when they were revealed. With each new magistrate, I felt as if I had to start from scratch. I had to get them to understand all over again the danger I was in and the level of violence to which Greg could stoop.

I asked for permission to speak and stood up. 'Greg has a history of violence,' I said. 'Scouts is unsupervised, the car park is pitch-black. It's not safe for me to drop Luke off there. There are not as many people around. It's not like cricket or football at all!' I had started to become emotional – my voice rose and began to quaver. I went on to inform the magistrate of the child pornography charges, the knife threat, the involvement of Child Protection and Greg's long history of violence.

Magistrate Holzer instructed me to sit down. Prosecutor Davidson turned around and motioned at me to sit back down, indicating my outburst was not helping my cause. But I was too far gone. I picked up my handbag, wiped the tears from my face and walked out of the courtroom.

Minutes later, I was in the foyer trying to compose myself when Prosecutor Davidson emerged. 'There you are!' she said. 'You got what you wanted. He's changed the wording on the IVO. You just had to stay.'

I looked at her, dumbfounded. She seemed to me to be implying that I had overreacted. No matter how well-intentioned she was, this woman knew little of my history. Because of a system that means she deals with possibly fifty cases a day, she could never be across the full details of them all. She probably had little appreciation of the journey I had been on to get to this point – to be sobbing uncontrollably in the foyer of a courtroom. Was she really thinking I had overreacted?

'What's the point?' I spat back at her. 'I mean, honestly. What is the point of all of this? It's not going to make a scrap of difference. I've been through all of this before and it doesn't change a thing. I might as well throw myself under a bus.'

'You keep speaking like that, Rosie, and I'll have to report it to the mental health team,' the prosecutor said.

'You cannot be serious,' I replied. 'I'm angry, and I have every reason to be angry. In fifteen minutes I'll be calm again. I'm not the one that needs mental health intervention. This is ludicrous.'

But the prosecutor was only doing her job in accordance with the law. So she went to find a police officer, who returned to speak with me to determine my mental state.

When he was done, I gathered my things and walked out of the courthouse.

In the car on the way home, I reflected on the catch 22 in which I found myself. If I downplayed the violence and threats, no one took them seriously. But if I became hysterical, I was written off as a melodramatic – or mad – woman. Decades of exposure to family violence had muted the official response to it, and I was suffering for that.

22

Holding Pattern

Winter turned gradually to spring, in that lazy, sometimes reluctant way it does in southern Victoria. I loved the beauty of the Mornington Peninsula. Those winding roads along dramatic coastline, the thundering surf on the ocean side, the quaint beaches on the bay side and the vineyards and rolling hills in between – it truly was a stunning part of the world in which I found myself. Moving to Tyabb had given me the taste of country that I needed to stay sane. After being raised on a farm, I needed that sense of space more than I was even properly aware.

As we started to shuck our winter gear and prepare for what can often be a searingly hot summer, I signed Luke up for cricket again. Luke was good at sport but not always the best. He loved to win and be noticed. He was proficient with a ball, had decent hand-to-eye co-ordination, for sure. But he was probably not going to be a prodigy, and when I thought about his future, I didn't see him walking out onto the pitch at Lords representing his country.

For that reason, I'd also enrolled him in a local, after-school drama course. He'd always shown a talent for performing. At his age, it was easy to confuse being a ham or a class clown with any actual acting or performing talent, but I figured it was good for him to know that there were other things in life than sport.

Luke took to the classes like a duck to water. I wouldn't go so far as to say he had found his calling, but certainly his weekly excursions into the world of the arts were an unexpected hit. Luke liked the stage and the stage seemed to like him back.

*

Dissatisfied with and distressed by the recent court ruling around Greg's access to Luke, I rang Child Protection to ask if they could help me take out a protective order for Luke. But they said they were unable to help me. They'd determined that I was a suitable protector of Luke's wellbeing and they were satisfied Luke was not in danger and therefore they had decided to close his file. Once again, I had turned to an agency for support, and once again they had left me stranded.

Because I was relatively sane (though my sanity was being sorely tested), and able to provide for Luke and give him a stable home environment (of sorts), I was being left to deal with the Greg situation by myself. I felt terribly isolated and that I was being unfairly punished because I wasn't a complete mess. I didn't want to be the one to confront Greg and tell him that he couldn't see his son anymore. I knew the violence of which he was capable: I didn't wish to be the brunt of it again. I wanted the directives to come from judges or police or child protection officers.

Also, and perhaps without being aware of it, I wanted validation from a third party – an authoritative third party – that Greg was dangerous, that he was a potentially damaging influence in Luke's life, and therefore, after eleven years of supporting his relationship with Luke, it was time to shut the door.

I received a letter from the family violence service in which they offered to arrange more counselling sessions should Luke or I feel the need for them. But I didn't want any more counselling sessions, I just wanted Greg out of my life. I could lie on a couch until the cows came home, pouring out my heart, but it wasn't going to remove the cancer that had taken hold in our lives. I just wanted someone to step in and excise it.

I felt that Greg had lived a really tormented life, and that everything he had ever loved or cared for was slowly being taken away from him. He was homeless, jobless and pursued by police. He had a serious marijuana habit, which was not only expensive to maintain but was messing with the little mental clarity he was holding on to. What shreds of dignity he had left were all predicated on an increasingly jumbled grab bag of religious zealotry, and even they were starting to look more frayed by the day as his mental state continued to unravel.

At the back of my mind, I harboured a faint hope that something untoward would happen to him. Not out of malice – because despite having every reason to despise him, I didn't – but rather out of pity. He was living rough in and around St Kilda, and the people he spent time with in hostels or on the streets were unsavoury to say the least: the chances of him encountering misadventure, I thought, were better than average. I never wanted him to feel any pain, but I felt it would have been a small mercy. It would have put him out of his misery.

He used to talk to Luke about how he was going to get an apartment and a job and how Luke would come to live with him. He would paint a picture of domestic harmony to which Luke had always been susceptible. But as Luke grew older, he began to understand — as I had from the outset — that it was never going to happen.

And it began to worry me how life was going to be for Luke when his dad was old and Luke was left to care for him. I couldn't even see how it was going to work when Luke was a teenager and Greg's mental state had deteriorated even further. The teenage years are when you traditionally push away from your parents, and I couldn't see how Greg would ever let Luke do that.

I remember around this time I went to a professional photographer and had a beautiful photo taken of Luke, and the photographer at the time remarked on how handsome he was. Like any mother, I loved my child no matter what: but also like any mother, I thought my boy was the most handsome young man around. And I was gratified by that in a strange way. The object of Luke's affection at Flinders College, a pretty little girl in his year, had done some modelling, and Luke — emboldened by the photographer's comments — began to entertain the idea of perhaps doing some modelling himself.

Greg shot down the idea immediately, telling him it was stupid. Likewise, when Luke had mentioned in passing that he might be interested in becoming a policeman, Greg launched into a rant against the constabulary, telling Luke no son of his would ever enter the police force. Greg always felt the need to control Luke and the direction of his life. There was no doubt, I remember thinking, they were going to clash when Luke got older.

Whenever Luke was really torn about his dad being unhappy — which was happening more frequently — I would say, 'You love your dad and your dad loves you. You'll always love your dad, but you may not always like what he does. And that's okay.'

If the letter from Child Protection had left me feeling abandoned once again, at least my opponent was starting to play by the rules. For the latter part of 2013, as spring turned to summer, Greg began attending football and cricket matches, in keeping with the parameters of the IVO. I was never sure where he had come from or where he would disappear to afterwards. We barely made eye contact, much less spoke to one another.

Greg would also occasionally show up to training mid-week. Because I hadn't stayed in Magistrate Holzer's courtroom long enough to hear his ruling, I wasn't aware that Greg was not supposed to be attending cricket practice. Any contact with Luke mid-week was technically in violation of the IVO. But I wouldn't find that out until many months later.

Still, for a good three months, I lived free from Greg's power games, without feeling as if I was constantly on guard or having to juggle his irrational behaviour. And it was such a relief. After all of the fear and pressure I had felt going into the court process, here at last was a sense that life could in fact be Greg-free. My strategy of holding him to account, of maintaining boundaries and pulling him up each time he crossed them, seemed to finally be working. I began to wonder why I hadn't tried it earlier. For the first time since Luke was born I felt free, and I even began to believe there was an opportunity for me and Luke to build lives that didn't have Greg's shadow permanently hanging over them.

We both benefited from that lack of stress in our lives. Luke began to excel at school. The stress of the previous twelve months had showed via behavioural problems at school. He seemed to be semi-permanently in the principal's office for being disruptive in class. But now, as the year drew to a close, he appeared to have turned a corner. Friends commented to me on what a difference they had seen in Luke and how much he had matured. I too had noticed a change in him. Like any mother-son relationship, ours was hardly all roses. We were exposed to one another almost constantly, and while we were very close, we had our disagreements. Like any eleven-year-old, he could at times be rude or arrogant towards me, or demanding or impatient, and he knew which buttons to press to upset me. But that was part and parcel of our relationship: I knew our ability to annoy one another was mostly because we were the closest people in one another's lives.

Overall, Luke was such a kind, sensitive boy he was always able to say: 'I'm sorry Mum, I shouldn't have done that – I was out of line.' And I was really proud of him for that. It showed a maturity beyond his years, and I always made a point of commending him on it.

I'd always feared that, as a single mother of an only child, I'd been too indulgent throughout Luke's life – and certainly plenty of people had offered up unsolicited advice to that effect – but as long as he was socially well-adjusted, I was simply happy that he was happy. That was, after all, the essence of my job as his mother.

Which is why, every single day, multiple times a day, I would tell him how much I loved him – how beautiful he was and how perfect he was to me. Not once in my life had my parents told me they loved me. I knew they did, on a fundamental level, but I'd never heard the words.

I knew I must have been doing something right as a mother when Luke started to talk about me one day becoming a grandmother. When I was younger, I had never even envisioned getting married, much less having a life with children in it. But Luke had a very clear sense that in his life there would eventually be a wife and children. And it was a massive comfort to know that, despite his unconventional upbringing, he hadn't been sufficiently damaged to believe that sort of normal life was unattainable. Certainly, looking back, the trauma I experienced as a young girl and the attachment issues I had subsequently developed had had a huge impact on my life (and the expectations I had of it). But this, apparently, was not going to be the case for my boy. Maybe I hadn't been such a rubbish mother after all.

Luke loved the company of girls and was really loyal in his affections. One of his friends found herself on the receiving end of most of Luke's attentions. I remember taking him to deliver a beautiful Christmas card he had made. I marvelled as he marched in and handed the card over to his blushing (but clearly very pleased) friend. Who was this child so in touch with his emotions and so ready to put them out on display? I couldn't have been more proud.

He also wrote her a letter that was a masterstroke of innocent childish seduction. I know, because he asked me to proofread it. He addressed his letter to her parents, telling them that there were three boys at school who were all interested in their daughter, but that he was by far the best prospect because he could do better cartwheels than the other two. He added that he had a particular advantage over one of his rivals, who spent 'far too much time brushing his hair'. He never did deliver the letter, and I still have it. Here is an excerpt:

> Hello T—— or Mrs or Mr W——
>
> I have loved you or your daughter for some time now and it turns out two other boys I know like her maybe three … I'm an active funny guy who can do a perfect cartwheel for a boy. I would take care of T—— as long as I live … So there you have it I am the one. Please send back.
>
> From Luke

Greg, to his credit, had taken extra special care to make Luke as worldly as possible. He spoke to him as an adult, chatted about life's big issues and spent hours with Luke in public libraries poring over encyclopaedias together. There were a lot of positives to their relationship. Even so, I knew that the best possible outcome at this point was for Luke to be removed from Greg's sphere of influence – and so I began to make enquiries about sending Luke to boarding school.

I had been kicking the idea around for a while and had even been in contact with a school in Sale, some 200 kilometres away. I reasoned that perhaps they could enforce the discipline that I had not been able to – and also keep Luke at arm's length from his father. Of course, when I mentioned the idea to Luke, he almost had a fit. He had no desire to move schools, or indeed move away from home. It became a moot point anyway: when I scanned the fee schedule, it became clear pretty quickly that it was an idea well beyond my means.

In the interests of continuing to expand Luke's horizons – and also just to take a break after a long and stressful year – I started planning for Luke and me to take a trip back to the UK for Christmas. I'd had a tough year and I craved the unconditional love and comfort that only family can give you.

Constable Topham and a few others had said to me in the previous few months that I ought to think about returning to England permanently – irrespective of Greg's wishes. And though I had no desire to break the law and live in the UK as fugitives, I was starting to accept I was going to have no peace from Greg as long as he was alive. And so England was firming up as a definite option. When I booked the holiday, I booked a five-week break. I wanted to have a comfortable period of time there to get a sense of what our lives might be like if we moved back to England. I also wanted Luke to spend Christmas with my family. I had a new little niece whom I barely knew, Luke had a lovely connection with my brother Terry, and I just thought it would be a good way to end what had been a tumultuous year.

It was during the flight booking process that I discovered Luke's passport had expired. And to apply for a new one, I would need Greg's signature. Spying an opportunity to once again exert influence over our lives, Greg steadfastly refused to sign the document. It wasn't so much an outright denial as a dragging out of the process in the full knowledge that the longer he could inconvenience me, the longer he could make me sweat. I made repeated requests for him to sign the form, to no avail. He would either not respond or give some vague reply about not yet having gotten around to it.

Luke, bless him, saw my distress and once again sought to shoulder some of the stress. 'Mum, you should just go without me,' he said one night, almost breaking my heart.

I told him I had no intention of doing that, and that I was sure his father would see sense and finally sign the form.

As the weeks ticked by and Greg showed no signs of cooperating, I contacted the Department of Foreign Affairs and Trade to enquire about securing an emergency passport. I was told they would consider it, but time was running out and I would need to submit the application straight away.

Another couple of weeks passed without any news. With tensions rising, I left multiple messages with the passport issuing office, but received no reply. Finally, when I got through to someone, I explained the situation and offered to send through the IVO to justify why I needed a passport to be issued without Greg's signature. I was told the application would need to be referred to Canberra for closer examination. Attempts were made by the passport officials to contact Greg – to no avail.

I finally told Luke I had no other choice than to ask him to go directly to his dad and tell him he really wanted to go to England. It was the first time I had ever purposefully put that sort of pressure on Luke, but I was desperate.

A day before we were to fly, Greg finally relented, scribbling four words on a plain white piece of paper: *'I give my permission'*.

Miraculously, the passport officials approved the application and we were off. I arrived at the airport a bundle of nerves. Once again, Greg had managed to manipulate me to the point of breakdown. As the plane lifted off, I felt a burden drop from my shoulders – and was hit by a moment's clarity. Getting away had been almost impossible: but mustering the willpower to get on the plane and come back was going to be even harder.

As usual, a smiling Josephine was at the airport to meet us. She'd drive three and a half hours to be there and would then drive us the same distance home, something I was eternally grateful for. I all but fell into her arms. It wasn't until I was with family, and could completely drop my guard, that I realised how exhausted I was. I spent the first few days at Dad and Josephine's house, curled up in bed with a book: just so delighted to not have to do anything. To not be responsible. To not feel as though I was permanently on guard.

Christmas was spent with Terry and his family. They lived in a converted barn and I remember Christmas lunch as just the warmest, most wonderful day. Luke really connected with his little cousin and deepened his relationship with Terry. It was lovely to watch him flourish under the attention of a positive male role model. At one point in the holiday, Luke returned there alone and spent a few nights in the company of his aunt, uncle and cousin. I couldn't have been happier.

We visited the National Space Centre in Leicester, where Luke tried his hand at being a weatherman in an interactive display: a role he hammed up as much as possible, true to form. We visited a zoo and laughed at the animals. We ate a pub meal with my brother Rob, who delighted in teaching Luke how to play pool at his local, and my brother James took Luke to a movie. Luke was in his element. He loved connecting with his uncles, and now that he was older and could hold his own he was developing a strong bond with them. In the loving glow of that unconditional love that can only come from family, I watched Luke flourish.

Meanwhile, I revelled in the fact that I was able to forfeit all decision making to others. I wasn't having to race from one after-school activity to another. I wasn't worried about the business. I allowed myself to completely disconnect and it was wonderful.

On New Year's Eve, I took Luke to the local pub with my brother James and his friends. Many people I had known since childhood had gathered to ring in the New Year and I would have happily stayed until midnight, but Luke was fading and so we returned to Dad and Josephine's house.

As we nestled in together on Dad's recliner and watched a DVD, I realised there was nowhere I would rather have been. The whole time we stayed at Dad and Josephine's, Luke and I engaged in a sneaky game of midnight corridor-crawling. Josephine – who disapproved of Luke sharing my bed – had set up two beds in separate rooms. Each night, Luke would wait until the coast was clear then sneak down the hallway and creep under my covers. And there together we would slumber until morning, when he would sneak out of my bed and back into his own.

Luke still had the endearing habit of needing to have his feet touch my legs before he was able to sleep. It was his routine, his comfort. And I became used to falling asleep with a pair of little feet touching me. Of course, the feet were getting bigger by the week – and we had agreed that by the time he was as tall as me, the co-sleeping arrangement would have to come to an end. He concurred, making like he didn't care either way. But there was still enough of the little boy in him that I could tell the idea of sleeping alone in his own room was one he was going to struggle to get used to.

It was with the heaviest of hearts that I said farewell to England and my family. It had been such a lovely holiday, not least because I had glimpsed what it would be like to have a life in which the spectre of Greg did not loom as a daily presence.

I had talked to Luke about moving to England on a more permanent basis. But he was not in love with the idea. He had a life and friends in Australia. England was nice, and being around family was a comfort all its own, but Tyabb was his home. And I had to admit he had a point. I wanted Luke to be around family – and to be allowed to mature without Greg in his life – but I didn't see how we would fit in, where in England we would live, and whether, in fact, we had the means or energy to pack up our life and start all over again.

What I did know for certain was that the experience of recharging my batteries had given me a renewed sense of energy and determination. I remember saying to one of my friends in the week we returned, 'I don't know what is going to happen this year, but I am not having the same shit year as I had last year. I am in a really good place and I intend to stay that way.'

*

We arrived back from England on 16 January 2014. It was midsummer and the heat was stifling. After five weeks in England, I had forgotten how bright was the Australian sunshine and how huge was the sky. Despite my misgivings, it was nice to be home.

I decided to take Luke to see the stage production of *Grease*. He moaned like hell about going to the theatre with his mother – but when he got there he loved it. I remember looking across at him in the dark, his face lit up from the reflected glow of the stage lights, and he looked so happy, so engaged – so alive.

Loath as I was to re-engage with the mire of the Greg situation, I worried there may have been a court case in my absence, and so I contacted the police. They told me that there had in fact been a court appearance, and that Greg had failed to show up. A warrant had subsequently been issued for his arrest.

Several months later, I would learn that, on 24 January, Greg's housemate went to police seeking an IVO, which was subsequently granted by a magistrate. I understand that he told police that Greg had threatened to cut off his head. Because of Greg's history of violence, four police officers were dispatched to serve the IVO papers, including an order to vacate the premises immediately. Police records from the day indicate that Greg reacted with typical belligerence, smashing a television on his way out. The senior constable in charge of the operation checked the LEAP database before arriving at the share house, but found no mention of the outstanding arrest warrant. Four policemen stood by and watched as Greg walked away.

Here again was this specific threat of heinous violence involving a knife. Here again were police being called to serve an IVO on a man with a history of violence. Here again, when confronted, was a man quite clearly in need of professional help.

And yet, here again, he was left to keep wandering the streets. At no point did anyone think I needed to know that Greg had threatened to cut off his housemate's head. At no point, apparently, did lights start flashing or red flags appear in the multiple police or court records that existed for Greg Anderson. Child Protection, which had closed Luke's file some four months earlier, had no idea that his father was threatening to decapitate a man. It was just another allegation recorded against a man who had committed a litany of offences, just another report to add to the ever-growing pile.

While we had been away in the UK, I had allowed Luke to have occasional phone contact with Greg. I felt it was a fair compromise. And what possible harm could come to Luke from a father more than 16,000 kilometres away?

But in the weeks after our return, Luke showed no interest in making contact with his dad. It was as if the time away had given him the opportunity to reflect and finally decide that he no longer wished to have his father in his life. Neither Luke nor I could have guessed what the ramifications of this shift in his attitude would be.

*

On the morning of Wednesday 5 February, the phone rang at home. I was surprised to hear the voice of DSC Cocking on the end of the line – it had been so long since we'd had contact.

'Rosie, it's Detective Cocking,' came the voice down the phone. 'I was wondering if you might know where Greg is living.'

'I'm sorry, Detective,' I said, biting my lip. 'I have no idea.' I hung up the phone, shaking my head in amazement.

Later that day, the phone rang again. This time it was Greg. 'Can you get Luke to call me?' he said gruffly.

I was taken aback. We hadn't spoken for months. Just hearing his voice set off a wave of fear. I did my best to sound nonchalant.

'Do you have a number he can call you on?' I asked. Greg passed on a phone number.

'Where are you living now, Greg?' I asked, never expecting a reply.

He told me the name of the street and the number of a boarding house he was staying at in Frankston, barely 20 kilometres away.

My hand trembled as I wrote it down.

Minutes later I was back on the phone to Detective Cocking. 'Andrew, it's Rosie Batty,' I said, my voice quavering. 'You won't believe who just phoned me and gave me his address.'

I requested that DSC Cocking let a small amount of time pass between receiving this information and arresting Greg, as I didn't want to make obvious to him that I had been the one to betray him to the police. I hung up the phone and felt relieved. At last, Greg could be intercepted at his home. Not at the cricket club, not in front of Luke and not in a way that would obviously implicate me.

Now, a reasonable person might assume that a policeman in possession of information about the whereabouts of a wanted man would take steps to immediately arrest that man. You would think perhaps a phone call might be made to the local police station, an order to arrest might be issued across the radio airwaves or even an email sent informing nearby police officers to attend the nominated address and apprehend the offender. This was, after all, a man facing eleven criminal charges who had no less than four warrants out for his arrest.

But no. No action was taken. DSC Cocking would later testify at the inquest that when he spoke to his superior, no decision was reached on what to do with the information I had provided them. He would tell a court that he decided not to arrest Greg in a timely manner out of concerns for my safety. He would tell the same court he thought he'd received the information a week later than he did, intimating that by honouring my request not to take action immediately left precious time for any meaningful intervention. My biggest mistake? Believing that the police were about to arrest Greg with a sense of urgency.

*

So it was with a certain amount of shock when, during Luke's cricket match at Tyabb oval the following Saturday, I looked up from my duties helping with mid-game refreshments to see Greg striding around the perimeter of the oval towards us. I tried not to show my shock, instead continuing to tend to the team as they sheltered from the midday sun.

Greg stood off to the side of the gaggle of kids and parents, clearly wanting to be part of proceedings, but not sure how to break in. At certain points, when Luke wasn't batting or fielding, Greg would take him to one side and engage him in quiet conversation. I remember feeling anxious that Greg was separating Luke from his teammates. But I told myself that he hadn't seen Luke for ages and was no doubt only snatching what little time he could to have a conversation with his son.

I could only guess at why he hadn't been arrested by the police. Either they had been to the boarding house and missed him there, or once again Greg had managed to squeeze through one loophole or another in the legal system I had long ago lost faith in. I thought for a moment about phoning the police, but knew it would only provoke Greg and potentially lead to yet another embarrassing and ultimately futile police intervention at cricket in front of Luke and his friends.

Two days later, the phone rang. I was in the kitchen, preparing dinner. Greg's voice came down the line. 'Can I speak to Luke?'

I thought for a moment of reminding him about the terms of the IVO – how even phone contact was not allowed. But I decided against it. I called out to Luke, who emerged from his bedroom, took the phone with an air of resignation and retreated to his room, closing the door behind him.

He re-emerged five minutes later.

'Is everything all right?' I asked, watching as he walked, shoulders slumped, into the living room.

'Dad's really not happy,' Luke said, plonking himself down on the couch. 'He's living in Frankston and he's not happy about the people he's living with.'

I nodded. There was a moment's silence.

'He said he was disappointed with me for not contacting him when we got back,' Luke continued, staring out the window.

'It's not your fault, Luke,' I started. 'There's a restraining order – your dad knows that.'

He looked across the living room at me. 'Mum. Normally it's me that hangs up on him, but this time he put the phone down on me.'

He looked confused and a little worried.

I didn't know what to say.

23

As my car pulls into the gravel car park at Tyabb oval, I'm struck by what a glorious summer's evening it is. The sky is turning a stunning cobalt as the day slips away.

Some of the kids are practising in the cricket nets while the dads help out. I see Luke there, still playing. Then, as I get out of the car, I see Greg. He's taking part, helping the other dads and bowling to the kids. He looks relaxed and happy. I'm pleased to see him behaving normally. Luke is happy to have him there too.

Other kids are packing their cricket bags and heading to the car park to find their parents. I see Cameron there, one of the fathers from Luke's cricket team – he's trying to corral his three boys from opposite ends of the oval.

I see Mariette, one of the other mums. She's dressed to the nines, having attended the Mornington Cup earlier in the day. And there's Liam, my neighbour Therese's little boy. He's waiting by the picnic table, near the kid's playground, watching for his mum to arrive. I ask him if he is okay, if his mum is coming. Therese is never late. He answers, telling me that she's on her way, and sure

239

enough, here she is. I joke with Therese about how it's usually me that's running late, and we stand and chat for a while. I think how nice it is to be part of a community: to be known. This is my home now; these are my people.

I'm listening to Therese speak and watching out of the corner of my eye where Luke is and where Greg is.

Luke comes running over to me, his face flushed from an afternoon of cricket practice. He looks full of life. 'Is it okay if I have a few extra minutes with Dad?' he asks.

'I guess so,' I hear myself reply. 'But five minutes is all. We've got to get home soon.'

I return to my conversation with Therese. After a minute or so, I'm suddenly aware that I can't see Luke or Greg. I interrupt Therese mid-sentence. 'I can't see Luke or Greg,' I say to her. 'Greg knows better, he's not supposed to take Luke anywhere.' I'm not panicked, but I am starting to feel anxious.

'It's all right, Rosie,' Therese replies, looking over towards the nets. 'They're over there.'

The nets are 50 metres away, partially obscured by a toilet block. From where I stand, I can make out Luke, in his yellow polo shirt, hitting balls as they come to him. He has a look of concentration on his face. Greg is bowling to him, out of my line of sight, obscured by the toilet block.

Therese heads home and I call Natasha to invite her over for dinner. While we're talking, I look away from the cricket nets for no more than twenty seconds. As I hang up the phone, I hear a scream. A man's scream. Guttural, agonised, primal. A scream of pure anguish.

Everything starts to move in slow motion.

Panicking, I run towards the cricket nets, where I see Greg hunched over Luke, who is lying limp on the ground. Greg is cradling Luke's head, rocking on his haunches, wailing.

Oh my God, I think. He's done a fast bowl to Luke and hit him in the head. He's knocked him out. The stupid bastard has knocked him out. He's really hurt him. He's really hurt him.

And my boy, limp in Greg's arms! My first thought is to get an ambulance. My boy is hurt. He needs help, and so I start running towards the clubhouse. Stumbling across the lawn, I punch at my mobile phone, trying to call triple zero. But in the panic, and with my head swimming, I don't have the co-ordination. I see Cameron and start screaming at him.

'Luke's hurt! Luke's been hit! You have to get an ambulance here now! It's bad! I know it's really bad!'

I'm telling myself it's just a knock in the head. Stupid fucking Greg has bowled too fast and knocked him out. He's just been hit by a cricket ball. I repeat it over and over in my head like a mantra.

Greg is there, Greg has the situation in hand, my job is to find help.

I can't stand still. I don't know where to go. Every part of my being wants to be with Luke, to be holding him, tending to him and telling him everything is going to be fine. But I can't bring myself to go near him. I'm terrified to get close. Terrified to learn the truth. Somewhere, in the depths of my consciousness, I'm thinking that if I can somehow keep distance between me and the reality of what has happened over there in the cricket nets, then it's a truth I can deny. As long as I haven't seen it – it's not real.

My boy. My baby boy.

And so I run. I'm screaming as I run. Confused parents watch as I run in a blind panic, as far across to the other side of the car park as it's possible to go. Right over to the wire fence that separates Tyabb oval from the adjacent paddock. Beside a tree, under an oversized bush – I need to put as much physical space as possible between me and those cricket nets.

There I stand, watching the road in a state of panic, waiting for the ambulances to arrive. Moaning, rocking, willing this all to be a nightmare from which I will wake.

I call Therese, whose car I saw pull out ten minutes before. I'm not sure why. I figure she's close by, she can maybe help direct the ambulance. Where is that ambulance? Why is it taking so long? My call goes through to voicemail.

I call Natasha. 'I don't think I'm going to be able to do dinner,' I hear myself say, fighting back tears. 'Something has happened. It's bad, really bad. Luke's been hurt. I think I'm going to have to go to hospital. Greg is here. He's hit him in the head with a cricket ball. It's bad, Natasha. I'm scared. It's really, really bad.'

She tells me she is on her way and hangs up the phone.

A man drives into the car park in a black ute. I have never seen him before. Seeing me, he stops, winds down the window and asks if I am okay.

I tell him there's been an accident. My son. Hit by a cricket ball. His father is there. I don't know where the ambulance is. He offers to go and wait at the road to direct the ambulance down the drive.

Minutes pass, I don't know how many. Each one feels like an hour. I am pacing, cursing every second the ambulance isn't there. Finally, I hear sirens in the distance.

Natasha arrives and crosses the car park towards me. 'What happened? Are you okay? Where's Luke?'

I have no words. She puts a comforting arm around me. I am shaking with fear.

I look across to Cameron, and he has returned to his car. He is herding his boys into the car, telling them to stay inside, to keep the doors closed. Why isn't he coming over here? Why hasn't he come to tell me it's all going to be okay? That it's just a knock to the head and all will be fine once the ambulance arrives?

I tell myself over and over that Greg would never hurt Luke. That Greg loves Luke more than life itself. That right now, Greg is over there comforting Luke, taking care of him. Like the time Luke fell off the monkey bars when he was little, and Greg bundled him up and took him to hospital. Or the time Luke fell as a toddler and hit his head on the corner of the coffee table, and Greg was there to comfort and calm him down and tell me to get ice. I will look back on this in an hour and laugh at how I overreacted. And yet, I cannot go near the nets.

'What's happening?!?' I keep shouting at Cameron across the car park. 'What's going on? Is Luke all right?'

I see the flashing red and blue lights of an ambulance as it races along Flinders–Mornington Road, then a plume of dust as it turns into the driveway.

The ambulance. I have something constructive to do at last. I will show them where my boy is, they will come and find that he is unconscious from a cricket ball to the head, and we'll go to hospital and everything will be okay.

I run towards them, frantically waving my arms, willing them to hurry up. As they drive towards me, they seem to slow down. 'Over there!' I am shouting. 'In the nets! My son! My son!'

As the ambulance drives past me, I collapse on the spot, my legs buckling underneath me, my body unable to cope. Natasha drops down beside me. She is urging me to stand up, to go to the ambulance. But I can't move.

'Come on, Rosie,' she says. 'We need to go and speak to the ambulance. To check up on Luke.'

But I want to leave the ambulance officers to do their job. I want to give them time to get to Luke and make everything all right. And so we sit, with the clubhouse between us and the cricket nets, and I am rocking and Natasha has her arm around me and I am numb.

I hear shouting coming from the other side of the clubhouse. And I am suddenly aware that the car park is full of police cars. I don't know where they have come from, and can't understand why they are there. Surely they haven't come to arrest Greg now. Surely they understand that the first priority is to get Luke into an ambulance and off to hospital.

None of it makes sense.

'Come on Rosie, we need to speak to the ambulance officers,' Natasha is saying. 'You have to get up.'

I know she is right but I still cannot move. My legs feel like lead. Natasha helps me to my feet and my first steps towards the clubhouse are tentative. I don't want to go there. I don't want to see.

As we round the corner of the clubhouse, we are met by a paramedic. She seems to panic when she sees me. She knows my name, but I don't know how or why. 'Rosie, you need to come with me, you need to move back, back behind the clubhouse,' she is saying. And I look at her, confused. There's nothing wrong with me. Why is she tending to me? Why isn't she in the nets tending to my boy?

'What are you doing? Why aren't you with Luke?' I begin.

She cuts me off. 'You can't be here, Rosie, you need to move back.'

Why are the police trying to arrest Greg now, of all times? Why aren't the paramedics in the nets with Luke?

If they arrest Greg now, I think to myself, it's just going to antagonise him and it won't be nice for Luke – here in public, at the cricket ground, in front of his friends. Luke will be embarrassed. So I start shouting at the police. 'Leave him! Just leave him! This is not about him! It's about Luke. Just let the ambulance get in there and help my boy!'

There is more shouting. I am forced to return behind the club house. I turn momentarily, and that's when I hear the gunshots. Two distinct cracks ringing out in the night air. I freeze on the spot. My mind seems to seize up. Because you can only take in so much – your brain can only process so much.

I hear a voice, I don't know whose, and it is saying, 'They've shot Greg, they've shot Greg.' And I am hit by a force I cannot describe. I slump to the ground. There in the grass, by the clubhouse, I sit, unable to speak, unable to move. Mariette hands me a cigarette and I smoke it.

*

At some level I know that the police are going to come and tell me that Luke is dead. I know it with a certainty but at the same time I refuse to accept it. I'm not in denial so much as being drip-fed by my mind, allowed to process only the bits of information that it feels my body is capable of dealing with. In the confusion following the shooting, police are running everywhere.

I look up to see Constable Topham. He kneels down, puts a hand on my shoulder and asks if I am okay.

'Paul!' I say, relieved to see a familiar face. 'There's been an accident. Some sort of mistake. Luke's hurt and they've shot Greg.'

He looks at me gravely, clearly being careful to choose his words. I look at him, confused.

'It's not looking like that, Rosie,' he eventually manages. 'There's pretty strong evidence to suggest it was no accident. He had a knife.'

I hear the words but am not able to process them. But what about my boy? My baby boy.

Shaking, I pick up the phone to call my friend Ben. I get his answering machine. 'Luke's really badly injured,' I say. 'Call me.'

And without anyone telling me, I know. I know that Luke is dead. Of course he is dead. He has to be dead. There is no other possible outcome. I feel numb.

Two police officers approach.

'Don't tell me,' I say, before they can speak, staring beyond them. 'You can't tell me. You have to tell Ben.'

I call my parents in England. It's early morning there. 'Luke's been killed. Greg has killed him. You need to come.' The words spill out of me. I don't remember their response.

I ask about Greg and someone tells me he's been seriously injured. 'Just let him die!' I say to no one in particular. 'For God's sake, just let him die. He won't want to be alive.'

A policeman called Wayne comes and sits down next to me. He puts a hand on my shoulder, a gesture of tenderness that I remember to this day. He didn't know me, but he knew enough to know not to speak. What words do you even use? At a certain point, he convinces me to get up from the ground and go and sit in the back of the police car. He explains we are all witnesses to a major crime, and as such, we all have to be kept separate until our statements can be taken.

I don't know how long I sit in the back of the police car. A matter of hours. My phone keeps buzzing with a barrage of texts and phone calls until eventually the battery goes flat.

I sit there thinking I should cancel the work appointments I had scheduled for the next day. And then I think how, in a matter of minutes, I have become one of those people; one of those horror stories. I've joined those ranks – of the mother whose three little boys were driven into a dam by her husband, of the mum whose little girl was thrown off the West Gate Bridge. I am one of those worst-things-that-have-ever-happened stories. That is my life now, it is my journey and there is nothing I can do to turn any of it back.

At some point, I need to go to the toilet. Wayne explains he has to escort me, and so he walks me into the clubhouse. As I enter, I am met with a wall of blue uniforms. Police seem to have materialised out of nowhere. There are plain clothes, uniformed and high-ranking officers, and I look on, bemused. What are they talking about? Why have they gathered in such numbers? Why, when Luke and I needed police to protect us, could we barely muster their interest, but now, when it is too late, there is a small army of them? I feel my hackles rise.

As I return from the toilet, I hiss at Wayne, 'I am not going to go back and sit in that police car not knowing anything while they all have their fucking arse-covering meeting in here. You go and tell them right now to come out here and you tell them to tell me what's going on, because if you don't I'm going to go in there and I'm going to be really angry.'

Wayne looks a little concerned and dutifully goes inside. I am seething. I *need* to know what's happening. This is my son! I *deserve* to know what's happening.

One of the senior police officers comes out to the car and explains that they have established a major crime scene. 'Luke has been killed, Rosie. And Greg has been shot. We need to do a thorough investigation.'

Tears run down my face as I nod.

After a while, I can sit in the car no longer. I walk back into the clubhouse and find the sergeant in charge. 'I want to see my little boy,' I say, choking back tears. 'He's all alone out there. I need to be with him.'

'I'm sorry, Rosie, but you can't go out there,' comes the reply. 'We're looking after him, I promise.'

'But I need to see him.'

'Trust me, Rosie, you wouldn't want to see him like that,' the sergeant responds. 'It's not how you should remember him.'

As I walk back to the car, I can make out the shape of a small body lying in the cricket nets. I can't go to him. I have to leave him out there in the cold. My boy. My baby boy. Alone out there in the nets.

24

Eyewitnesses

Tyabb oval is your typical playing field in semi-rural Victoria: a patch of manicured brown-green grass set among the paddocks that encircle the township. There's the Ivor Ransom Scoreboard at one end of the oval, and large metal signs around the oval's fence advertising the Kings Creek Hotel (Bingo on Thursdays), the Peninsula Motor Inn and Harvey Smash Repairs.

Families from the area spend lots of time driving to and from the Tyabb oval, and standing on its sidelines. Sheltering from blazing summer sun during the cricket season and shivering on the periphery during the cold winter mornings of the AFL season. It's a safe place, for the most part. A place where the wholesome practice of junior sport is carried out year round. It's not the sort of place you expect your child will witness a murder.

Of all the unbearable details of that night, 12 February, easily one of the worst is that the only eyewitness to Luke's death was an eight-year-old boy. He had left his cricket bag at the nets and had gone back to collect it while his dad, Cameron, waited in the car park.

The little boy ran, screaming in a wide-eyed panic across the grass to his dad. 'The man hit the boy! He hit him with the cricket bat. He hit the boy in the yellow T-shirt in the head.'

As Cameron would tell me later, it took a moment for him to register. At first, he thought his son was telling him he had been hit by a cricket bat. But that made no sense. He was panting there in front of him, looking perfectly normal. Then he looked across to the cricket nets and saw Greg kneeling over Luke, who was lying prostrate and motionless on the ground. Cameron says he looked on in confusion as I ran towards him, screaming for him to call an ambulance. He called triple zero, telling them to send an ambulance immediately, then he saw me fall down, get up, fall down again, wailing, yelling for anyone to help.

Having dispatched an ambulance from Frankston, the ambulance officer asked Cameron to go to the nets and report back on the extent of Luke's injuries. I was screaming about a cricket ball to the head; his son had come running with a story of a father hitting his son with a cricket bat. It was all happening against the backdrop of a normal summer's evening of cricket practice, and none of it made sense.

Cameron approached the cricket nets and came within 5 metres of Greg, who had gotten up to his bag then returned to sit down next to Luke.

'Is he okay?' Cameron asked, following the prompts of the ambulance dispatch officer. 'Is he breathing?'

Greg turned and, upon seeing Cameron approach, jumped to his feet and charged at him, shouting at him to stay back.

Cameron recoiled, horrified not only at having Greg run at him, but also at the sight of Luke, lying in a pool of blood.

'Is he okay?' he asked again.

'He's fine,' Greg replied. 'He's gone to heaven now.'

Cameron was in shock – now suddenly party to a horror that had nothing to do with him. He was simply taking his boys home from cricket training.

When finally the ambulance arrived – having initially gone to the wrong oval in Tyabb and then missed the turn-off to the cricket club – two paramedics leaped out and made towards the cricket nets. Greg wouldn't let them anywhere near Luke, threatening them with a knife. They retreated to their ambulance and waited for the police to arrive and contain the situation.

Police reports from the night record that when the police arrived, they jumped from their cars and ran towards the cricket nets. Upon seeing them approach, Greg got up from the nets and met them halfway across the lawn between the nets and clubhouse, covered in blood, knife in hand.

'Drop your weapon and get on the ground!' they screamed at him, drawing their guns. Greg continued to advance on them.

By now, there were four or five police officers and multiple cars. The scene was a blur of sirens and flashing lights and shouting.

Brandishing the knife, Greg ignored police commands to get down, to drop his weapon. One of the police officers pulled out his capsicum spray – but it dissipated in the wind and had no effect.

'Drop your weapon! Get down on the ground!'

Greg kept advancing. He lunged at one of the officers. Two shots rang out in the night. Greg fell to his knees, then collapsed on the ground, felled by a bullet to his chest. The police officers approached, one of them kicking the knife to the side, guns drawn and pointed at the hulking man writhing on the ground in front of them. He had been shot, but was still thrashing. It took several police and paramedics to subdue him and restrain him until the police helicopter arrived.

'Let me die! Just let me die!' he protested as paramedics tended to him.

When finally the paramedics reached Luke in the cricket nets, he was dead. He had been dead for almost thirty minutes. One of Greg's shoes had been placed beneath his head, one of Greg's shirts placed over his head.

Greg was airlifted to hospital and admitted to emergency surgery. He died just after midnight.

*

I still feel sick about whether Luke knew what was about to happen. If he did, why didn't he run? Why didn't he scream out? Was it because Greg was his father and he trusted him implicitly? If Greg had said, 'Turn around, Luke, and look the other way, we are going to go to another world together' – was that something he would have done? Was there any fear? Was there a moment when he wondered where his mother was, and why she wasn't there to protect him? It's a thought that horrifies me and will haunt me for the rest of my days.

I am only grateful that I didn't see it happen. I don't know what force in the universe made me turn my back on the cricket nets at the moment Greg killed Luke, but I will be eternally indebted to it. Had I seen it coming, had I realised what Greg was about to do but been powerless to get there in time to do anything about it – I would be living a whole different sort of horror.

As it is, I already torture myself daily with the what-ifs. What if we had stayed home from training that afternoon? What if I had put my foot down and said no to the extra five minutes of practice in the cricket nets? What if we had never returned from England? What if I had never met Greg?

'It was premeditated,' the homicide detectives all told me on the night. 'You did nothing wrong.'

But what if Luke knew it was coming? What if he was in those cricket nets, even momentarily aware of what was about to happen? What if in that moment of fear he looked for me and I wasn't there to save him?

I didn't read the autopsy report, because I knew it would be too distressing. But I was assured by those who did, and those I trusted, that Luke would have lost consciousness from the initial blow to the back of his head. He would not have felt a thing. He would not have been conscious when his father cut his throat.

It's funny how in the most awful of circumstances you can find comfort. No matter how unspeakably heinous the situation, the human spirit finds consolation in the smallest of things. The smallest of mercies.

25

The Morning After

Around midnight of the night Luke was killed, I was taken to Mornington Police Station to give a statement. The police had offered me the opportunity to put off giving my statement until the following day – but I wanted it all recorded, I wanted it out of the way. Even in the depths of shock and despair, I knew there needed to be a reckoning – and the process had to start straight away.

And so I sat in an interview room with two detectives and I talked. And I talked, and talked and talked. They wanted the whole story from the beginning. Where and how Greg and I had met, what the nature of our relationship had been, exactly what I had witnessed at Tyabb oval.

At some point while I was giving my statement, displaying a kind of out-of-body composure in the face of events that should have rendered me speechless, Greg died on the emergency operating table. Doctors had tried to save him from the injuries sustained by the gunshot wounds, but they were unable to. A small mercy for all concerned.

Early the next morning, I was dropped home in a police patrol car. Lee was awake, waiting for me to return. I floated in a kind of daze into the house and opened a bottle of wine. Lee looked at me as if to say, are you sure that's a good idea? At this time of the morning? And I threw him back a look that said, I don't give a fuck what time of the morning it is, I'm having a drink. I sat at the kitchen table with Natasha and Lee and, still in shock, we drank the bottle.

I must have taken myself off to bed and fallen asleep at some stage. When I woke up, I was still in my clothes from the day before. I became aware that the house was filled with people. I came out of my bedroom, still dazed and confused. Silence fell as I walked into the room, my hair a mess, my clothes crumpled, my face puffy from crying. Someone offered me a cup of tea, another asked if I wanted something to eat. I batted them both away. I didn't want anything. I curled up on the couch cuddling Luke's SpongeBob SquarePants soft toy, half-listening to the hushed talk around me.

Everyone was in shock, all speaking about how unexpected it was that Greg had killed Luke in such a violent way. And all I remember thinking was, well of course Luke had to die. As Greg's world had continued to contract around him, as I had started to pull away from his influence and control, as Luke had begun to show signs of wanting to put some distance between himself and his father, there was never going to be any other outcome. Greg had killed Luke to make me suffer. It was his final act of control and power. While I had clung for so many years to a desperate belief that Greg would never hurt Luke, it was obvious to me now that there was no other possible outcome.

At a certain point I tuned in to a conversation that a group of my friends were having about what to do about the media pack that had assembled outside my front gate. One of them volunteered to go out and tell them there was no comment to be made, that I just wanted to be left alone.

And I remember sitting up and saying, 'Hang on a minute. You're trying to make decisions about what? On my behalf? Without me? No you're not. If anyone is going to deal with the media it is me. This is happening to me. He was my son, this is my pain. I won't have anyone speaking on my behalf.'

The room was stunned into silence. It was only day one and people were already struggling to come to terms with my style of mourning. The tiptoeing around, the walking on eggshells: I knew it was well-meaning and I appreciated the concern, but I just wanted people to act normally around me. I craved conversation, even banter, not just respectful silence. This was my home, not a funeral parlour. I needed my friends to be friends. To cajole and make inappropriate jokes. To stop modifying their behaviour as if I had become a completely different person. I was more than aware of the tragedy that had befallen me. I didn't need it amplified with cloying behaviour. It was my son who had been killed, so I would be the one to set the tone for how I would grieve that loss, not anyone else.

And so, horrified at the thought that someone else would speak on my behalf, I went outside towards the waiting media pack. I had no idea what I was going to say. I was just determined to get out there and speak. I mean, what could possibly happen? It wasn't as if the twenty journalists out there, with their cameras and notebooks and iPhone recorders, meant me any harm. I figured they had come all this way, they were out there trying to do their job, I would simply walk out and thank them for coming and tell them that I just needed to be left alone. My philosophy had always been, whether it was a colleague or a tradesperson who has come to fix something at your house, just let people do their job properly.

I would learn months later that I had deviated from the playbook when it comes to these things, and that this split-second decision would set in train another series of events that would completely change my life. Apparently, accepted practice in these situations is for a member of the bereaved's family to come out, make a statement and send the journalists back to their respective newsrooms.

As I approached, cameras were pulled up onto shoulders, microphones were extended in expectation and notebooks were primed. What I didn't know at the time was that none of the assembled reporters knew that I was Luke's mother.

As one of the reporters would later tell me, it was only as I started to speak that it began to dawn on them that I wasn't a family representative, but in fact the mother who had just witnessed her son being murdered. I was too dazed and confused to really register any reaction among them, but people have told me the effect was electric.

My friends started to walk towards me to try to form some sort of protective shield around me. But this was my journey, this was my pain. I had spent a lifetime standing on my own two feet, and that wasn't about to change now. I hadn't planned to say anything other than 'thank you for coming', but as I stood there, I felt the need to account for myself. Out of respect for Luke's memory, I wanted them to know a little about his and my story.

And so the words just started tumbling out.

'No one loved Luke more than Greg,' I began, fighting back tears. 'No one loved Luke more than me. We both loved him. I did what I believed was in the best interests of Luke. He was a little boy in a growing body that felt pain and sadness and fear for his mum. And he always believed he would be safe with his dad. And he would have trusted Greg.

'If anything comes out of this, I want it to be a lesson to everybody. Family violence happens to everybody, no matter how nice your house is or how intelligent you are. It happens to everyone. And this has been an eleven-year battle.'

I finished speaking and everyone had fallen silent. I thanked the reporters for their understanding and turned to walk back inside. I had no idea what time of the day it was; I had no idea what I had said. All I remember thinking afterwards was: God, I hope I didn't say something stupid.

Looking back, I was clearly in shock. You're in a state where you don't really know what you are doing or why you are doing it. Those first few days were all a blur. I can't remember the chronology of anything. Days turned into nights, and nights somehow turned back into days. I spent most of the time curled up on the couch hugging SpongeBob. I didn't change my clothes for three days. People kept trying to get me to eat. I think I may have nibbled on a strawberry, but I wasn't hungry. I don't know why people feel the need to feed you at moments like that. The last thing you feel like doing is eating. It was not like I was going to starve. But I guess it gives them something to do. To make sure 'you keep your strength up' – even though you feel like there's nothing in life worth keeping your strength up for.

I would wake up and there would be people at the end of the couch, or sitting around my bed. Each time I came out to the living room, the house would be filled with more people and more flowers. And over the course of the next two or three days, I told and retold my version of events at Tyabb oval, probably just trying to make sense of it all myself.

There were so many people at the house that my friend Molly

went out and brought in one of those big hot-water urns, and someone else went out and bought a load of new coffee mugs, because I didn't have enough. And everyone just came and went, to support me, to support each other.

Somehow, and I don't know how people knew, but they all got the message that I wanted people to come. If they were friends and they wanted to see me, or mourn Luke, I made it clear that they should feel free to come. And so they did. It was a stream of people. Anyone who knew me in any way, shape or form came. My friends were obviously there, but also people from the cricket club, representatives of the school, the local church, Luke's AFL team. His death had touched people in a fundamental way: the flowers and tributes poured in as complete strangers mourned the death of a little boy they didn't know, but whose brutal passing had touched the humanity in all of us. Mourning the boy killed by his father at cricket practice, mourning for God only knows what personal tragedies his death had reminded them of.

Lee had been to my doctor to get a script for painkillers, and when the thoughts in my head became too loud and the simple act of being awake proved too painful, I took them and fell into a fitful sleep. But there was no respite in sleep. I would dream of Luke. I would wake and wonder why his feet were not touching mine in the bed. And then it would hit me and I would wish I were dead. Death was preferable to enduring another waking hour knowing that I had lost my little boy for good.

And then I received a call that someone needed to identify Luke's body. Again, a host of friends stepped up, all offering to undertake the onerous task. But I was determined to do it myself. He was my son. I was his mother. I felt like it was my duty. As a parent sometimes you just have to step up to the plate and do the things that are tough. I had been there for him from the very beginning of his life, and I wasn't about to abandon him now at the end of it.

I asked my friend Jill to come with me to the morgue. Of all my friends, she was the most level-headed and sensible. I didn't need histrionics, I just needed calm. And so we drove in to Melbourne together, located the morgue and went inside. After a series of formalities, we were led down a maze of corridors and into a dimly lit room. And there he was. He was just lying there, looking like he was asleep. It was my Luke, but it wasn't him. There was a glass screen separating us. He was lying on his back so that I could see his face in profile. He had a white cloth around his neck. He didn't look battered or bruised, as I had feared he might. There was no obvious sign of the trauma he had suffered to the back of his head. It was him, but without the essence of him.

I remember talking to him, telling him how I would miss his spaghetti legs on me in bed. I sat in the half-light, telling him about the fuss that was being made over him, the flowers, the cards, the people who had come to the house to celebrate his life. I told him how his dog, Lily the golden retriever, was missing him, how she pined for one of his cuddles. I told him how the PlayStation hadn't been turned on for days, and joked that it must be a new record. I told him how sorry I was. How, as his mother, I'd only had one job to do in life: to protect him. And how I had failed. And how I would have to live with that for the rest of my life.

I talked to him for quite a bit, and I could have gone beyond the screen, but I didn't. Because I would have been tempted to touch him. And I knew that if I did, he wouldn't be Luke.

I wanted to sit there and talk to him all day, but I knew I couldn't. I knew I was going to have to muster the strength to leave. I took one last longing look at my little boy, then turned and walked out the door.

26

Saying Goodbye

No mother should have to attend their own child's funeral. It's fundamentally wrong: a complete inversion of the natural order of things.

The days that followed Luke's death were a blur. I couldn't tell you what happened on any particular day – I was barely aware if it *was* night or day. I floated through most of it buffeted by well-meaning family members and friends, and incapable of making a decision or much in the way of coherent thought.

My family arrived from England and they stepped into the roles of protectors and providers, gracefully receiving the waves of visitors who continued to arrive while creating a protective cushion around me. All the people in the world who meant something to me had gathered because the one person in the world who meant the most to me wasn't there anymore. Faces I hadn't seen for years appeared on my doorstep. The natural instinct was to be pleased to see them, to want to catch up – but I was barely lucid for most of that time. Or if I was, it was only in bursts, before the grief would rise up and engulf me all over again.

Thankfully, the school stepped in to start organising the funeral, which was a godsend. I had neither the capacity nor inclination to do it myself. The funeral planners came to the house and, in that softly spoken way they have, ensured my input into the funeral arrangements was relatively painless. Nothing was too much trouble; everything I suggested was a good idea. We talked about yellow being Luke's favourite colour, and Mick the funeral parlour man told me that a yellow coffin was absolutely doable.

'A bright yellow coffin?' I asked, hardly believing it.

'As bright as you want it to be, Rosie,' Mick replied. And I remember thinking, Luke would be pleased with this.

Then Mick asked me if there was anything of Luke's I might want to him to wear – and I didn't hesitate. Since he had been given an animal-themed onesie for his eleventh birthday, barely a day had passed when he hadn't worn it. He loved that thing. There was no other choice, so I went and grabbed it. And because I didn't want my boy to be in there alone, I gave Mick one of Luke's SpongeBob soft toys to go in the coffin with him.

Talk turned to music: specifically, which songs I wanted played. It seemed like an odd conversation to be having: what one song can possibly encapsulate a life? Capture a mood? And so I resorted to the songs I had chosen to be played at my own funeral, years before, when I had written out a will. Because it was always going to be me, not Luke, for whom music was going to be played at a funeral.

'Amazing Grace' was an easy choice. It was my dad's favourite hymn and had always held a special place in my heart too. Louis Armstrong's 'What a Wonderful World' would, I thought, capture something of the innocence and wonder that I felt Luke represented. There was a poignancy to it that I knew would form the perfect musical soundscape to the montage of photos that was being prepared. And finally – in a complete rejection of convention – the Bruce Springsteen version of the Beatles classic 'Twist and Shout'. It was easily my favourite song in the world. I had seen Springsteen perform it in England when I was younger and it had stayed with me. And while I felt that it was the song I wanted to play at Luke's funeral, it didn't seem proper somehow.

I looked sheepishly at Mick. 'That's maybe not appropriate, is it?'

'Why not have it on the way out, as we're walking out of the church?' he replied. And it seemed like a good idea. It was to be a celebration of Luke's life, after all.

A day or so later, some people came from the funeral home to collect photos to create a montage to play at the funeral. I had forgotten they were coming. There were so many people in the house, I had barely had a second to myself. I was momentarily thrown: suddenly possessed with the importance of this task, wanting to get it right, annoyed with myself for forgetting, panicked that I would choose the wrong selection of photos, stressed with all of the people in my house: people whom five minutes before I had been thanking for being there to support and care for me. The only constant in those days after Luke's death was my inconstancy. My moods swung, my patience with people ebbed and flowed, my forbearance wavered. But people were kind and patient with me. I was the bereaved mother.

I scrambled through old photos of Luke, curating a selection that I thought would best represent his life. And I began to worry I wasn't going to get the mix right, that this was somehow going to be a letdown for Luke. It was his day, after all. But finally, I realised that it didn't matter. Whichever photos they took, whichever they chose to use, they would all end up painting the same picture – a portrait of a beautiful boy gone too soon.

The administrators at Flinders College, who were doing everything they could to help, had taken charge of organising all of the logistics. They had suggested using the school chapel for the funeral service itself – accessed only by family and close friends – and opening up the school gym for members of the community and public who otherwise wanted to pay their respects. I had no idea how many people would come. I was already overwhelmed by the number of friends and family who had descended – my brain honestly didn't have room to consider that their ranks would be bolstered significantly by people I only vaguely knew or didn't know at all.

The school undertook to liaise with the funeral parlour so I didn't need to get involved, and even managed the media interest. Again, because I had been in my bubble since Luke's death, I had no idea the nerve it had touched around the country. Since my impromptu appearance for the TV cameras the morning after Luke's death, friends had worked assiduously to shield me from the subsequent barrage of media requests. I had unwittingly created national interest in my son's death, and consequently his funeral was going to be big news.

I remember waking up that morning and thinking, I don't know how I am going to get through today. But I know I have to. I have to survive today and I want to absorb and remember this day in its entirety. This is Luke's day. This is his funeral. And I felt that if I let myself go, if I let emotion overwhelm me, I would never collect myself again; I had to get into a zone and stay in that zone, because I wanted to share this day, I wanted to be a part of it. I wanted to be able to remember and embrace it.

The house was full of my immediate family: Josephine's friends and family from New Zealand and my immediate family from the UK had all assembled. Everybody wore yellow. My brothers went out and each bought a yellow tie and I borrowed a yellow jacket. Everyone had a splash of yellow. We looked at the meaning of the colour yellow and it was so poignant – joy, happiness, intellect and energy. It was so special and so right.

As the hour of the funeral approached and we all gathered in the living room, there was a sense that we were all steeling ourselves to face an ordeal. We all knew what we had to do and we prepared ourselves to do it. The British stoicism seemed to kick in. The stiff upper lip. The determination to get the job done and not let the emotion of the moment overwhelm us. To break down would have been to let down the side.

A limousine came to collect us and we all travelled in it together, down the hill to Flinders College. It was a damp morning – grey and drizzly. I remember pulling in to the school and seeing all these people walking across the grounds. There were cars parked all up the street, just waves and waves of people making their way solemnly to the school gym. And I didn't properly register how many people there were, because I was so focused on maintaining composure, but I had a sense of this great body of people already assembled in the gym and scores of people still walking across the oval – all wearing a yellow ribbon, a yellow shirt, a yellow scarf.

As I walked into the chapel, I saw the coffin and had to steady myself. There he was, my little boy. The bright yellow coffin, crowned by a spray of yellow roses and gerberas arranged in the shape of a cross. Atop the coffin was one of Luke's large SpongeBob plush toys, and a beautiful portrait of my Luke, the one we'd had taken only a year earlier. Professionally lit and effortlessly handsome, he smiled out at the congregation. I put my head down and made my way to my seat at the front of the chapel.

As we waited for the service to start, I knew I needed to look anywhere but at that coffin if I wanted to keep it together. And so I craned my neck to take in the congregation. The chapel was packed. There were people there from far and wide. People I hadn't seen in years. People I had no idea had even known about Luke's death much less known they were going to make the journey to his funeral. There were friends from Darwin, friends from Sydney. I saw friends who lived on the Gold Coast, friends from Queensland. People had come from everywhere to be there for Luke. People from my past, people I'd worked with twenty-odd years ago, people I had only had the briefest of associations with. I didn't get a chance to speak to all of them but I saw them all, I noted their presence and it gave me enormous strength. There were neighbours, cricket mums, Scouts dads and, of course, Luke's friends. The whole school was present in the school gym, mostly in the company of their parents, alongside a good proportion of the greater Tyabb community. Some people had driven for hours, from the other side of Melbourne. They had never met me or Luke, they had never before been to Tyabb. But for that morning, they were connected to this community, shaken by the senseless death of a little boy at cricket practice.

My friend Kirsty, who plays with the Sydney Symphony Orchestra, had flown down to play a piece on her violin at the funeral. She composed herself, looked at me and smiled then began to play Jules Massenet's 'Méditation de Thaïs'. Notes from a single violin wafted out over the congregation – not too forlorn but appropriately melancholy. It was a beautiful, special moment.

The pastor, a man called David who had been recommended to me, led the service and hit all the right notes himself. It was a perfectly balanced ceremony: with enough of a religious overtone to suit the surroundings, but not so much that it became overbearing. After years of being exposed to Greg's extreme religious convictions, Luke had developed his own relationship with God. He had believed in God, and spirituality had been an important part of his life. It seemed appropriate that God figured prominently in his funeral. Josephine had suggested including the poem 'Reason, Season, Lifetime' in the funeral booklet, and I found myself focusing on it as David spoke.

Somehow – and I don't know how – I was able to stay composed. It wasn't easy but I did feel that huge need to stay in control of myself, because I really did want to be able to look back and know that I was present, that I was fully there, that I absorbed every single moment of that day. I came close to losing it completely when the first bars of 'Amazing Grace' were struck. I felt a wave rising in me, a wave I knew would drown me completely if I allowed it to crash, and so I pushed it down. Inside, I was howling – wrenched apart with pain. On the outside, I maintained composure. I held it together for Luke.

Josephine took to the lectern and spoke beautifully; my brother Terry did too. I got up and read Psalm 23, 'The Lord is My Shepherd', the same psalm that had been read at my mother's funeral. It was important to me that my parents contributed to the funeral proceedings; I wanted them to feel that they had a voice too. It was their goodbye to their grandson as much as it was my farewell to my son.

Matthew, my friend Leonie's husband, spoke brilliantly. The school principal gave a moving speech. The school made a video of the ceremony, something I have never watched. Perhaps one day I will. One of the teachers photographed the entire funeral and put together a beautiful album. At first I thought it was a macabre memento but I've since come to appreciate it as a sensitive record of this most important occasion.

By the time we stepped out of the chapel, it was as if we had been transported to a completely different day. The grey clouds and drizzle had given way to blazing sunshine. Luke's coffin was carried from the chapel by his uncles and our neighbour Chris. I walked in step behind them, reaching my arm up to touch the coffin as it went. I don't know why. I just felt this urge to touch Luke – to make sure he knew I was with him.

And then there were the moments where I felt like it wasn't happening. That this couldn't be happening. Surely this was some sort of silly nightmare from which I would wake in a cold sweat. No mother should have to say goodbye to her eleven-year-old boy forever. It didn't seem possible to me that Luke – my Luke – was really in that yellow coffin. My little boy, wearing his onesie, clutching SpongeBob – being carried aloft by his uncles on the way to being cremated.

We got into the car and followed the hearse as it wound its way steadily towards the crematorium. As we drove, my family made small talk around me as I just focused on Luke's coffin up ahead. SpongeBob smiled goofily out the back window at me, and it made me smile. It seemed so appropriate, because it was just a little boy in there, a gorgeous little boy who still enjoyed SpongeBob and hadn't properly left his childhood behind. Upon arriving at the crematorium we were ushered into a little chapel and invited to say our final goodbyes. I had said a hundred final goodbyes at this point and was determined not to be overcome by the emotion of this moment. And so I approached the coffin, laid my hand gently on it, closed my eyes and said a silent farewell. A brief ceremony was held, none of which I remember. It was just immediate family and some very close friends. We were asked if we wanted to say anything and there was silence. There was so much to say, but no one felt able to speak. Finally, I spoke. I don't remember a word of what I said: just a simple goodbye to my son. And a reminder that I loved him more than life itself.

I couldn't stand and watch the coffin disappear behind the curtains. It was too painful to even contemplate. And so, as I had done in the morgue only days before, I took a deep breath, turned and walked out.

The wake was held at the Tyabb Cricket Club. The club had kindly given over the premises for the occasion, and it could not have been more perfect. Everyone was there. People from the local community, all the friends and family who had travelled from far and wide. The sun was belting down and people spilled out from the clubhouse and onto the oval itself. Local cafés and restaurants had donated all the food, a brewery had donated kegs of beer and Mornington Peninsula vineyards supplied wine. The generosity was overwhelming. I remember feeling so touched and thinking, how can I ever repay these people? How can I ever repay them for what they're doing for me and Luke today and have done since his death?

To this day, I still don't know how it all came together – who had organised it, which people had driven it – because I still wasn't in a place to really take it all in. It all just happened. The mood was, if not ebullient, at least upbeat. Luke had touched so many people in his short life, this was a celebration of him. It was a cleansing of this place too, of sorts. A reclaiming of it from the horrible cloud that hung over it.

I remember having so many people come to me to talk that I never got into the clubroom. I know there was no point at which

I didn't have a glass in my hand. And I didn't get around to speak to everyone, because it all happened in such a blur, but I noted all of the people who had come from far and wide and will be forever grateful to them for their support.

In the weeks immediately following Luke's death, I was inundated with flowers and cards from people all over the country. People I had never met before but were moved by my and Luke's story to send flowers, a note or a sympathy card. Every day for weeks I would get huge piles of cards in the mail. Some were addressed to 'Rosie, c/- Tyabb Cricket Ground', others to 'Rosie, Flinders College' and many still bore the simple address of 'Rosie, Tyabb'. Every single one of them reached me. As did the hundreds of bouquets of flowers, some from the top local florists, others hand-cut and hand-delivered. More flowers than I had space to accommodate. There were flowers on the back patio, the front patio, all over the house. And more cards than I could read. I used to scoop them up and put them in a special basket that someone had given me expressly for that purpose.

In the fullness of time, I would sit down and open and read each card. Beautiful poems, heartfelt messages of sympathy, complete strangers pouring out their hearts, writing lengthy letters about how deeply affected they had been by Luke's death and my apparent stoicism in the face of it. If only they had seen me behind closed doors. I tried my best to send a personal, handwritten reply to each card and bouquet of flowers I received. I just felt such an enormous debt of gratitude. I wanted everyone who had reached out to me to know that I didn't take any of their kindness for granted. Even now I still feel that I haven't told enough people how much I appreciated what they did. That I've missed people out who I should never have missed out. That I still need to thank every single person even if I don't know who they are because every single one of their gestures, no matter how large or small, made the world of difference to me.

At some point during Luke's wake, I became aware that numbers were thinning, and I became aware that the junior players were arriving to start their regular, scheduled cricket practice. And I took a moment to stand and watch quietly as training began. And while it could have triggered a rush of negative emotion, I derived a sort of comfort from it. Comfort that this summer ritual continued. It was a perfect summer's evening on a nondescript oval in a tiny corner of this sprawling country, and cricket practice was underway. Just as it would be underway on countless other ovals in countless other towns all over the country. And I felt happy that people were getting on, that normal service was being resumed, that despite the fact my world had been shattered irreparably, everyone else's was continuing to turn. There was, oddly, a sense of comfort in the constancy of it all.

It was now early evening and as I looked around, I noticed my family had all retreated home, as had the New Zealand contingent. Even Rosemary, a friend of mine from Sydney who had come down expressly for the funeral and was staying at my house, had headed back with them. A core group of my Tyabb friends were settling in, and it was only when Rosemary came back to the clubhouse to find me that I realised I ought to head home. It wasn't fair to leave her to deal with the extended Batty clan on her own.

So I gathered together a handful of friends and we went back to my house, where we carried on drinking and sharing stories. Evening turned to night and one by one, people left. Rosemary excused herself, saying she had an early flight the next morning, and went to my room to go to sleep. I sat up talking with my brothers, all of us becoming increasingly loud and unintentionally belligerent.

And I guess there was a point where we had been talking and emotions had been stirred up, and I remember being really upset and angry and shouting at them. All of a sudden my dad came storming out from his bedroom, telling us all to get to bed. We were suddenly five years old again, shrinking from his raised voice and skulking off to our rooms.

After a day spent holding it in, my outburst with my brothers had been little more than a release. An irrational emotional response to an imagined slight over which I ultimately had no control. And so I crawled into bed after everyone had gone to sleep. I had just buried my son. I had just experienced my own son's funeral. And I felt so desperately alone, so desperately alone. I didn't know what to do with myself here alone in the dark, finally unable to keep it all at bay. No more distractions, no more people, no more events. Just me and the darkness.

And my friend Rosemary had anticipated this. That's why she had come from Sydney and offered to sleep in my bed. Because when everyone else had gone to sleep, she was with me on the night of my son's funeral, and she held me while I sobbed. We went to sleep holding hands. That closeness I'll never forget of being with someone rather than having to be alone – that was special.

27

Change

When I reflect on the last eighteen months of my life, I'm struck by what a remarkable ride it has been. In a short space of time I've become a household name. Rare is the occasion I can walk through an airport these days and not be stopped by a complete stranger. Sometimes – and disconcertingly – they will ask for an autograph, while other times they will excuse themselves for approaching me and tell me how much they admire me. Other times still they will ask me for a hug, or use the occasion to tell me about their own experience as victims of family violence.

I have become a lightning rod for people and their myriad problems. And I don't say that with anything other than the utmost humility. It is humbling in the extreme to have people entrust you with their darkest stories. It also takes a toll.

In the year and a half since Luke died, I've been named Australian of the Year and feted by a prime minister. I've been indirectly responsible for the establishment of a royal commission in Victoria into family violence. I have been appointed co-deputy chair of the Council of Australian Governments' advisory panel on family violence. I have spoken to the country's top CEOs, addressed the National Press Club and met people from all over the country at speaking engagements that have taken me from far north Queensland to suburban Perth. I've lost count of the number of media interviews I have done. From *Four Corners* to *The Today Show*, from stories by Helen Garner in *The Monthly* to appearing on the cover of *The Australian Women's Weekly*. It's been a tumultuous, extraordinary, slightly surreal time.

I have a kind of fame – but for all the wrong reasons. I am a strange sort of celebrity – but because of how I got here, it's a celebrity status that nobody wants.

I am the person that no one says no to. I am the bereaved mother whom everyone indulges, because there but for the grace of God go us all. I was a mum in middle-class suburbia, in a nice house, raising a little boy at a nice school. I was everyone and no one. And now I'm Rosie Batty. No one would swap places with me for even a second. People sometimes talk about how strong I am. How brave. I'm not sure about that. I don't see myself that way. All I can do is go forward. This is the journey I am on. This is the direction I have decided to take my life in. I no longer have a son to live for, and so I fill my life with creating a legacy for Luke.

I was a mum, that was my meaning and purpose. That's why I did everything. Chose a lovely school, a lovely neighbourhood, made sure that Luke had great male role models in his life, made sure he explored every opportunity he wanted to in terms of team sports, Scouts, swimming and drama. I just wanted him to be happy – to try to make up for the black cloud hovering over us that was Greg.

Anyone who is a parent knows you get up in the morning, you go to work, you do all the things you do because you want your kids to have a good life. But my boy has gone now, and I don't have a job to go to. So I have to replace that absence with another reason to get up in the morning, to fill my time with being busy with things that mean something. I have a different purpose now. I may only make a little difference, but a little difference is a start.

When I stood on the podium in front of Parliament House in Canberra to accept the award of Australian of the Year, I dedicated it to Luke. Because everything I do is for him. So that I don't forget him. So that his eleven years in my life – on this planet – will count for something. So that no other mother has to suffer the same fate as me.

Am I deliberately keeping busy to keep the grief at bay? Perhaps. Am I terrified that when my tenure as Australian of the Year finishes, the phone calls will stop, the speaking invitations will dry up and the doors that have hitherto flung open whenever I knocked will remain stubbornly shut? Most definitely. But in the meantime, I feel like I have found my calling. Out of the most tragic event imaginable, I have found purpose. And if people want to think that makes me a bad person or some kind of oddball, then there's not a lot I can do to change their minds.

Part of the reason I think I seem to cope far better than people expect – and far better than I ever would have expected I could – is because I have this new sense of purpose in my life. If, by raising community awareness of family violence – and getting men to recognise that this is a very basic issue of gender inequality – I manage to help one woman, then it will have been worthwhile. If I serve as inspiration for only one victim of family violence to summon the strength to call a crisis line and take steps to remedy her situation, then I will have achieved all I set out to do.

Of course, if, along the way, I also play a part in changing legislation or shifting societal attitudes towards family violence, or thoroughly reviewing the way we fund and support frontline family-violence service providers – from emergency shelters to counselling services – then that is a good thing too. Because it is fundamentally unacceptable that we can't live in our own homes safely, that people who are close to us can terrorise us and make our lives miserable and we are not doing enough about it. I hope I have forced that uncomfortable truth out into the open.

For you only have to consider the statistics to understand what a pressing problem family violence is for this country. One woman almost every week dies at the hand of a current or former partner. One in six women will be a victim of family violence in their lifetime. And of these one in six, at least half of them have children in their care. If we had one woman a week dying on the public transport system, we would be up in arms – so why aren't we similarly horrified about family violence deaths? Is it simply because they go unreported? Largely overlooked by law enforcement, widely dismissed by our judicial system and routinely written off by our media as 'just another domestic'?

If we were to broadcast the family-violence death toll on the TV news each night, like we do with the road toll, would that shock us into understanding how prevalent this violence is and how pressing is the need for us to do something about it? If we were to put up posters, like we do with road safety campaigns, would that work? And why do we put so much money into those kind of campaigns and virtually nothing into a far bigger, far more pernicious problem?

I would never seek to diminish the suffering of others, but isn't it telling that the nation can get behind a one-punch (coward's punch) campaign – and in one state, at least, completely overhaul the liquor licensing system – and we can't even speak openly about the problem of family violence?

It's not a problem that is going to be solved by one woman. Nor indeed by one government advisory panel or department. It's a whole-of-society problem that requires a whole-of-society solution.

The former governor-general Quentin Bryce recently delivered a damning report into family violence in Queensland. Called *Not Now, Not Ever*, it found that 180 cases of family violence were reported in Queensland every single day. Speaking to the report and its findings, Bryce said: 'The truth is that domestic and family violence is caused by unequal distribution of power and resources between men and women. It's about the rigid gender roles and stereotypes that characterise our society.

'For all of us, we must be asking ourselves, "What can we do as neighbours, family and friends? What can each one of us do about this appalling scourge in our society?"

'We don't want to confront these things, we want to turn away and say, "That's not my business," but it certainly is everybody's business.'

This is why I have established the Luke Batty Foundation. This is why I have launched the Never Alone campaign. So that we can start to have the conversations that will finally drag this issue out of the shadows. And that is why I speak out and tell my story. I've spoken at more than 110 events to more than 35,000 people since January 2015. I know that my and Luke's story is just one of many, many stories of family violence out there, and I know some people are critical of me, saying that maybe I'm too much in the public spotlight, or that I should grieve in private. But I'm not going to do that. And I will not let my grief limit or define me. For reasons that are beyond me, I am the one that people seem to want to hear from. And I know – people tell me – that I inspire them and give them courage. But what people don't know is that speaking out also empowers and inspires me. It's bittersweet, knowing this has happened because of Luke's death, but I feel I am making a difference. That gives me the impetus to keep going, which is important, because my sense is that if I keep doing this, and keep the public spotlight on the issue of family violence, things will change. Because they have to change.

Ken Lay, the former Victorian police commissioner and my co-chair on the advisory panel on family violence, and the former senator Natasha Stott Despoja, chair of the family-violence advocacy group Our Watch, gave a joint address to the National Press Club last year. Ken told how for many years violence against women has been one of Australia's filthy little secrets. Natasha called it a national emergency. In Australia, it is both.

I sat with Quentin Bryce in her Brisbane office recently. It was just after her report had been released in Queensland. In anticipation of my arrival, she had baked a delicious date and walnut teacake. As well as being whip smart and determined, she's a generous woman and an excellent cook. She congratulated me on the momentum I had helped to create around the subject of domestic violence in this country, but worried that it could dissipate just as quickly as it has developed. And I share her concern. Today's headlines can so easily be tomorrow's fish and chip wrappings. And we owe it to our mothers, sisters and daughters to make sure that doesn't happen. We have a once-in-a-generation opportunity to make some real change – but we need to pull together as a society to make it happen. Because while I can travel around the country speaking at every community event on the calendar, while Ken and I can chair an advisory panel and do interviews, and while Quentin Bryce can author reports and campaign, real change will only come about when society accepts this is a fundamental, entrenched, systemic problem. And just as importantly, when governments prioritise it as an issue, when legislators start to craft new laws or alter existing ones to properly deal with it, and when – crucially – we have greater accountability of perpetrators.

Because the way things are now: we are enabling the violence. For as long as we as neighbours or family members or friends continue to turn a blind eye or, worse, write off incidences of family violence as 'just another domestic', then the physical assaults, the psychological torment, the unfettered harassment and the killings will continue. The media has a role to play here too. How many times have you watched the evening news and seen the murder of a woman in her home downplayed as a 'domestic dispute' – as if death at the hands of a partner is somehow less serious?

Murder is murder. Is it any less terrifying if it is committed by someone you know intimately? I'd suggest it's quite the opposite.

We talk a lot in this country about the war on terror – and certainly, the eradication of international and home-grown terror threats is a worthy cause. But what about the terror that one in six women are living daily? What about the terror that means they are too scared to leave the house or too scared to go home? What about the terror that seizes them every time their partner walks in the door – never knowing what mood he might be in, what eggshells will have to be trod, what evasive action they are going to have to take to protect themselves? Or worse, protect their children?

What about the terror of the woman who is too scared to leave because either she or her children have been threatened with death if they do? Or the terror of the woman who has been so totally stripped of financial independence that even if she wanted to leave, she wouldn't have the means? What about the terror of the woman whose partner has so carefully, methodically, isolated her from her friends and family that she wakes up one day and realises she has nowhere to go – no one to turn to?

Another thing we need to address is this simplistic idea that women in family violence situations only have themselves to blame, because, after all, why don't they just get up and leave? I hear it all the time. I've heard people say it about me. And it makes me so, so angry. The ignorance from which this attitude stems is frankly staggering.

I rather famously had a stoush live on air with a TV presenter who, in a throwaway comment that was breathtaking in its ignorance, suggested that there were no excuses for women victims of family violence – especially those with children – to stay in a relationship. 'They just need to leave,' he said.

So let's just firstly call this what it is: it's victim-blaming. Once again putting the onus on the victim to remedy the situation. Inherent in that is an acceptance that men are fundamentally violent, fundamentally incapable of controlling their base instincts, and therefore it is up to women to take all the precautions and accept all the responsibility. It is up to the woman to report it to police, to pursue it through the courts, to take out an IVO and report again to the police when it is breached – as it almost inevitably is. It's up to the woman to go into a refuge, to change her identity, to flee interstate or overseas. All of which means leaving behind your friends, family, your home, your job, your community. And all the while, the perpetrator is allowed to get on with his life, to go down to the local pub and, without a word of protest from his mates, describe himself as having 'women troubles'.

More crucially, let's pause for a moment to think about this notion of 'leaving'. As anyone who has worked on a family-violence crisis helpline will tell you, that's when victims are at their most vulnerable. The point of leaving is when perpetrators of violence are at their most dangerous and unpredictable. That's why Greg killed Luke. He had come to understand that both Luke and I were no longer under his control. He began to appreciate that I was no longer in fear of him – that we were pulling away. And so he killed our son – in a final act of control and vengeance. He killed Luke so that he would win, and so that I would suffer for the rest of my life.

So the next time you are reading a story in the newspapers or watching or listening to a story on the TV or radio about violence perpetrated on a woman, apply a little bit of critical analysis. Is there an undertone that because the girl was wearing headphones as she walked through the park in daylight, she somehow had it coming? Is there a suggestion that a woman's decision to walk across a park at night on her way home from work means she deserved to be stabbed to death? Is there an intimation that the short skirt or the fact she had one drink too many automatically means she forfeited any rights to be treated as a human being and deserved to be raped?

We tend to sometimes focus in a sensationalistic way on the details of individual acts of violence without joining the dots to a culture of gender-based violence. And think also about the way the media is quick to assign a narrative to a story, irrespective of the bald facts. I am reminded of the case of the farmer in rural New South Wales who murdered his wife and three children before turning the shotgun on himself. Was he decried in newspaper headlines as a mass murderer? No. He was eulogised by the media as a hardworking farmer who had battled bravely with the burden of caring for a brain-injured wife. His decision to put bullets into his three kids and his wife was reported on as some kind of act of humanity. I have also seen atrocious headlines that openly disrespect victims. 'Monster Chef and the She Male' springs to mind. We need to challenge this every time. Perpetrators must be held accountable for their actions. Women are not to blame.

According to VicHealth's latest attitude survey, a significant proportion of Australians still excuse, trivialise and justify violence against women. A growing number of Australians think that a victim is at least partially to blame for an instance of domestic and family violence. One in six think that women who say no really mean yes. Attitudes among young people are particularly bad. According to recent research commissioned by Our Watch, one in four young men believed that controlling and violent behaviours are signs of male strength. One in six people aged twelve to twenty-four believe women should know their place. If we want to tackle this violence, to stop it before it starts, we need to tackle these attitudes and beliefs in our schools, in our homes, around our dinner tables. And men, especially, bear the brunt of the responsibility here. Men are especially sensitive to the approval and respect of their peers. If you are a man and you hear a friend or associate talking about controlling behaviour or violence against a woman in any kind of boastful way, you need to challenge it. You need to tell them that what they are doing is not okay. To not do so is to be complicit in the violence itself.

Importantly, what we also need is a greater appreciation of – and greater funding for – the frontline service providers: the women's shelters, the helplines, the people who go to women's homes and physically extract them from situations of extreme violence and danger. I have been to several of these frontline service providers and have stood by and watched trained professionals field calls from women in various states of terror from all over the country. I have watched a large TV screen in a call centre show the number of women on hold, waiting to speak to a professional. Women who have already taken a huge step by dialling the number – who then have to sit on hold. And I have watched with a sinking heart as some of those calls drop out before a counsellor can get to them.

Last year alone, the government's 1800 RESPECT helpline missed an estimated 18,000 calls because of a lack of adequate resources. That's 18,000 women whose cries for help went unanswered. One of them may have been your sister, your mother, your daughter.

Resources in these frontline services are stretched, counsellors working around the clock to meet demand. And like doctors in an ER, they are forced to make decisions on the spot about which cases are in most pressing need of the finite resources that are available. Does the professional woman in the city who says she has been threatened with violence but insists on downplaying it take precedence over the mother of two in a rural outpost who is calling for the fourth time that month following a sustained history of violence? Do they allocate what meagre resources they have to getting that rural woman and her children on a charter flight to the nearest urban shelter as soon as possible? Or do they put that money into expanding the number of beds available in the overstretched, under-resourced women's shelters that already exist? It is not uncommon for these helpline counsellors to work fourteen-hour days, carefully listening to each caller, methodically assessing the level of risk, prioritising dwindling resources and doing their best day after day to ensure what little money they have is spent in the most efficient way possible. And all the while, the calls keep coming. The number on the TV screen showing the women on hold ticks inexorably up.

Once we have looked at this first-responder side of the family violence equation, we need to review what happens next – inevitably at the judicial level. What happens when, once a victim has summoned the courage to stand up to their partner, she finds herself in front of a magistrate? Is she going to be means-tested for Legal Aid, as I was, no matter her situation? No matter that the very finances on which that judgement is being made might be controlled almost wholly by the man who is abusing her? If she gets to court, is she going to be treated with disdain by an out-of-touch judiciary long used to categorising domestic violence situations as low-risk and relatively minor in the scheme of things, legally speaking? Is it acceptable that magistrates seem to believe that an IVO is worth the paper it is printed on? Or that some judges (not all, but definitely some) have so many ingrained prejudices when it comes to women victims of family violence that their response to it is negligent at best and criminal at worst? Is it okay that our court system routinely minimises risk to female victims of family violence and fails to recognise the red flags that continue to put women and children in grave danger?

And what of the Family Court, this most influential institution whose deliberations and decisions cannot be reported on by the news media? Go to the United States, and stories of family disharmony and domestic violence appear regularly in the news media. Why? Because the media there is not subject to the same constraints when it comes to reporting on matters before the Family Court. Assuredly, some of these rules exist in Australia for very good reason: there are often excellent reasons for not reporting on custody disputes, reasons that usually involve the privacy and welfare of any children involved. But what we lose is a most important sense of transparency and accountability when it comes to the activities of the Family Court and the Federal Circuit Court. And as a society we need to ask ourselves if this sort of secrecy is part of the problem. Often victims' experiences are not reported in the media because the people involved cannot be identified. This makes it too difficult for the media, which, frightened of being sued, puts such stories in the too-hard basket.

These are the sorts of questions we need to ask. And if I achieve nothing else in my tenure as Australian of the Year – or beyond that, as an advocate for change in the way we deal with family violence in this country – then forcing these issues out from the shadows will have been a job well done.

Isn't it terrible that your young son might think it is okay to be violent and controlling because it's a sign of strength? Or that it's okay for your daughter to accept controlling or derogative behaviour or the occasional slap because her partner's drunk and he apologised? We need to challenge these attitudes each time they arise so our children grow up understanding there is no grey area when it comes to family violence. It is not okay in any of its forms. Not ever.

So much of it is entrenched gender inequality. As men and as women we are born with our views of life, from the moment we take our first breath. Men have their male sense of privilege and entitlement, and that's the lens through which they view life. They don't know any different. As women, we know our place. And I'm not suggesting centuries of gender roles and stereotypes can be overturned in a couple of years: but certainly acknowledging that disparity is a start.

Think of it as a basic economic issue, if nothing else. Police commissioners around the country estimate that 40 percent of their forces' time and resources is taken up dealing with family violence issues. And that's not to mention the time and resources dedicated to the issue in our courts and public health systems. Think of how fruitfully these resources could otherwise be deployed.

Because the sad reality is it's far more common to be affected by family violence in this country than not. That's what I realised after Luke died. Even the children who were close friends of Luke's and who came from great homes and lovely families have now had their entire world rocked because, not only did a friend of theirs die, but he died at the hands of his own father. Some of those kids were playing cricket with him earlier that same day. That suddenly makes the world a very dangerous place for a small child in a very safe community in a lovely little pocket of Victoria.

I remember in the weeks after Luke's death, one of my friends told me about an exchange she had with her son. She and her ex-husband had always struggled to agree on access visits, and there had been instances of arguing in front of the children. And her son spoke about Luke and asked her if she thought his father might do the same thing to him. She was horrified. She told her husband, and he was devastated. But it forced him to take a look at his actions and assess the impact it was having on the people closest to him.

We all need to take a look at ourselves. Because change begins with each one of us.

28
Grief

Monday 11 August 2014

My first journal entry since Luke's death. Don't know why I haven't written before now – just haven't made the time or wanted to connect with myself this way until now.

What am I feeling today? Today has not been so painful, but when I'm on top of a meditation hill and see the sky and clouds, mountains and vast beautiful scenery, I feel the pain. The huge sense of loss.

Where is Luke? Is he high above the clouds, looking out safely from a tree way up where no one can see and where he is safe from the world?

Why can't I reach out to touch him? To call out to him. To laugh with him. To get cross with him. To just enjoy his presence. I know why I haven't written before now – it's too painful. Too real. Too raw. I WANT HIM BACK!!! I so want him back.

I talk out loud to him all the time – and that helps. I have tried to remember all the holidays we've had, the trips to England. It fills me with so much pain I think I might burst.

I can only bear to think about all those things so much.

When will I ever be able to remember him without so much pain? When will I be able to see a photo of his beautiful blue eyes and gorgeous face without sobbing out loud? When will I stop feeling this pain?

It is too hard. I am better to be busy and distracted – only letting bursts of grief to break through occasionally throughout the day rather than letting the grief consume me.

I feel cheated that all my memories of Luke will be forever painful. That the photos and videos I have will always bring tears.

Why did I never sit with Luke and share all our photo albums together? I know he looked at them alone sometimes without saying.

I do wish that I had thought to make the time to do that.

All the videos of his life too. I guess you think that one day you will, but there's no rush. Then it's too late and now the thought of watching them is too painful. But still. I have them for one day. One day when the pain isn't so intense. But how long will it take? How long will it be before my entire day is not spent thinking of Luke and feeling the pain of his loss?

All the things I shall no longer be able to share and all the things I shall no longer be able to do. I am no longer a mother and it hurts like hell.

Why me? Why Luke? Fucking, fucking Greg.

How could he have done this? I still feel no hatred — just total sadness. Disbelief. Sadness and more sadness.

When will it fucking end?

*

I have not yet had a moment where I have been inconsolable over Luke — where I have just fallen apart. I know I did when my eighteen-year-old cat died, but it hasn't happened yet over my son. So whether that is still to come, I don't know.

The body is quite an amazing instrument. When I met Gill Hicks, the Adelaide woman who lost both her legs in the London bombings, I was struck by what an incredibly strong, positive person she was. And she told me it took her seven years before she became inconsolable — before her body allowed her to process the full enormity of what had happened to her. Before then, she figured, her body had decided she wasn't up for it. She wouldn't have been able to handle it. And I wonder if that is the same with me. I wonder if perhaps at some level, my body knows that the horror of what I have experienced is so great, that I need to put a certain amount of time between myself and my loss before it will allow me to completely break down.

I believe, if it happens to me like that, it will happen when it is safe for me to do so, when I can cope with it. I am not in denial; I am not disengaged. But there is a point that I can't get past. I can start to feel emotional and I can start to tear up, but I can't seem to let myself go. I am so busy holding back this wave of emotion that my body is scared is going to drown me. I wonder when I am going to stop constantly thinking about Luke.

Because even when I am not thinking about him, I am thinking about him.

And then there are the small mercies. I didn't see Luke be killed. I think about women like Ingrid Poulson. She came across the bodies of her children and father just after they had been murdered: I am grateful that that is something I have never had to deal with.

I think of the pain the Morcombes have to deal with – the fact that Daniel was kidnapped and probably in fear of his life for hours before he was killed. And I am grateful that Luke's death was instant: that he would not have been in pain and if there had been fear, it would mercifully have been fleeting.

And I think of the mother of Darcey Freeman, who was thrown off the West Gate Bridge by her father, and the mother of those three Farquharson boys who were driven into a dam by their father: and I am grateful that Greg is dead. I don't think I would cope if Luke was dead and Greg was still alive.

So you do look at these things – these small mercies – and say, yes I was in the worst situation in my life, but I am still grateful I was spared a lot of other pain. For how else do you go on?

I've only ever taken a few sleeping tablets, and those in the weeks immediately following Luke's death. I was offered valium, but I worried that, once I started it, I might not ever get off it. I chain-smoked in the weeks immediately after his death, and I remember drinking a lot more than I usually would but, even then, I wasn't writing myself off. I'm still on my anxiety medication, the same one I have been taking since Greg's harassment of me really escalated. But otherwise, I am medication-free.

I don't live in a vacuum. I'm aware that some people find my reaction to Luke's death unusual. As if there is a 'usual' way to react in my situation. They point to my extraordinary performance in front of the TV cameras the morning after Luke's death, and they say there's something not right about that woman. They look at me standing up to receive awards, like Australian of the Year, or make speeches about family violence to auditoriums full of people, and they think I'm cold or unfeeling or robotic. They don't see me crying myself to sleep every evening. They're not with me during those moments – and they happen every day – when I am overcome with such grief that I have to take myself off somewhere for a quiet cry.

The irony, of course, is that, when it comes to my feelings, I am a private person. Whether it's through being raised by a father who is not demonstrative, or because of a lifetime spent trying not to allow myself to be vulnerable, I'm not much for wearing my vulnerability on my sleeve. Open and honest, yes. But outwardly demonstrative, no – that's not my style.

I've spoken to friends in the media about it, and they point to Lindy Chamberlain, and the trial by media she endured because she refused to grieve in a way the Australian public thought she ought to. But there are no rule books for people like me. It's not as if there is a set of accepted behaviours for mothers who were 50 metres away when their ex-partner brutally murdered their son. I cope as best I can, feeling my way as I go.

There isn't a day goes by that I don't miss Luke. And it's a pain that can be triggered by the most mundane things. A trip to the supermarket when I automatically reach for the cereal he used to like or the bananas he used to eat. A visit to a café where a mother is cradling a newborn. The sight of Luke's former classmates, trooping up the hill to school – marching on into their respective futures. The wave will come crashing down, and for a moment, I am breathless and drowning. Until I can see the surface and I swim back up for air.

Of course, there are times when I lose it completely and take down anyone who happens to be in my vicinity. Sometimes the trigger is obvious, sometimes it is seemingly trivial. The only constant is that when the fall comes, it is spectacular and can leave those in the line of fire licking their wounds. Like the poor shop assistant on the day before Luke's funeral when I couldn't find the shoe I wanted in my size. Or the hapless stylist at a magazine photo shoot who had brought the wrong size clothes. Or the person who happened to be using a leaf blower outside my house, or the friend who was using a vacuum in my house in the days after Luke's death. At the time, it seemed perfectly reasonable for me to scream and rant and rave at them all. But in hindsight, I realise it wasn't. Even now, eighteen months later, I spend every moment of every day suppressing something, be it a fleeting thought or a flood of tears. It is so constant I don't even know I'm doing it. And then, sometimes, it all just bubbles to the surface and I explode, bringing people down around me. I'm not especially proud of it, but nor am I in a position to really control it. I am suffering from post-traumatic stress.

Six months after Luke was killed, I went to a health retreat in the Hunter Valley. It was one of those places where you leave your phone at the door and spend a week detoxing: undertaking classes and diets and exercise regimes to hopefully find again whatever equilibrium you may have lost. People kept telling me I needed to 'take time to grieve', as if I had been spending my days since his death wilfully ignoring the fact my only child was no longer in my life and had been taken from me in the most heinous of circumstances. I knew my body was drained, I knew I was physically and emotionally exhausted, and so I thought two weeks spent eating well, doing exercise and otherwise being still – away from home and in an environment

291

purpose-built for taking stock – could be just what the doctor ordered. It turned out to be all of that and more, and I emerged two weeks later, if not a different person, at least a marginally less damaged one.

But what I wasn't prepared for was being in the company of people who didn't know my story. And being confronted by the simplest of questions. I had spent six months surrounded by friends and family. Or if not friends and family, any number of people who life had sent my way expressly because of Luke's death: journalists, politicians, social workers, domestic violence campaigners. So it was confronting to sit at dinner with fellow guests at the health retreat and be asked the questions strangers ask one another when they are thrust into a situation of forced intimacy.

'So Rosie, tell us about yourself. Do you have any kids?' came the enquiry one night from someone sitting at the next table.

I was stumped. It was the simplest question in the world, the most innocuous of enquiries – and yet it took my breath away. Being a mother had been a fundamental part of who I was. Was I still a mother? And if I was no longer a mother, what was I? An ex-mother? A former mother? What did I answer?

'Yes, I do. I mean, I am. I mean, I did have kids. A little boy.' I heard myself reply to confused looks, the usual wave of emotion rising in me. 'But he passed away.'

Did I have the energy to go through with an explanation? Could I face the trauma of going over it all again with relative strangers? And if so, to what possible end? I had been here before. I would explain what happened, I would watch as these people struggled to know how to respond and then I would feel obliged to ease their discomfort by telling them it was fine – when patently it was not.

And so I learned to modify my small talk, to only reveal to strangers what I felt capable of dealing with on any given day. Sometimes it felt bad to deny I was a mother, as if I was somehow dishonouring the memory of Luke, but for the sake of expediency – and my own mental wellbeing – it was occasionally easier just to let it go.

*

Luke's old school, Flinders Christian Community College, is only half a kilometre from my home. Down a gentle hill, past the neatly kept gardens of my neighbours, set at the top of a series of nearby paddocks that stretch to Tyabb and roll eventually down to the sea at Hastings. Every morning around 8.30 am and every afternoon around 3 pm, I see kids in uniform walking past my front gate. I know the uniform well – white shirt, grey shorts. I used to wash it twice a week, hang it from my clothesline out the back. The kids are also familiar to me – faces from Luke's class. Except that they are all changing slowly: morphing from children to teenagers. All gangly limbs and maturing features. All getting on with the business of growing up and becoming adults, fulfilling the potential their parents have spent the past thirteen years nurturing. And it is a peculiar kind of torture. I think of my Luke, frozen in time. Forever eleven – never to go through puberty, never to have another growth spurt, his face never to shuck off the softness of boyhood as he develops into a man. Never to don a backpack and take off around the world, never to experience the highs of first love, never to have his heart broken.

While I was initially comforted on the day of Luke's funeral to see life go on for other parents and children, I found myself

293

resenting other parents for many months afterwards. I would be angry that they dared go on with their lives when mine had been placed in limbo. It used to upset me that other mums and dads blithely went about the business of raising their kids in my orbit. How could they be so insensitive? But then I realised how unreasonable I was being and that, if I was to have any peace, I needed to confront this irrational feeling and come to terms with the fact that while my world has been brought to a standstill, everyone else's has to go on.

It makes me wonder whether it's better to stay here in Tyabb, where at every turn there is something to remind me of Luke, or move somewhere where I won't be constantly reminded of him. Every time I look at the pool in the backyard, I think Luke will never swim in it again. Every time I drive past the basketball courts, I think Luke will never shoot hoops there again. Every time I pass his bedroom, I think Luke will never sleep in there again. And it's the silence that slowly eats away at me. A house that was once full of noise now lies mostly silent. I sometimes feel like it is closing in on me. How can I stay here with his memories haunting me daily? But then how could I ever move on and leave them behind?

Because that's what is scary too. The idea that with every day that passes, he dims a little in my memory. My recollection of events gets foggier. In fact, it is my greatest fear. That, one by one, the memories are going to fade and this most perfect creation of mine – this most wonderful light that I nurtured and gifted to the world – will be forever extinguished. And it terrifies me. Sometimes I even have the strange feeling that he was never here. Stop the clocks. Stop the clocks.

I am constantly being told – sometimes by complete strangers – how remarkable has been my strength in the face of this tragedy, because apparently the 'normal' reaction, whatever that is, is to be racked with bitterness and anger. But what kind of a way is that to lead a life? We are so used to people feeling that they need to hold on to their anger and be unforgiving, but that just slowly eats away at you. Being forgiving doesn't mean you accept what has been done to you, it just means you can let go of what has happened, because at the end of the day you cannot change it. The alternative, after all, is to be consumed with anger – and what purpose does that serve?

I don't know what the truth is, beyond finding a truth for yourself. Finding your own individual spiritual path. I've read quite a lot of Buddhist philosophy, and I think I have mixed some of that in with my Church of England and Catholic school upbringing to come up with my own unique blend of Rosie Batty life philosophy. And as for my spiritual beliefs – well, I believe in reincarnation. So if you opt out, you've only got to come back and repeat the life. You'll have to deal with it eventually.

We are all on a journey, and we all have things to learn. None of us knows what is around the corner, and it's what you learn from the experiences that life deals you that defines that journey. In my case, that's whether you gain wisdom and insight or whether you stay bitter and angry.

People ask me all the time: 'What do you think about Greg?' And the truth is, I don't think about him much at all. I don't hate him. I just don't waste any time or energy thinking about him. I did have one conversation recently with his brother – he called me without realising it. It was one of those things where he had hit a wrong number in his phone, and I called him back without knowing who it was. We ended up speaking for a while, and I said how bad I felt for him and his mum and dad, because Greg's family has been inadvertently caught up in all of this too. It's not their fault. They live in a small country town and they carry the stigma every day. I think they were selective about what they chose to be aware of with Greg and his behaviour, but Greg was their son and brother. No matter his crime, he was once a baby that his mother cradled. I know it cannot be easy for them.

One of the things I am proud of is being respectful towards Greg. There is nothing to be gained by defiling his memory. If I think anything at all about him, it's that he and I were both failed by the system. That whatever intervention occurred – from a law enforcement and mental health perspective – it was ultimately too little, too late. And so finally, I have come to accept there was nothing more I could have done to prevent Luke's death.

I had been through the courts, I had taken out the IVOs. I had exhausted all legal options and even considered running away to England. I tried to manage Greg myself, and when that failed, I got the law involved and did everything the police and courts subsequently told me to do, naïvely trusting that the system would protect me. That it would protect Luke. But we were both simply victims by association of someone's mental health problems. And there are a lot of people in that position today. They have a tormented journey with no respite – and that's a national tragedy.

That's where the coronial inquest was good for me, as taxing as it was. It set out in black and white the sequence of events that led up to Luke's death, and analysed the journey I had been on in the previous eleven years with Greg, and helped me come to understand that there was nothing more I could have done.

I have learned a lot since Luke was killed. I can see more clearly the trap I was in. Do I have regrets? Yes. Would I have done things differently a second time? Absolutely. Would things have turned out differently if I had? Maybe, maybe not.

You cling to the things that make living each day bearable. And for me, one of those things is the fact that Luke's murder was a premeditated act. It was Luke's last night of cricket training for the season. Greg didn't know when he would be seeing Luke again. He had emptied his bank accounts, packed up all his belongings at the share house. When he set out that afternoon for Tyabb oval, he had no intention of ever coming back. If I hadn't said yes to Luke spending five more minutes in the practice nets with his dad, I suspect it would have happened some other way, in some other place.

Whenever I thought about Luke being in danger in Greg's presence, especially since the knife incident, I had envisioned scenarios involving the two of them alone. Maybe he would drive off, put a hose from the exhaust pipe into the car and kill them both that way. That was why I'd fought so hard to restrict Greg's access to Luke in potentially dangerous situations. But it never occurred to me that he would kill Luke in the way he did. In broad daylight, in a public place, in front of mums, dads and kids. In front of me.

But I look back now and I can see that Greg had lost control over me and Luke was starting to pull away from him. To Greg's mind, I was winning. He killed Luke as the ultimate act of vengeance. He killed him so I would suffer for the rest of my life.

*

I've gotten past the deep, deep sadness – the trough that I was in for the first year after Luke's death. I'm no longer traumatised by what happened to Luke. The circumstances of his death, the meaninglessness and horror of it, no longer consume my every waking thought. And it did for that year, when it was hard to simply get through every day. But I feel like now I have turned a corner.

Now, if I find myself getting melancholy, it's about what I was unable to give him. I'm sad about the life I wasn't able to offer him. I'm sad I wasn't able to build for him the close-knit nuclear family that I too had missed out on – and that I have spent a lifetime observing from afar and coveting. More than anything else, I wanted him to know the unconditional love of family. But at the end, and despite all my efforts, it was just him and me.

The real tragedy for me is that, despite appearances, I am not unusual. My situation, while extreme, has simply captured the national imagination because of the way I chose to react to it. For reasons I have yet to properly understand, I have garnered all this attention and won all these awards, but there are a hundred, maybe a thousand Rosie Battys out there right now. Women who are being terrorised by family violence, women who are victims of a partner's descent into mental illness. And the system is treating them in the same inadequate way that it treated me.

This is what spurs me on. This is the reason I get up out of bed every morning. I lost my son – my only son. And he was my reason for being. So now I have a choice. I either shrivel up and let his senseless death defeat me, or I stand up and use the platform I have been given to try to ensure no other woman in Australia suffers the same fate as me. Because no mother should have to feel this pain.

Epilogue

In May 2015, I was asked to take part in a Women of Letters event in Melbourne. The concept is simple. A group of women – of varying degrees of prominence or notoriety – are invited to an event at which they read out a letter they have written to a prearranged theme. I was invited to come along and read out 'A Letter to the Me That Never Was'. This is what I wrote.

Dear Rosie,

I write to you first of all as Rosie, the little girl that really was once upon a time, over forty-five years ago. The little girl growing up on a farm with two younger brothers and a dad that you loved but just didn't know how to get close to you. The dad who worked hard and read his newspapers but didn't know how to hug you, encourage you or tell you that he loved you.

The little girl who was six years old, enjoying school and making new friends. Learning how to read, to add and subtract, and beginning to discover the bigger world outside. The little girl whose life was turned upside down forever when her mummy died.

The little girl who watched her mummy taken away on a stretcher, into the ambulance and never to be seen again. The little girl who didn't get to say goodbye, to hug her or to tell her that she will love her and remember her forever. The little girl who didn't even know that her mummy had died and wasn't at her funeral to share the grief and sadness with everyone else. The little girl who couldn't believe that it really was her mummy that had died, trying desperately to believe that they had mixed her mummy up with someone else and that she would return again one day – that is, until she saw with her own eyes that big black gravestone and knew she would never return again. Ever!

And now I write to the 'me that never was'. The me that never got the opportunity to know what it would have been like to have my mother be my best friend. To share my life through its ups and downs and to comfort and support me like other good mums do. And I don't doubt that my mum would have been my best friend and the best mother that I could have ever wished for.

The 'me that never was' who never got to see my mum become a grandmother, to grow old and to laugh and cry with. The mum that isn't here now when I need her the most. The mum that I never had time to get to know and only have distant, dim memories of. So the 'me that never was' will never know how different my journey through life would have been if my mum had lived. If my world hadn't been shattered from that point on, and the fear and loneliness that crept into my life, separating me from everyone, would last forever.

You see, I can't help but think that the 'me that never was' would have been so very different if my mum had lived. If she had been there to nurture, protect and love me. To laugh at me. To laugh with me. To shout at me. To encourage me. To argue with me. To debate life with me. To be a part of my life that I could always trust and depend on, no matter what. To help me understand my emotions and teach me how to express them. To be there for me no matter what.

You see, 'the me that never was' could have made so many different choices if she hadn't died. Would I have been drawn into a pattern of unhealthy relationships with men? Men who drank too much, men who were weak and sucked my strength from me. Relationships that failed because I shouldn't have been in them to start with. You see 'the me that never was' would have walked past those relationships and recognised that they were set to fail. The 'me that never was' would have confidently aimed higher and been able to identify a partner who I could trust and see a future life together with.

But you see if I had got to be 'the me that never was', I wouldn't have met Greg. I would have walked away when I first saw the signs of abuse and violence. I would have run a mile in the opposite direction never to see him again. Because I deserved better!

A man who couldn't hold down a job. A man who couldn't keep friends. A man who sabotaged every area of his life through his delusion and paranoia. That had no money and no prospects. A man who had spent twenty years repeating the same mistakes and never taking any responsibility for his own behaviour. Projecting blame onto me and everyone else. Staying in total denial, never gaining wisdom or insight into his actions and the harm that he caused – no matter what challenges he had to face. I definitely deserved better.

You see, because the 'real' me, the little girl who 'really' was, gained way more than her fair share of empathy, compassion and understanding because of losing her mum. These are great qualities and qualities to be proud of. But these very positive characteristics made way too many allowances, were way too forgiving and allowed way too many men over the years to hurt and disappoint me. But then if I hadn't met Greg, if I hadn't believed at some very early point in our relationship that I loved him and wanted to be with him, then I wouldn't have had Luke. So, now that I reflect, I'm glad that I lived the life I've lived and never was 'the me that never was'. Because I had Luke.

Rosie

Postscript

It's August 2015, and I am about to send this book to the printers. I'm at the end of another manic week that comes at the end of eight months of manic weeks.

Since I was named Australian of the Year in January, my life has been a whirlwind. I have travelled the length and breadth of this beautiful country and met many inspiring, wonderful people. I've spoken to gatherings everywhere, from small groups in country town halls to conferences of two thousand people. I've addressed everyone from nurses, midwives, teachers and students to legal professionals, judges, politicians and business leaders. I've given the keynote address at the National Press Club, appeared on the ABC TV program *Q&A* and undertaken more media interviews than I can count.

It has been incredibly rewarding, but sometimes I stop and wonder if I'm making a difference at all. Certainly, for all the support I have received – and it has been both immense *and* immensely gratifying – there have also been critics and detractors. I've become something of a lightning rod – an easy target might be a better description. I understand that comes with the territory when you become a public figure, but it still hurts when people – sometimes in the public sphere – cast aspersions on my motivations and my integrity, despite knowing very little about me. That stings.

Over the last eighteen months or so I've also become a magnet for every woman who has ever suffered violence at the hands of her partner. Wherever I go, they come to me in waves, wanting to share with me the intimate details of the horrors they have endured. They need to talk, to confide in me. And often they are horrors they have never shared with another human being. I am now a psychologist-by-proxy to thousands of Australian women who feel I am giving voice to their silent suffering. They write me their stories in email and letters. And while it is humbling and their stoicism drives me on to make the most of this platform I have been given and effect real change, it also takes a toll. Because, invariably on my travels, I go back to a hotel room on my own where, after the applause has long since dissipated and the well-wishes of strangers have stopped echoing, it's just me and my thoughts.

It's a funny thing, this Australian of the Year award. While it's easily the greatest single honour I have received in my life, it's also an enormous burden. I feel a massive sense of responsibility to make it count, to use every second of my year in the spotlight.

And that can be exhausting, not least because it's a job that comes with no support staff, no monthly stipend nor even, for that matter, a rule book on how I should conduct myself. It's just me and my mobile phone and my personal email address and a daily tsunami of demands.

So there have been moments when I have felt completely overwhelmed and wondered if I have the energy to go on. But that's always when the universe smiles. The gods of compassion always seem to find me when I am at my lowest and most exhausted. And that's invariably when I receive a letter like the one below.

Dear Rosie,

I want to thank you for your bravery and commitment, even if thanking you for losing a child and rising above it just doesn't seem right ...

I also want to share a story with you. My nine-year-old son came home from school, telling me he had to do a project on his 'hero'. At first, he mentioned Tim Cahill (he is a boy who loves his soccer), and so I asked him to go to the computer to see what information he could find and what aspect of that puts Tim into the 'hero' status. After about ten minutes, my son returned and said, 'Mum, I've decided Tim hasn't done anything heroic, but Rosie Batty has and I want my project to be on her.' My jaw fell to the floor – what nine-year-old boy gives up the opportunity to discuss a sporting person? I asked him what he knew about you and he said: 'Well, her son was killed by his father when they were playing cricket and then she became Australian of the Year.' Google does provide children with so much ...

In any case, whilst he was amazed at your strength, I asked him exactly what it was that made you a 'hero'. His response was quite simply that through your profound loss, you have created so much hope.

I have attached his project to show you that you have reached the heart of a little boy, who idolises his parents, and thankfully lives in a safe and secure home. As much as we all want to protect our children, you are right: domestic violence does occur everywhere. To create hope in the hearts of little people and victims is an immensely heroic thing to do, so THANK YOU.

So this is my promise to you, to Australia, to all the abused women and children out there. I might just be a suburban mum but I will keep talking out about this issue, for as long as I can, for as long as I'm asked to. I will keep showing up, and asking difficult questions, and challenging us, as a society, to do better. Because I can. And I know *we* can do better.

And my message to all Australians is to stand up and say no to family violence, wherever it is, whatever form it takes, whomever it affects. We need to pull together to overhaul our court system, our policing, our support services, education. We need to prevent family violence before it starts and name it, shame it and take immediate action when we see it. No ifs, no buts. Because our future, and our children's future depends on it.

NEVER ALONE ♥ luke batty foundation

Never Alone is a campaign by the Luke Batty Foundation.

We will stand with the women and children affected by family violence so that they are supported in the community and have a powerful voice in the corridors of power.

Never Alone will build a groundswell of support for victims that will make it impossible for family violence to be ignored any longer.

We will not tip toe around the issue of family violence. We will say the things that make people feel uncomfortable.

Never Alone will bring people together. We have a vision that change is driven through the eyes of the victims, with a force of supportive people behind it.

We understand that family violence can happen to anybody and that we all have a responsibility to help end this epidemic.

Recently, we handed over a weighty petition with over 13,000 signatures from Never Alone supporters to every state and territory leader, calling for compulsory respectful relationships programs in schools.

They were receptive but we have to keep the pressure up to make sure it happens. Let's make sure the funding and further development of state-wide roll out models are top of the agenda for every state and territory education minister too.

To stand with us, visit www.neveralone.com.au

TIMELINE

2001: Rosie falls pregnant to Greg.

20 June 2002: Luke is born.

July 2002: Greg becomes angry with Rosie, picks up a wooden chest and threatens to throw it at her. Rosie is advised by Victorian Legal Aid that she cannot return to England with Luke to live without Greg's permission.

January 2003: Greg threatens Rosie with a large urn and aims kicks at her head.

March 2004: Rosie is advised by Victorian Legal Aid that Greg has a right to see his son.

June 2004: During an access visit, Greg pulls Rosie's hair and threatens to kill her. The following day, Rosie seeks and is granted an intervention order forbidding Greg from seeing or speaking to Rosie, but not restricting his access to Luke.

June 2005: Intervention order expires.

December 2005: Rosie relieves Greg of duty to pay child support, hoping that by relaxing financial pressure on him, his attitude towards her may soften.

April 2006: Family Court orders Greg can have continued access to Luke, including overnight on weekends.

June 2006: Greg attacks Rosie, pushing her into a wall and telling her, 'I would like to knock you into next week.' Rosie calls police. No charges are laid.

May 2012: Greg threatens to hit Rosie with a glass vase at her home. Luke witnesses the attack. Greg is arrested and taken to Frankston Hospital for psychiatric assessment. A new intervention order names Rosie and Luke as protected persons. Police refer case to Child Protection.

June 2012: After assessing the case, Child Protection advises Rosie that Luke is not at significant risk of harm and no further action is warranted.

November 2012: Greg downloads child porn to a USB key at a public library. He is later charged for the offence. Privacy laws mean Rosie is not informed.

January 2013: Greg still has court-ordered access to Luke on weekends. During one handover, Greg tells Rosie, 'I would really like to kill you' and 'I can make you suffer.' Rosie reports the threat to police, who arrest Greg the following day. Greg is remanded in custody and charged. The following day, Greg is released on bail.

February 2013: Courts issue another intervention order against Greg.

April 2013: Greg fails to show at court to face threat-to-kill charges. Rosie testifies to court that during a recent access visit, Greg showed Luke a knife and said, 'It could all end with this.' Warrants are issued for Greg's arrest. All access to Luke is suspended. Greg is living in his car.

7 May 2013: After police have trouble locating Greg, Rosie informs police that Greg is likely to show up at Luke's footy training. Police tell Rosie to call triple zero if Greg appears. Greg appears the following night. Terrified, Rosie calls triple zero – only to be told by local police that warrants for Greg's arrest have not been received. Rosie is hysterical.

10 May 2013: Rosie attends Frankston Magistrates Court to seek a variation of the intervention order. Greg is not present. Rosie says she has lost faith in the system. Court officers report her as being a 'complete mess'.

21 May 2013: Rosie informs police that Greg will be coming to footy training again the following night. Greg shows up briefly but police are busy with other matters and unable to attend.

29 May 2013: Greg is arrested by police at Tyabb oval. In custody, he responds aggressively to police, saying God will 'get' them.

11 June 2013: Greg faces court and is granted bail. Matter is adjourned until 3 July. Rosie says she is scared for her and Luke's safety.

3 July 2013: Greg applies for a variation of the intervention order.

22 July 2013: Magistrate orders Greg to have access to Luke on weekends at football, cricket or Little Athletics – only when others are present. Rosie breaks down at court.

25 July 2013: During counselling, Luke says he is not afraid of his father, but worried about the safety of his mother.

September 2013: After another court hearing to tighten the intervention order, Rosie breaks down and tells Child Protection she is at the end of her tether, requests they take out a protective order for Luke.

16 October 2013: Child Protection close file on Luke Batty.

10 December 2013: Rosie takes Luke on five-week holiday to UK to visit family.

17 January 2014: Greg fails to appear at court to face child porn charges.

24 January 2014: Greg's housemate applies for an intervention order against Greg.

28 January 2014: Warrant is issued for Greg's arrest – for breach of bail conditions.

5 February 2014: Police contact Rosie asking if she knows Greg's current address or whereabouts. She doesn't. That same day, by coincidence, Greg calls Rosie, in breach of IVO. She elicits his address and passes the information immediately to police.

8 February 2014: Greg attends Luke's cricket match. Later that week, Greg phones to tell Luke he was living with people he does not like and was upset that Luke had not contacted him on his return from the UK.

12 February 2014: Greg attends Luke's cricket training at Tyabb oval and kills him. Greg is shot by police while confronting them with a knife and dies early the next morning in hospital. At the time of his death, Greg was facing eleven criminal charges and had four warrants out for his arrest.

ACKNOWLEDGEMENTS

The journey of grief is not easy. Not for me and not for those sharing my journey. I thank everyone who has been able to weather the storms and stick by me no matter what.

To my brothers, who share my pain and understand my loss like no one else. To my dad, who would do anything to help me and take away the pain.

To Michelle, Sam and the wonderful Richardson family for their open door, home-cooked meals and for being true friends in every sense. To Mel for her big heart. To Ben, who has always known what to say and how to make me laugh. To Lee for being able to stick around when the going was so very tough. To Flinders Christian College for helping me with Luke's funeral and for making sure it was such a very special day. To the Tyabb Cricket Club for their support and helping me with all the arrangements for Luke's funeral. To the Salvation Army, friends and everyone in the community for the home-cooked meals, toilet rolls and never-ending compassion that helped me in those very early days. To everyone for the cards, poems, flowers and letters. Knowing how much you all cared and were there to support me through those first few months of intense grief was overwhelming, but showed me that humanity knows no limits.

To Lisa for helping me when I've been at my most vulnerable, for sharing some amazing experiences and helping me gain my confidence.

To Charandev for being such a wonderful person and being there through Luke's inquest. You are such a gentle caring soul and I feel so very privileged to have been able to get to know you. To Justin for being my right hand and my confidante – I could never have achieved what I have without you. To my new friends in the family violence sector – I have learnt so much, and without your professional insights and support I would not be where I am now.

To Sue, Mike and David for believing in me and joining me in Canberra to share that very special evening when I became Australian of the Year. It was an evening we will never forget.

And to Bryce, whose friendship I treasure and sense of humour I value. I am so very pleased you chose to help me write my book.

RESOURCES

The pernicious thing about family violence is that victims of abuse accept the behaviour that they have been conditioned to believe they deserve. Their self-esteem is so completely worn down over years and years of abuse – be it physical, psychological, financial – that they sometimes barely even recognise they are in an abusive relationship.

The bottom line is that violence is never okay. You don't deserve it, and whatever your partner might tell you, you are not the cause of it.

What is family violence?

Too many Australian women and children experience violence every day. Domestic or family violence is one of the most common forms of violence against women and their children in Australia, and can take a number of forms, including:

- physical – for example, slapping, hitting, choking, stabbing
- sexual – for example, rape, harassment, being forced to watch pornography
- emotional or psychological – for example, isolating the person from friends, family or culture, threats against children, threats to commit suicide or self-harm

- economic – for example, withholding money, controlling family finances, taking out loans in a partner's name without consent
- stalking – for example, repeated following, watching or harassing.

The cost of violence against women and their children to the Australian economy in 2009 was $13.6 billion. It's calculated to rise to $15.6 billion by 2021–22 without the right preventative action.

Getting help on domestic violence for yourself and others
If you or someone you know is in immediate danger, call 000 in Australia or 111 in New Zealand immediately. Help is available from many services in Australia and New Zealand. The following family violence services are gateways that can put you in touch with the best service for your needs, or can provide a listening ear.

Australia – National
1800 RESPECT (1800 737 732)
Available twenty-four hours a day, seven days a week.
www.1800respect.org.au
The National Sexual Assault, Domestic Family Violence Counselling Service is a free and confidential telephone and online service for any Australian who is experiencing or has experienced domestic or family violence and/or sexual assault. Translating and Interpreting Service: call 13 14 50 and ask them to contact 1800 RESPECT.

National Relay Service: for callers who are deaf or have a hearing or speech impairment: visit www.relayservice.gov.au and ask them to contact 1800 RESPECT (1800 737 732).

TTY/voice calls: phone 133 677 and ask them to contact 1800 RESPECT (1800 737 732).

Speak and Listen users: phone 1300 555 727 and ask them to contact 1800 RESPECT (1800 737 732).

Luke Batty Foundation
www.lukebattyfoundation.com.au
Helping women and children affected by the trauma of family violence.

Our Watch
www.ourwatch.org.au
Our Watch has been established to drive nationwide change in the culture, behaviours and attitudes that lead to violence against women and children.

Women's Legal Services Australia
www.wlsa.org.au
This is a national network of community legal centres that specialise in women's legal issues. They provide advice, information, casework and education to women on family law and family violence matters as well as provide advice on more general legal issues.

The Men's Referral Service
1300 766 491
mrs.org.au
The Men's Referral Service provides anonymous and confidential telephone counselling, information and referrals to men to help them to stop using violent and controlling behaviour.

What Men Can Do

whatmencando.net

This site provides information on how men can respond to and prevent men's violence against women.

Kids Helpline

1800 55 1800

www.kidshelpline.com.au

Australia's only free, private and confidential, telephone and online counselling service specifically for young people aged between five and twenty-five.

ANROWS

www.anrows.org.au

Australia's National Research Organisation for Women's Safety Limited (ANROWS) is an independent, not-for-profit company established as an initiative under Australia's National Plan to Reduce Violence against Women and their Children 2010–2022.

Lifeline

13 11 44

www.lifeline.org.au/Get-Help/Facts---Information/Domestic-Abuse-and-Family-Violence

Among its crisis support services, Lifeline deals with domestic and family violence.

APPS

Daisy

Daisy connects women who are experiencing or have experienced sexual assault, domestic and family violence to services in their state and local area.

iMatter

An app to help young women understand the warning signs of abusive and controlling behaviour in relationships as well as promote healthy self-esteem.

Australia – States and Territories

AUSTRALIAN CAPITAL TERRITORY
Domestic Violence Crisis Service ACT
02 6280 0900
www.dvcs.org.au

NEW SOUTH WALES
Domestic Violence Line
1800 65 64 63
www.domesticviolence.nsw.gov.au

NORTHERN TERRITORY
Dawn House
08 8945 1388
www.dawnhouse.org.au

QUEENSLAND
DV Connect Womensline
1800 811 811
www.dvconnect.org/womensline

SOUTH AUSTRALIA
Domestic Violence Crisis Service
1300 782 200

Domestic Violence and Aboriginal Family Violence Gateway Service

1800 800 098

www.gatewayservices.org.au

TASMANIA

Family Violence Response and Referral line

1800 633 937

www.safeathome.tas.gov.au/services

VICTORIA

Domestic Violence Resource Centre Victoria

03 9486 9866

www.dvrcv.org.au

The Domestic Violence Resource Centre Victoria (DVRCV) provides training, publications, research and other resources to those experiencing (or who have experienced) family violence, and to practitioners and service organisations who work with family violence survivors. The website is an excellent resource for anyone seeking information or help.

Safe Steps

1800 015 188

www.safesteps.org.au

Safe Steps is the 24/7 Family Violence Response Centre that offers a comprehensive range of intervention, support and advocacy services for women and children experiencing violence and abuse from a partner or ex-partner, another family member or someone close to them.

WESTERN AUSTRALIA
Women's Domestic Violence Helpline
08 9223 1188 or 1800 007 339

New Zealand
Women's Refuge National Crisisline
0800 REFUGE (0800 733 843)
Available twenty-four hours a day, seven days a week; call toll free from anywhere in NZ. (If you're in Auckland you can also call 09 378 1893.)
www.womensrefuge.org.nz
Provides information, advice and support about domestic violence as well as help in a crisis.

Shine
0508 744 633
9 am to 11 pm, seven days a week.
www.2shine.org.nz
Domestic Abuse Helpline for anyone living with abuse. The website includes information on how to stop someone knowing you have been seeking information online about domestic violence.

Family Violence Information Line
0800 456 450
9 am to 11 pm, seven days a week, with an after-hours message redirecting callers in an emergency.
www.areyouok.org.nz
Provides self-help information and connection to appropriate services.

OTHER RECOMMENDED WEBSITES

www.familyservices.govt.nz

The Family and Community Services site has a directory of social services in each community.

www.justice.govt.nz

The Ministry of Justice site has information about protection orders.

www.nnsvs.org.nz

The National Network of Stopping Violence site has a directory of local services.